EVERY WOMAN
HAS A RIGHT TO KNOW
THE DANGERS
OF LEGAL ABORTION

every woman has a right

to know the dangers of legal abortion

ann saltenberger

AIR-PLUS ENTERPRISES   GLASSBORO, NEW JERSEY

CONTENTS

DIAGRAMS
AND ILLUSTRATIONS

ACKNOWLEDGEMENTS

The researchers whose works are included in this text deserve the deep appreciation of all whose lives their experience and knowledge touch. Special thanks to Dr. Willard Cates of Atlanta, GA and Dr. Richard Watson of San Francisco, CA for their helpful suggestions.

Thanks also to the many friends without whose help this book would not have been possible: Denise Cocciolone, Kay Moughan, Maxine Lombardo, Mary Joseph, Betty LaRosa, Ann Smith, David Nesbitt, Gert Capone, Kara Eustace and, most especially, my mother, Ann McF. Montchyk, R.N., M.S.N. and my husband Jim, whose patience, thoughtfulness and love have sustained me through many dark hours and bright hopes.

PREFACE

Legalized abortion has been with us for a decade—it was first liberalized in Colorado in 1967—but most people still have little or no knowledge about how it affects women, couples, families, society.

Over the years, myths have grown about abortion—some good, some bad. Most erroneous. This book is meant to lay to rest some of those myths, and to bring forward previously published but little known information.

With this knowledge consumers as well as educators, legislators, consumer advocates and journalists who are often called upon to evaluate abortion for themselves and their various publics, will be able to speak with more authority on the subject.

NOTE TO SECOND PRINTING

Since this book was first published, readers have asked if abortion has not become "safer." We looked at the 1982 abortion statistics from the State of Michigan for an answer. Women who procured abortions that year were divided into eight categories by age (under 15 years, 15-19, 20-24, etc.). Of these, Michigan records that the largest group of women sustained the largest number of complications. The second largest group suffered the second highest number of adverse effects. The third biggest group had the third biggest incidence of complications. The same was true of the fourth, fifth and sixth groups, and even the seventh and eighth groups. So are the women of today enjoying safer abortions? On the contrary, the women of today are learning that pregnancy termination by the brute force method is, to put it bluntly, brutal. When some women have abortions, some women have complications. When more women have abortions, more have complications. When a considerable number choose to abort, a considerable number are adversely affected. Whenever a great many women induce abortion, a great many get hurt. But whether the ratio remains constant, rises or falls with passing time and the refinement of abortion techniques is irrelevant, since we are dealing not with statistical abstracts but rather with serious medical complications which endanger individual women. [311]

The American Journal of Nursing recently asked readers to test themselves on their knowledge of the effects of induced abortion on future child-bearing. The choices were an increased risk of later pregnancy failure, problems such as ectopic pregnancy and premature delivery in a later pregnancy, and scars on the womb which might lead to an improper placement of the placenta and intrauterine adhesions. Were a nurse to answer based on a reading of leading women's magazines or the popular press, her answers probably would be far off the mark. But if her knowledge was based on the medical reports cited in this book, her answers would be that all of the above are serious complications which arise following induced abortion. [312]

This book is not a statistical record of the *incidence* of complications, but rather an exploration of the *incidents*, the women, and the unfortunate consequences of their choice to abort. The women whose stories are told herein learned from experience that a preborn is not a disposable commodity, and that an abortion, far from being a "simple, safe procedure," is in reality a surgical downpayment on a whole new set of problems.

"The American woman certainly has the right to know the risks to her health and well-being and future reproductive capabilities as a result of abortion."[103]

1

TO THE WOMAN CONSIDERING ABORTION

Although more than one million American women each year have undergone abortions since they were legalized in 1973, there is only one you. This book is dedicated to those women who have submitted to abortions, but most especially it is dedicated to you. Their experiences are the source of the material for this book; you are the *reason* for it. It has been written so that you might not casually accept abortion imagining that because it is legal it is also safe.

A few years ago I nearly became an abortion statistic. Thirty days after my son was conceived, I became very ill. My husband and I had been involved in a cross-country motorcycle race the day before. I was fine. The sun was bright, and a warm breeze kept us company all day. We returned home tired but happy, and excitedly discussed our outing before turning in for the night. There was no hint at that time of what the next day held.

I awoke feeling groggy; my whole body ached. When I tried to get up, pain sliced through my forehead. Knowing I was pregnant, I had been anticipating the onset of morning sickness, so I thought, "Oh, well, I guess today's the day," but the nausea never came. Instead, by evening I had begun to run a low grade fever. The next day I made an appointment with my family doctor. When I saw him that evening, my temperature was up around 101°F and I felt truly lousy. I nearly passed out in his office. I remember lying on the examining table hearing him say "rebound tenderness" while nurses scurried to find someone to watch my two little girls. I was rushed to the hospital.

13

My blood count was all wrong. They thought I had a tubal pregnancy, so two x-rays were taken. After what seemed like an eternity in the emergency room, I was sent, half conscious, to a room where an electrocardiogram was taken. One test followed another that night, and the next day, and the next. The x-rays did not show a tubal pregnancy; all the other test results were negative. Maybe I had leukemia? They did a bone marrow test. Painful, but negative. On and on it went, while at home, strangers were caring for my children. I wanted out!

And suddenly it was over. I woke up feeling rested, refreshed, well. Whole. I got up; it was 4 a.m. I put on my robe and walked down the hall to the nurses' station. Having never seen me erect, they were amazed. "What happened?" they all asked at once. "Why aren't you in bed? Don't you feel sick?"

"It must be the Four O'Clock in the Morning Instant Cure," I told them. "I'm fine."

When my doctor examined me at 9 a.m. he agreed that I was, indeed, well enough to go home. He offered to drive me himself.

An hour later the green, sun-drenched farmlands of South Jersey were slipping past the car windows. I settled back into the plush seat and relaxed. But Dr. L. was tense and I soon found out why. "I know you're the wrong person to say this to," he began (I had already begun to garner a considerable reputation for my research into the effects of artificial pregnancy termination), "but you really should have an abortion." His words chilled me. A dim horror twisted up my spine and exploded in my brain. "This can't be happening to me," I thought. "Not *me,* not *my* baby."

His words had continued, unheard. I tuned in as he was saying something about my probably having had a viral infection, and German Measles is a viral infection, "and we all know what German Measles does."

"Yes, but it only does it to 25% of preborns. You're not going to tell me that part, are you?" I thought, but I said nothing.

He droned on. The x-rays. X-rays do horrible things: twist developing bodies, destroy forming minds. No doubt about it, he was sure, this baby would be retarded or deformed. Not worth worrying over. Not worth saving. Rx: abort it and forget it. (Oh, but doctor, could I scrape it from my mind as easily as you could scrape it from my body?)

His car stopped in front of my house and I got out, no longer feeling fine. Stiffly I walked up the brick steps. The house was strangely quiet; I was alone with my fears.

I sat down with a cup of coffee to ponder my choices. I could panic, blindly accept my doctor's dictum, and abort. Or I could think about it, find out what kind of damage my new little one might have suffered, how he could be helped, how I could carry a pregnancy for eight more months not knowing whether I'd give birth to a healthy, normal child or one who would be severely handicapped. Could I withstand the overwhelming fear those eight months would undoubtedly bring? Or should I abandon hope and resort to the quick fix of an abortion?

Webster's New Collegiate Dictionary—abort: to miscarry, to bring forth stillborn offspring, to cancel, to stop in the early stages as a disease. A disease? A preborn is not a disease. Even a diseased preborn isn't a disease! And diseases can be cured. Maybe there was a cure for *my* disease (Webster's—disease: trouble, a condition that impairs the performance of a vital function). Thinking is a vital function and the paralyzing fear of producing a severely malformed or retarded child *was* impairing my ability to think, to reason.

So let's be reasonable, I thought. Let's begin at the beginning. Forget the baby and concentrate on me; that's easy, I'm here. What do I stand to gain by abortion? I do not become the mother of an unknown factor. What do I stand to lose by aborting? Intangibles—my self respect, maybe a very nice kid, perhaps my husband would divorce me or my mother would hate me. Tangibles (now here's the bottom line)—I could lose my ability to have another child; I could be seriously injured; I could lose my life.

What had I learned in three years of studying the effects of legal abortion? That there are myriad complications and that there are no guarantees of safe passage. No doctor, no hospital, no clinic can guarantee a woman she will survive a legal abortion. They don't even promise she'll be able to walk out afterwards. No thanks. I'm too important to me, I thought. I know too much about legal abortions to risk my life letting them do that to me. There had to be a better way, and I was determined to find it.

I began with an embryology textbook. I wanted to find out what part of the preborn is developing on the 31st day after conception—the day the x-rays were taken (because that was where the surest danger came from). I learned his body had been growing and changing from the moment egg met sperm, the moment my child's life began. He had a rudimentary nervous system, a beating heart, pulsing blood and on that very day his brain was the part developing most. His brain. That could go two ways, if indeed it had been affected. Super dumb or super smart—which would it be? I decided to hope for the best and plan for the worst.

I contacted the Association for Children With Learning Disabilities and St. John of God School for the Retarded. I learned that they wanted to start working with infants almost as soon as they are born; this ensures the child will attain his highest possible potential.

Another important stop was Birthright, an emergency pregnancy service that supports women through crisis pregnancies. There I found shoulders to cry on (and cry I did, amply) and understanding, hope, and people who thought I'd make it. I was told I was a person of worth and dignity; that I was special and important, that I could find the courage to carry my baby to term. It's not hard to believe in yourself when someone else believes in you; those are the kind of people I found at Birthright.

Now that I was not alone, I could begin to see through the confusion caused by the pressures on me. My physical condition fluctuated as greatly as my emotional state. I became jaundiced, turned yellow, and itched like a sheepdog with fleas. I got a severe case of hay fever and took nearly a dozen different, prescribed medications trying to clear it up. And the blood tests! Every week, a blood test. It wasn't long before my veins were so scarred a scouting expedition was needed to find a place to draw blood. One day I had driven miles to a different city for my blood test. I was miserable, sitting in a self-pitying stupor in a tiny white room, waiting for the vampire, uh, technician, to come when into my mind on greased ball bearings slid the thought, "If I were here for an abortion, this would be the end of the pain. It would hurt just a little more, then it would all be over." It would be so easy. Or would it?

Between the womb, where the preborn lives, and the vagina or birth canal, is a little-known organ called the cervix. The cervix is sometimes called the neck of the womb because it's long and narrow. It is also closed very securely. If the womb can be described as a balloon filled with air, the cervix would be the part that is tied tightly, so that what is in it can't get out. In natural termination of pregnancy (when the baby is supposed to come out) this long part becomes short, and its closedness opens up allowing the baby to pass through. But in artificial termination of pregnancy, this tightly closed part has to be forced open. This is done by shoving rods through it: first a slender one, then a thicker one, and so forth and so on until the opening is wide enough to allow insertion of the tools that will take the baby out. Sometimes one of these rods will accidentally be shoved through the side of the cervix causing bleeding. Many times even when no accident happens, this rough treatment damages the muscles that hold the cervix closed, and so permanently weakens them that they can never support the weight of a baby beyond the third, fourth, or fifth month. Then the woman miscarries. And miscarries again. And again.

I thought about never having another baby. I definitely was not ready to make that decision and even less ready to have the reality of such a situation thrust upon me months or years after a "quick, simple, safe legal abortion." I thought about the many people who had read the booklet I wrote describing the dangers of legal abortion and who had written saying they were glad to have concrete proof an abortion was bad for them. What would my actions be saying to them if I succumbed to the lenis lure?

I thought about the "counselor" in the abortion clinic, smiling from ear to ear while she tried to hide a blood splatter on the side of her skirt. I know the one thing she never says to any woman who goes in there; she's always so happy to take your money, but she never says, "Sweetie, did you know you could go out of here feet first with a sheet over your face?" Was I ready to lay my life on the line just to get rid of some pain? Maybe death hurts more. No thanks.

When I left the lab that day I was committed to continuing my pregnancy. I still had times of depression, but the hopelessness was gone. And although I still had periodic pain, I also had laughter, and friends, pretty maternity clothes, and dreams about the little boy I would play with and hold.

Now, eight years later, it's spring again. The sun is shining and the breezes are warm. And Jimmy is seven and healthy and strong, full of fun and questions and tricks. Appearance: beautiful; neurological evaluation: normal; intelligence: superior.

Public interest in abortion has, for a decade, centered on advocacy. Superficially it appeared to be advocacy of women, but increasingly it tends toward advocacy of abortion per se. Our openness to the lenitive possibilities presented by modern technology must be tempered by some hard-nosed skepticism. The willingness to ask hard questions has evolved, in part, as we have developed our understanding of abortion. The answers to those questions may very well sober our confidence in a procedure which, admittedly, sometimes goes wrong.

In the spirit of the sunshine laws, many states and localities are attempting to have informed consent legislation enacted which would require abortion providers to tell a woman the truth about pregnancy and the possible effects of forced termination. Everywhere that such consumer protection bills have been introduced, the people who promote and profit from abortion have fought against them. Often their fight has been successful, and the woman considering abortion has been denied her right to freedom of information about what is involved. While those who promote abortion may be able to influence the legislators, they can't suppress the facts which are available—more than 125 case histories and 225 medical reports are cited in this book. Until now this knowledge has been scattered, and not easily accessible to those who need the facts most—women who are considering artificial termination of pregnancy. This book may be read and used by many people, but it is intended especially for *you.*

Women and girls who become pregnant consider abortion believing that it restores them to their physiological and psychological condition preceding the conception.

BUT THINK:

How safe is an induced abortion?
How does induced abortion affect subsequent pregnancies?
Should it be a matter of concern to a future husband?
Are others in the family affected?
Should you submit to this, or any surgery, before knowing all the dangers?

CAN STATISTICS SUPPLY THE ANSWERS?

The exact incidence of any given complication following induced abortion is unknown. Accurate statistics are not available for a variety of reasons:

- many women do not know the name of the doctor who performed their abortion

- the abortionist is often not the doctor who sees the complications (some clinics have standing instructions that doctors not be interrupted with phone calls from patients[243] even though the woman may be calling to report serious symptoms)

- women who need emergency medical attention usually go to nearby community hospitals; less than 40% ever return to the original clinic[105, 270]

- an infection or other illness or damage may not be recorded as abortion-related by the attending physician

- selective under-reporting of deaths may occur[231]. One investigation revealed that although the state health department could quote statistics on the race, age and marital status of every woman who had received an abortion since 1973, it didn't know how many had died from their "safe, legal abortions"[241]

- there are no federal laws or state regulations requiring reporting of complications or even deaths from legal abortions that can force a doctor to report something he chooses to conceal

- office-based first trimester abortions are usually not reported to the Center For Disease Control (CDC)[231]

- post-abortion followup may be brief or non-existent or relegated to a doctor not immediately involved with the procedure (many and often serious infections of the urinary system and other urological problems go unreported in such instances)[104]

- it is very easy to miss morbidity (complications), especially ambulatory morbidity, in the absence of long-range postabortal documentation, which itself is hindered by women giving false addresses, subsequently moving or having their phones disconnected, desiring privacy, or just not caring to divulge painful details of their abortions

- the CDC, charged by the federal government with responsibility for recording abortion statistics, relies on individual doctors, clinics and hospitals to report complications that follow legal abortions. The reliability of their information, therefore, is only as good as their reporting

19

system. When even *deaths* may not be reported, "official government figures" for complications reflect only an unknown portion of the total. CDC's data is incomplete and hence unreliable in that no substantive conclusion about the relative safety of legal abortion reached from their data can have statistical accuracy

• ultimately, when you're dealing with a human life, you don't quote statistics. You can't say to a woman, when resuscitation fails, "Sorry, honey, you were the one percent."

What we are exploring is not a statistical record of the incidence of complications, but the results obtained from the observation of individuals and representative groups of women who actually underwent legal abortions. Because of the inability to follow all, the total number of women affected by any given complication is actually greater than the number of instances mentioned, although how much greater we do not know. There may also be more complications which are not recorded here.

Your concern for your own well-being makes knowledge of what others have experienced—what they have endured as a direct result of their choice to abort—invaluable to you in your decision-making. These girls and women faced a new frontier, not as brave and hardy pioneers, but as emigrants clutching at a hope to shield them from their reality. They faced unknown, unheard-of dangers and hardships, and many did not survive. In learning what legal abortion did to them, you realize the dangers that face you as an individual, dangers which may affect or alter your body, your health, your life.

You cannot make an intelligent decision when you lack vital facts. You cannot make a free choice based on assumptions and empty clichés. You cannot give informed consent to this surgical procedure unless you have become aware of all the known complications.

"Unfortunately, because of emotional reactions to legal abortion, well-documented evidence from countries with a vast experience of it received little attention in either the medical or lay press . . . The public is misled into believing that legal abortion is a trivial incident, even a lunch-hour procedure, which can be used as a mere extension of contraceptive practice. There has been almost a conspiracy of silence in declaring its risks . . . This is medically indefensible when patients suffer as a result . . .

"In view of the incidence of sepsis (infection) in this and other reported series it is irresponsible to advocate out-patient or lunch-time abortion without adequate post-operative medical or nursing supervision."[21]

2

THE BOTCHED LEGAL ABORTION

We're all familiar with the term "safe, legal abortion" and with the posters and buttons linking "keep abortion legal" with "safe"; and we've been lulled by this concept into the thought that in clean and cheerful surroundings our pregnancies can be terminated quickly and effectively, ensuring our swift return to normal routines. This lenis lure draws many unsuspecting women into grim situations where they become the helpless victims of botched legal abortions. For even in antiseptic surroundings, attended by a competent and experienced abortionist, a woman's supposedly simple surgery can become an ordeal of nightmare proportions.

Sondra's* botched legal abortion at a leading clinic left her "totally and permanently incapacitated." According to the statement of eight doctors filed with the Court, Sondra—once attractive, intelligent and looking forward to the future—now has the abilities of a 2 to 3 year old and will require constant care for the rest of her life. Five civil lawsuits totalling over $7 million in damages pend against the large abortion chain responsible for Sondra's condition; three other suits have been settled out of court.[106]

Twenty-one-year-old Tamara*, described by her doctor as "previously healthy," was in the 15th week of her first pregnancy when she had an abortion by Rivanol installation and catheter insertion. A few hours after the procedure she began to vomit and developed total anuria (complete urinary suppression). She was treated with dialysis but urine production did not begin for six days. After getting off to a slow start, she went into a polyuric phase which lasted a week, after which she returned to normal.

Because of the seriousness of this complication, an investigation was carried out which showed the hospital pharmacy had distributed a 1.0% solution of Rivanol marked 0.1% which means Tamara received a dose ten times stronger than needed.[215]

Mrs. Claudia Lott brought her abortionist to court in a $1.5 million suit against one of Texas's oldest abortion clinics. Fearful that medication she had received during a gall bladder operation might have harmed her preborn infant, the 20-year-old mother called the Reproductive Services Clinic and was advised by a counselor that the baby she was carrying probably would be deformed. That opinion, given by a non-professional without examination or testing, so alarmed Mrs. Lott that she agreed to an abortion. During the operation, her uterus was perforated and the artery to the womb was severed. She suffered extensive hemorrhaging, lost more than one-third of her body's blood and nearly bled to death. No whole blood, plasma, or emergency equipment was on hand at the clinic. Not until afterward, while Mrs. Lott was in the recovery room, did the abortionist ask her and her husband why they had decided to seek an abortion.

Later the doctor went home, where he received the call that Mrs. Lott was bleeding heavily; he began his drive back to the hospital *three hours after* the damage had been done. On arrival a nurse told him Claudia was "just a turkey" (medical slang for someone faking pain or symptoms). The doctor found Claudia lying in a pool of blood, in pain, nauseous, and vomiting. But instead of calling a Dallas Fire Department ambulance with its trained paramedics from just six blocks away, he called a private ambulance that took 40 minutes to arrive; moreover, the private ambulance had no emergency equipment. It carried Claudia past two hospitals enroute to Methodist where the doctor had privileges; there he discovered the extent of the damage—the hole in the uterus and the cut artery. Claudia's womb had to be removed; a young wife's fertility was tragically taken from her.

In court, in response to questions about normal routines at his clinic, the abortionist testified that when things were going smoothly there would be only a minute or so between one operation and the next. He testified that the first time he saw Mrs.

24

Lott was in the treatment room outside the operating room (she was accompanied into surgery by a clinic counselor, not a nurse, who prepared her for the abortion). It was like an assembly line: reviewing what was done in the moments between patients, the legal abortionist listed removing gloves and bringing women out and in. When asked if he didn't also wash his hands between surgeries, the doctor answered that they didn't scrub between procedures; sterile gloves were in, but hand-washing was out! The outraged prosecuting attorney asked if it hadn't been in the 1800's that the medical world learned of the need for antiseptic procedures. The abortionist's reply was a barely whispered "yes."[107]

"The surprising number of maternal deaths and near deaths following legal abortion complications should alert all who do these operations that they are not to be undertaken without the same degree of pre-operative evaluation and post-operative care rendered to other gynecologic procedures."[103]

3

FATAL
COMPLICATIONS

INTRODUCTION

Deaths from legal abortions are a problem people don't like to admit exists. There are, however, many factors, alone or in combination, which can make legal abortion lethal. Chief among these is the fact that inducing abortion means going against the flow of nature, interfering with a natural environment, bringing to an abrupt halt a complicated process designed by nature to be on-going.

"It's unfortunate, but it's happening every day in Chicago and you're just not hearing about it," said Michael Grobsmith, chief of the Illinois Department of Public Health's department of hospitals and clinics, commenting on the circumstances surrounding the June 14, 1977 death of Barbaralee Davis a few hours after undergoing an early abortion at Hope Clinic for Women in Granite City.[108, 109] Although she complained of weakness and pain after the abortion, Barbaralee was sent home. She needed help getting into the car and lay on the back seat all the way. Alone in her bedroom, she quietly bled to death; her body was found less than 12 hours after her legal abortion. An autopsy revealed a rip in her uterus; an artery had been cut and two quarts of blood lay in her pelvis. Imbedded in the wall of her womb were a face and part of a spine. A $1 million lawsuit for wrongful death was filed by her parents against the doctor and clinic.

Barbaralee's tragic death gives us some insight into the

27

mechanics of legal abortion fatalities. The cause of her death, a hole in her womb (caused by the abortion) which the doctor knew nothing about, is fairly common as a responsible factor. Other complications may prove equally lethal; these will be examined on an individual basis.

The fact that she died following suction abortion, the method most often performed, is not unusual either. Each abortion procedure is known to carry its own inimical dangers; some of these procedures and their particular consequences are probed in depth in this chapter.

Still other factors influence the safety of legal abortion. Location and timing, the use of anesthesia or laminaria, unscrupulous physicians (who always seem to have flourishing practices, often in more than one clinic, town, or even state), and error on the part of doctor and/or patient, may direct a fatal turn of events.

Further, this chapter touches on the broader spectrum of fatalities: conditions complicating pregnancies, the special problems of teenagers, ectopic pregnancies, the strangely rising death rate, and the comparisons one hears to the safety of childbirth. Together the collective knowledge of many professionals and the experiences of many women will bring to the reader understanding of the threat of abortion: when legal means lethal.

COMPLICATIONS THAT CAUSE DEATH

MISCELLANEOUS

Death may be caused by a variety of complications including cardiac arrest (heart failure), hemorrhage, infection[50, 51], inflammation of the heart[253], water intoxication, septic shock and disseminated intravascular coagulation, amniotic fluid embolism, salt poisoning and swelling of the brain.[227] At times, the exact cause of death following legal abortion may not be determined, and it will be classified "unknown" as in the case of Diane S. of Chicago.[253]

DAMAGE TO THE WOMB

The womb, or uterus, is a woman's principal sex organ and the natural environment of her developing offspring. A perforation of the uterus can be a cut, rip, gash, gouge, hole or rupture inflicted by a qualified, competent doctor using a dilator, curette, forceps or other surgical instrument.

Molly*, a tan, blonde newspaper reporter in her early twenties, had a D&C abortion performed in her doctor's office at 17 weeks' gestation; she went home and died of a perforated uterus.[126]

Darlene*, a single woman 26 years old, died of a ruptured uterus from a nozzle instillation of poison sodium hydroxide solution. An autopsy revealed gangrene of eight feet of her intestines.[117]

HEMORRHAGE

Massive, uncontrolled bleeding is an all too familiar spectre of legal abortions:[253]

Evelyn D., 38, died of a hemorrhage after an abortion at a legally-operating clinic.

Julia R., 20, bled to death following an abortion at the same clinic.

Dorothy B. suffered the same fate.

Sandra Lynn C., a 35-year-old mother of four, died of blood loss from a punctured uterus within hours of her legal abortion.

Registered nurse, Dorothy M., apparently underwent two incomplete abortions at a legally run clinic. She died of excessive bleeding.

INFECTION

"Infection is the main cause of death associated with legal abortion in the United States."[271] Infection was the leading cause of abortion-related deaths of 104 women in a CDC report.[113] In another study "documented incomplete abortion caused each of the four deaths from infection."[231]

One of 13 women aborted with a 50% glucose solution died of infection.[214]

I. B., age 28, died following an abortion at 17 weeks from septicemia and bronchopneumonia.[126]

K. H. was 42 when she underwent abortion at 26 weeks gestation; she died of septic endometritis, shock and pulmonary edema.[126]

Lea* delivered 36 hours after saline instillation; she had normal temperature after the abortion. Yet despite antibiotics given to prevent infection, she developed chills and a fever of 106°F. She died of staph infection nine days after the abortion.[227]

Tammy* had four operations after her saline abortion in an

attempt to empty her womb; she was bleeding severely. In none of these surgeries did she receive general anesthesia. Acute peritonitis (inflammation of the membrane that lines the abdominal cavity) with bowel perforations (the bowel is adjacent to the womb and in the "line of fire" of any instrument going through the womb) took her life.[227]

In another case of infection, Sonya* delivered spontaneously 12 hours after saline instillation and was sent home 14 hours after delivery. She received oral antibiotics as a routine management. Nineteen days later she was readmitted; she had been bleeding for two days. Her womb was the size of a 12 weeks' gestation and purulent material seeped from it. Curettage yielded large amounts of placental tissue. The next day, when her temperature went to 104°, she was given more antibiotics; but it went up still higher, to 106°, and Sonya went into shock. Despite treatment with all available medical means, her life could not be saved.[227]

EMBOLISM

An embolism is an obstruction of a blood vessel by a foreign substance: air, fat, tissue, or a blood clot.

The case of E. R., age 22, illustrates a bizarre accident, which need never have happened, due totally to the error of hospital personnel. Her ten week pregnancy was due to be terminated by suction, but someone misconnected the tubing, forcing air under pressure into her womb when the machine was turned on. Massive air embolism immediately resulted and frantic attempts to revive the woman failed. She died two and one half months later without ever regaining consciousness. [62, 103, 113]

Adella* lived for five days after a legal clinic abortion created a blood clot that ended her life.[253]

Known or suspected amniotic fluid embolism accounted for 17 deaths in a five-year period. [271, 310]

"Pulmonary thromboembolism is a serious complication of induced abortion"—a blood clot to the lungs which can appear from two to fifty days after the abortion. In one group of abortion-related deaths, fatal pulmonary embolism was the second most common cause of death, taking the lives of 10 out of 104 women;[113] gestation at the time of fatal abortion ranged from 8 to 15 weeks.

Marla* was 23 years old. During the eighth week of gestation she underwent an elective abortion by suction curettage with abdominal tubal ligation under general anesthesia. Eight days later she collapsed and was pronounced dead on arrival at a local hospital.[113]

Kathleen* was 31 years old when she had an abortion by sharp curettage during the eighth week of pregnancy; she did well until 38 days after the procedure when she became nauseated and developed chest pain. Because of increasing difficulty breathing, she was admitted to a hospital. An electrocardiogram demonstrated right heart strain. Despite receiving heparin, two hours after admission she died of respiratory arrest.[113]

Seventeen-year-old Linda* began using oral contraceptives immediately after undergoing a suction curettage abortion of her first pregnancy at nine weeks. Fourteen days later swelling and pain developed in her left leg; she was admitted to a hospital with a diagnosis of thrombophlebitis and heparin therapy was begun. On the 17th hospital day she suffered pulmonary embolism; six days later she died of cardiac arrest. It is possible that the oral contraceptives, and not the abortion itself, may have been responsible; however, if she had carried the pregnancy instead of aborting it, the particular events that led to her death would have been avoided.

By the age of 44 Carlene* had carried four pregnancies and had been taking the pill for 16 years when, for reasons of her own, she discontinued it. Within two months she became pregnant, but at eight weeks' gestation she chose to undergo a hysterectomy abortion. Eight days after leaving the hospital she collapsed suddenly and died of a massive pulmonary embolus.[113]

Nineteen-year-old Sheila*had extra-amniotic instillation of prostaglandin F2α augmented by oxytocin, completed after 37 hours by sharp curettage with the use of general anesthesia. She suffered a cardio-pulmonary arrest 30 minutes later. She lay dying for five days; death was attributed to multiple pulmonary emboli and electrolyte imbalance.[113]

Knowing the warning signs of pulmonary embolism may help protect a woman from a similar fate. Obesity, diabetes, peripheral artery disease, malignancy, varicose veins, oral contraceptive use, blood type A, age 27 to 30 and older, even the increased bed rest a woman may want after an abortion may increase the risk of pulmonary thromboembolism. The presence of *any* of these warning signs should alert both patient and doctor to the possibility of post-operative thromboembolism if the woman risks the abortion.

Marla, Kathleen, Linda, Carlene and Sheila all had documented risks. However, although caution is required in these circumstances, the presence of a risk factor is not in itself the sole source of danger, for even completely healthy women with no predisposing factors can die of pulmonary embolism following a legal abortion:

According to her doctor, 35-year-old April* had no risk factors prior to abortion, which was done by suction curettage in the tenth week of gestation. She had her tubes tied at the same time under general anesthesia. The procedures went smoothly, without any postoperative complications. Twelve days later, April was found unconscious in her home and was dead on arrival at the local hospital. Pulmonary emboli were found at autopsy.

This risk, seldom revealed to women considering abortion, is widely recognized in medical circles and attacks about 200 aborters each year.

With or without the presence of pre-existing complications, "even though we utilize general principles of care thought to minimize the risk, a certain number of tragic deaths from massive emboli are *inevitable.* "[113]

LETHAL ABORTION PROCEDURES

INTRODUCTION
Deaths can and do occur from every method of inducing abortion; certain procedures manifest their own characteristic complications. Utus paste and laminaria tents, for example, are specifically mentioned as the two methods of termination carrying the highest risk and it is deplorable that the number of deaths attributed to the introduction of a paste into the uterus during legal abortion has risen from two in the three years before legalization to *seven* in the three years after! "Induced abortion will never be without some risk."[118]

SALINE
Saline, or salt-poisoning abortion, also known as "salting-out," is a method used after the 14th to 16th week of pregnancy when the fully-formed swimmer is surrounded by sufficient fluid to facilitate the infusion of a 20% salt solution.

The woman lies down on a table and her hospital gown is lifted above her waist; thighs and genitals are covered with a towel, leaving only her pregnant stomach exposed. After this area is washed with germ-killing solution and a pain-killer is injected, a very long needle pierces the skin near the belly button and is driven through the abdomen into the womb and amniotic sac (the bag of water surrounding the swimmer). If the preborn does not push the needle away (which they are often known to do), about one hundred and fifty cc's of his fluid environment are removed to be replaced by the deadly saline solution.

Sometime during the next hour comes the most difficult part (and the part most likely not to be told to the woman considering abortion). More difficult than making The Choice, more difficult than seeing that huge needle bearing down on the stomach, is the time when the saline begins to affect the preborn and s/he begins to react to it with the basic tools of survival used by every living creature—fight or flight. The preborn kicks, thrusts, and writhes. Soon, since s/he can neither fight the poison nor run from it, the convulsions begin. The death throes of the preborn can be very uncomfortable for the mother; she can both feel and see them. There is no escape for her, either. After the preborn dies, labor begins, followed by delivery of the infant and the afterbirth (that is, if all goes according to plan).

Saline abortion is second only to a heart transplant as elective surgery with the highest fatality rate.[235] In an analysis of 446,052 legal abortions, it was reported that the saline abortion mortality rate was seven to nine times greater than for first-trimester abortions; infection following saline instillation was the single most frequent cause of death.[296]

Another major complication is coagulation changes resulting in disseminated intravascular coagulation (DIC).[296] Questions about the safety of saline abortion have been raised because serious hemorrhage from DIC is relatively common; indeed, according to recent reports, DIC regularly follows saline abortion.[39]

Reinforcing its lethal potential is this report of a maternal death directly attributable to DIC: twenty-one-year-old Sandy* developed this hemorrhagic syndrome ten hours after the saline was put into her. While her body was in this condition there was massive bleeding in her brain. Doctors worked vigorously to reverse the condition, but by the time they were successful, irreversible brain hemorrhage had already occurred. Within 36 hours of the saline procedure, Sandy was dead. This death, together with previous reports of serious hemorrhage, raises the question of the safety of saline abortion as an elective procedure.[39]

Shock as the result of a gangrenous ovary was listed as the cause of death of 20-year-old Alma* who had undergone a legal saline abortion.[55]

At 37, Terri* had no health problems when she went for a saline abortion at 15 weeks gestation. She soon developed hypernatremia (salt poisoning) with swelling in her brain leading to convulsions, prolonged hypoxia (lack of oxygen), renal failure and aspiration pneumonia. She died ten days later.[65]

C. R., 31, underwent saline abortion in a hospital twelve weeks into her pregnancy; she died of pulmonary edema and cardiac arrest.[126]

In one group of women killed by saline abortions, the main factors leading to death were complications secondary to incomplete abortion with bleeding and infection, complications which arose from the use of agents to shorten the induction-to-abortion time, complications secondary to preexisting medical conditions which were not compatible with this method of abortion, and salt poisoning:

Grace* was readmitted 24 hours after saline instillation with a 104° fever; she continued to bleed after delivery. Her uterus was vacuum aspirated following which she was treated for septic shock and diminished urine output; she died within three days of her abortion.[277]

Elaine* became comatose one and one half hours after saline instillation. She convulsed eight and one half hours later and lived only six hours after that; she died of salt poisoning.[227]

Dolly* delivered 29 hours after her saline abortion was begun; the placenta had to be removed surgically. A known asthmatic, she was given adrenalin for wheezing fifty minutes later, but the respiratory distress was too much for her and her heart stopped. Death may have been due to a severe asthmatic episode or water intoxication.[227]

Maria's long, exhausting abortion experience ended in her death, which may have been due in part to the great quantity of fluid put into her system:[227]

hour   0—saline infusion
hour 18—intravenous infusion of 1000 ml of 5% glucose and water with 40 units of oxytocin
hour 40—having received 3000 ml of fluid and 120 units of oxytocin, Maria went into convulsions
day   5—delivery finally took place
day 10—Maria succumbed to bronchopneumonia and cerebral necrosis (death of the brain tissue)

Sometimes a woman will opt for abortion without her husband's knowledge. One husband did find out, too late. Malcolm G.* found his wife Betty* bleeding and unconscious on the bathroom floor; when he turned her over, he saw the bottom and chest of a baby protruding from her vagina. The 23-year-old mother was dead on arrival at a nearby hospital. She had undergone a saline abortion in New York City where she had given a fictitious name and address. Ignoring instructions to return to the hospital when labor began, she went home to Massachusetts. Her death was attributed to massive blood loss.[124,227]

Since 1974 women have been strongly advised against undergoing saline-induced abortion with oxytocin augmentation. This warning, formerly issued only to mothers with several children, is now being given to *all* women. The combination of saline and oxytocin can cause rupture of the uterus; if not recognized and treated in time, it can be fatal, as these two cases show:

Willo*, a healthy mother of two children in her mid-twenties, underwent elective abortion by saline and oxytocin. Thirty-two hours later she was still in labor, agitated, and complaining increasingly of pain. In the next three hours Willo's vital signs decreased and her heart stopped beating; she was revived and taken to the operating room where exploratory surgery revealed her womb had been savagely torn as the preborn was rocketed into her peritoneal cavity. Damage to the uterus was so severe that it had to be removed. Taken to intensive care in a coma, Willo died five days later without regaining consciousness.[122]

Twenty-nine-year-old Prentice*, mother of three, died from a ruptured uterus despite the fact that "the uterus was explored manually and no defect was noted." Her doctors now strongly caution that all women who receive oxytocin during labor—

35

regardless of the number of previous pregnancies or how far the gestation is advanced—be closely observed for possible uterine rupture.[122]

PROSTAGLANDIN

Prostaglandins are a family of naturally-occurring compounds that have the ability to contract isolated smooth muscle; the uterus is such a muscle, and contractions are the means nature uses to push the infant from the womb. Contractions can also be induced with prostaglandins, but unlike saline, this method does not directly kill the preborn, so the birth-like abortion of a living infant may result. Much remains unknown about prostaglandins' effects on the body, but because its action is systemic, the woman's entire body is affected.

Hopes that the use of prostaglandins would avert renal complications in legal abortions were dimmed by the report of six deaths following second-trimester prostaglandin abortions. One of the victims was a 33-year-old woman who died of overwhelming infections complicated by coagulation defects and renal (kidney) failure.[129] Another woman choked to death on bloody vomit (fully 50% of all PGF2α abortions cause vomiting[130]). The other unfortunate women died of anmiotic fluid embolism/water intoxication/cardiac arrest, respiratory arrest after injection of a pain-killing drug, bleeding in the brain after a hypertensive crisis, and heart failure possibly due to pulmonary embolism. The doctors reporting these deaths warn that the use of PGF2α for a second-trimester abortion creates risks of both morbidity and death.[129]

The Upjohn company, which manufactures abortifacient prostaglandins, knows about the complications that take lives, but somehow the knowledge of this threat doesn't always reach the woman before she makes her choice. The package insert accompanying PGF2α warns against its use in hypertensive patients; warns that it can cause a hypertensive crisis which in turn causes bleeding in the brain and death. Because of the painful labor (contractions of the uterus resulting from PGF2α) there is *often* a need for intravenous narcotics which, in turn, can cause a fatal respiratory arrest. PGF2α can also cause cardiac arrhythmia; two confirmed deaths have occurred from sudden cardiac arrest at the time of instillation, and at least four cases of myocardial infarction associated with the use of PGE2 suppositories have been reported, two of which were fatal. [131, 294]

36

Prostaglandin may not be safer than other methods of late abortion.[294]

According to the Center For Disease Control, the manufacturer of prostaglandin agents recommends they be used only in a fully equipped hospital. One doctor's disregard of this warning may have contributed to his patient's death.

At 35, Aliza* was married and the mother of several children. Two months after having x-rays of her gall bladder (which were normal) she learned from her doctor she was two months pregnant. Although no one could know for sure whether she had even been pregnant when the x-rays were taken, she was counseled on the potential risk to the preborn of x-ray exposure. She elected to terminate her pregnancy, but for unknown reasons delayed four weeks.

The author, having endured that same "counseling" from a physician following x-rays in early pregnancy, can attest to its effective impact in frightening a woman into a possibly unwanted abortion. The author has experienced that conflict of emotions and agony of indecision which must affect any woman who has borne children, felt them move within her, been part of that unique intimacy uniting a mother and her preborn child, and who has been pressured into believing that this little one within her now isn't worth saving and should be aborted. Aliza's delay can easily be understood as the natural reluctance of a mother to abandon her nurturing role and consent to the destruction of a child her every instinct insists needs special protection and care.

In the doctor's office, 15 weeks pregnant, Aliza was prepared for intraamniotic instillation of prostaglandin F2α. Within five minutes of instillation she became nauseous and vomited. A few minutes later she collapsed. Unconscious and with no pulse she was given CPR and rushed to a nearby emergency room. There, for 90 minutes, they tried to resuscitate her.

Intensive efforts to save her life continued that day and the next, but Aliza was unaware even of the birth-by-abortion when it happened on the second hospital day. She was eventually transferred to a university general hospital but her condition never improved; five months elapsed before she died. Autopsy attributed death to a pulmonary embolus, and brain damage due to lack of oxygen. Sudden collapse is a serious and totally unpredictable consequence of abortifacient prostaglandin use.[24]

37

One cannot help but draw a comparison between Aliza's experience and that of the author. Two mothers in the same age group were counseled by doctors to abort preborns supposedly endangered by exposure to x-rays. The one who chose abortion lost her own life as well. The one who chose life, lives. Knowledge of the dangers of legal abortion may save lives by enabling women to judge abortion too unsafe a risk. When a woman can connect with her community's considerable resources of concern and support in carrying a crisis pregnancy, she need not feel so socially aborted that she will submit to lethal surgery.

HYSTERECTOMY AND HYSTEROTOMY

A problem exists in choosing the method of second trimester abortion. On the one hand, both saline and prostaglandin are labor-inducing and will subject women to a transient additional cardiac (heart) stress.[129] On the other hand, the surgical methods aren't risk-free either. The death rate inherent in hysterectomy abortion is one hundred times greater than for first-trimester abortions, by analysis of 446,052 legal abortions.[296]

Even women who have hysterotomy (a mini-cesarean section) aren't safe; a team of doctors reported two deaths among 171 terminations by vaginal hysterotomy and one death out of 69 women undergoing abdominal hysterotomy.[28] One death that occurred during a hysterotomy was caused by heart failure;[65] another woman died of pulmonary embolism.[123]

Hattie* developed disseminated intravascular coagulation within three hours of hysterotomy; during the next 24 hours she received 23 units of blood. Hattie lingered eight days before dying.[65]

Loretta*, a 26-year-old social worker who was 19 weeks pregnant, had a hysterotomy abortion; chronic pelvic inflammatory disease was encountered. Peritonitis developed and Loretta died despite massive antibiotic therapy.[51]

Lewanda*, 42, had her hysterotomy at 12 weeks gestation; she died in a coma of cardiac arrest and pulmonary edema.[126]

Twenty-five-year-old Gretta's* 18 week pregnancy was ended by hysterotomy. The complications that took her life included mitral insufficiency, ventricular fibrillation and anesthesia reaction.[126]

ABORTION AND STERILIZATION

Deaths related to legal abortion have risen steadily with the rising number of abortions performed since legalization. Mortality was nine times higher for abortions with sterilization than for those without. This high death rate bears upon the fact that in almost two-thirds of abortions with sterilizations, either hysterotomy or hysterectomy was required. Whenever possible, these surgical procedures should be avoided, as they significantly increase the risk of the abortion.[118]

OTHER FACTORS INFLUENCING
THE DANGER OF LEGAL ABORTION

LOCATION

Legal abortions can be performed in hospitals, doctors' offices, storefront clinics, anywhere an abortionist decides to set up shop. There are no regulations controlling or even guiding the circumstances under which first trimester abortions are performed—nor can there be, as long as the Supreme Court decisions of 1973 stand. Within two years of those infamous decisions, nonhospital facilities emerged as the principal providers of abortion services in the United States, raising important questions concerning their safety.

Some critics of nonhospital abortion facilities have speculated that, because they lack blood banks, staff skilled in resuscitation and surgical facilities to deal with emergencies, the risk of death and serious morbidity may be substantially higher in nonhospital settings.

Documented or suspected pulmonary emboli, reactions to anesthesia and heart failure accounted for most of the deaths among hospital patients in one comparative study; in the nonhospital group infection and reactions to pain killers predominated. Besides these four, hemorrhage was common to both groups as a cause of death: in each group one abortion patient bled to death despite the availability of blood for the woman in the hospital.

Inadequate resuscitation equipment may contribute to the greater number of anesthesia and analgesia deaths outside of hospital facilities.[231]

TIMING

Timing is unquestionably a factor affecting the safety and mortality rate of legal abortions. Timing is important in terms of the gestational age of the preborn, the duration of the abortion itself, and the delay in followup.

The older the preborn gets, the larger s/he becomes, and the more difficult to remove through the fiber-thin cervix. Within six weeks features emerge, and the ten week old preborn is a recognizable, if rudimentary, human. The relative risk of dying approximately doubles for each two week delay after eight weeks of gestation.[271] In a two year period eight women died from D&E abortions performed after the 12th week of pregnancy.[275]

If too much time elapses after the initiation of the procedure, there is an increased danger of hemorrhage and infection plus an increased possibility that more dramatic, radical methods of termination will need to be employed. On the other hand, if abortion is brought about too rapidly, an added incidence of mechanical disruption of uterine tissue is likely plus an increased risk of heavy bleeding;[267] there are doctors who, instead of taking the fifteen minutes necessary, execute suction abortions in an excruciating two minutes. Other doctors fail to allow ample time for pain-killing drugs to take effect.[241]

In one study 43% of the abortion deaths occurred on the day of abortion, 4% on the second postabortion day, 22% on the third, and 30% thereafter. Earlier patient followup and prompt intervention during the critical period from the time of induction to three days afterward might prevent many of the more serious complications. Routine contact of all women within several days prompts early detection of pelvic infection, thromboembolic disease, and other dangerous conditions.[231]

LAMINARIA

A number of abortionists have begun inserting laminaria (seaweed) into the cervix about 24 hours prior to the abortion; as the laminaria expand, the cervix (hopefully) will be opened gradually and without damage. This tedious treatment is not always successful; sometimes forced opening of the cervix is necessary anyhow; sometimes other complications develop. One team of doctors reported the deaths of four women out of 128 legal abortions using laminaria tents.[28]

40

ANESTHESIA

The rich supply of blood around the uterus during pregnancy facilitates the absorption and toxic effect of locally-injected anesthetics. Among 74 women killed by legal abortions, complications of anesthesia ranked third among the causes of death; paracervical anesthesia used for first trimester abortion claimed these five lives:[90]

Letitia*, a 21-year-old mother, chose to undergo abortion at 12 weeks gestation. For anesthesia, the doctor injected epinephrine-free lidocaine to produce a paracervical block. Before cervical dilatation could begin, the woman convulsed several times and her heart stopped. Resuscitation failed to revive her.

Michelle*, an 18-year-old with no known allergies, underwent suction abortion at 10 weeks. The procedure was uneventful until, near the end, she convulsed twice and died.

Cheryl*, a mother of four in her twenties, went to her local clinic for suction abortion of an eight week pregnancy; within seconds of injection of the anesthetic she reported not feeling well. Complaining of being cold and short of breath, she became agitated and pale and had involuntary twitching of her face and arms. As her blood pressure fell she began coughing up blood. She was transferred to a local hospital where she died the next day.

Seventeen-year-old Liza* had a suction abortion in a doctor's office at 12 weeks of pregnancy; when the doctor injected lidocaine paracervically, Liza went into convulsions. Despite external cardiac massage, she was dead on arrival at a nearby hospital.[132]

Justine*, a 29-year-old mother of two, nine weeks pregnant, died suddenly of respiratory arrest during a suction curettage. Blood pressure had become unobtainable shortly after intravenous administration of anesthetic. Resuscitative efforts failed.[51]

Two women are known to have died of oxygen starvation during abortions due to improperly administered anesthetic.[113]

Most deaths from paracervical anesthesia used during legal abortion are due to physician error[231], again proving that when it comes to abortion, legal does not mean safe.

UNSCRUPULOUS LEGAL ABORTIONISTS

Washington, D. C. doctor R. J. S. agreed to a half-million dollar out-of-court settlement after admitting his negligence caused the death of a 16-year-old patient. Rita McD. died of blood poisoning and shock about four days after he performed an incomplete abortion on her, a practice repeated *deliberately* on Medicaid patients as a means of raising the bill.

This abortionist apparently placed as little value on the lives of his patients as they did on the lives of their preborns: the medical licensing board revoked his license for allowing a semi-literate assistant to perform surgery on women with unsanitary instruments reused so often that the tips of them were broken off. Conditions in the clinic failed cleanliness standards: in some cases dirty cotton swabs were put back into a bottle to be reused.

The investigating commission found that young Rita died because her doctor used an under-sized suction device which could not sufficiently remove all parts of the preborn; the tissue remaining in her womb became infected.[114] Rita's fatal experience demonstrates that legalization of abortion is powerless to prevent an unsuspecting girl from becoming the victim of an unskilled abortionist working in unsanitary facilities.

Another prominent profiteering legal abortionist has been arrested at least 16 times. Following numerous malpractice suits, the insurance coverage of Dr. M. V. was cancelled resulting in his personal payment of a substantial out-of-court settlement following the death of one of his patients—a teenager who went into a coma during the course of a legal abortion and was left unattended for 12 hours. She was pronounced dead on arrival at a nearby hospital.[115]

PHYSICIAN AND PATIENT ERROR

What determines who will die from a legal abortion? Fate? Chance? Neglect? It is certain that cooperation between doctor and patient can reduce the opportunities for fatalities to occur. Both must do their part to ensure the safety of the operation and the health of the woman.

In performing saline-amniotic fluid exchange, as with any other minor surgery, rigorous attention must be given to sterile procedure. For her part, the woman must be honest with her physician, prompt in reporting what may be serious symptoms, and thoroughly precise in giving her medical history. Failure to take these precautions led to the death of a girl within days of her eighteenth birthday.[228] Here is a chronological account of Lisa's story:

Day 1—Lisa* is admitted to an out-of-state hospital for termination of a 16 week pregnancy by saline-amniotic fluid exchange. Unknown to her, the doctor's methods are slightly different than his colleagues'—minor differences which eventually produce major disasters.

Day 2—After a labor lasting 22 hours she delivers; eight hours later Lisa develops a fever and is injected with an antibiotic.

Day 4—Lisa leaves the hospital with a temperature of 102⁰ and a prescription for an antibiotic.

Day 5—She returns to her home state and consults her local physician because of fever and generalized aching. Unaware of her recent abortion, this doctor gives Lisa an injection of penicillin.

Day 6—The fever persists and Lisa sees this doctor again; she receives a second injection.

Day 7—Returning to the doctor's office, Lisa complains of shaking chills; her temperature is 101⁰. Now she tells him of her recent abortion; hospitalization is recommended.

Day 8—Upon admission to the hospital Lisa's temperature is 106⁰ and she's in shock. Blood tests reveal a staph infection resistant to a variety of antibiotics including the penicillin she received from her local doctor. Vigorous treatment is begun in an effort to stabilize her condition.

Day 12—Despite all attempts to save her, Lisa dies.

An investigation was carried out in response to her death. Causes of fever included retained placenta and operative removal of it. Infection may have been introduced at the time of the abortion by: improper application of antiseptic solution to the anticipated puncture site; introduction of the amniocentesis needle through an unshaven or minimally prepped area; by laying down the syringe on a possibly contaminated towel; by exposure of the saline to room air or to other equipment previously used during the procedure.[228] Had the abortionist been more scrupulously attentive to sterile technique or had Lisa informed her family doctor of the abortion when she first saw him, this tragic death may have been averted.

CONDITIONS COMPLICATING PREGNANCY
Even for the woman with a condition complicating pregnancy, abortion may be a perilous choice that does more harm than good.

43

A doctor who left his hospital career in Denmark rather than submit to oppressive liberal abortion strictures, states that "After many years' work in several large gynecological hospitals, *I have never yet seen a woman's life in danger, necessitating an abortion.*" He goes on to say, "I have seen two extremely sick women offered abortions because of serious heart-lung disease; both refused, and both delivered normal children, normally. When a doctor declares that the patient's life is in danger because of a pregnancy and an associated disease, that is his clinical *opinion. There is no absolute indication for a legal abortion in such circumstances.*"[101]

Rhondine*, 23, was ten weeks pregnant when she had a suction curettage abortion in a hospital. She died of sickle cell anemia aggravated by surgery and possible infection.[136]

Twenty-year-old Pamela* was a blue-eyed brunette with a fragile, china-doll complexion, and a congenital heart ailment. Classically heart disease is considered to be a major risk factor for the development of thromboembolic disease. Because of her condition, an abortion by suction curettage with concurrent abdominal tubal ligation was performed in the eleventh week of gestation with the use of general anesthesia. The sterilization procedure was complicated by an inadvertent incision into her bladder which required suturing; post-operatively Pam received heparin (an anti-coagulant used to prevent embolism). Over the next twenty-four hours she suffered chest and dull epigastric pain. Because of abdominal bleeding, heparin therapy was stopped and an exploratory surgery was performed, to no avail. Her condition deteriorated through nausea, vomiting and chills until, five days after the abortion, she died.[113]

A woman known to have epilepsy was given oxytocin 10 hours after saline instillation; 26 hours later the membranes ruptured spontaneously. Although Claire* was in severe pain, delivery was uneventful. Manual removal of the afterbirth, however, was followed by convulsions and death.[227]

A 31-year-old mother with a fibroid uterus underwent hysterectomy abortion. Everything seemed fine until 5 p.m. on the sixth post-op day when she cried out with severe abdominal pain, vomited, and said she was blind; she had trouble breathing and went into a coma. Efforts to revive her failed and she died an hour later. Autopsy revealed paralytic ileus and enlargement of both large and small bowel; infection was rampant in her abdominal organs, lung and brain. Intestinal contents had entered her lungs and partially digested them.[111]

Certain renal diseases are thought to worsen in pregnancy and in one case a "therapeutic" abortion was advocated to "rescue the kidneys." Unfortunately for the 21-year-old girl who had mild lupus nephritis, even "therapeutic" abortions are not without risk of complications. Jill* underwent a saline abortion in the 19th week of pregnancy and within four hours was in a coma and bleeding internally. Subsequently she stopped breathing, received six units of whole blood and various other medications. The coma became progressively more profound and even delivery produced no improvement. Soon she was dead, her death classified as preventable. Her doctors now feel that even though there is a threat of lupus crisis in the first trimester, medication may get a woman through her pregnancy safely. They realize the threat of crisis at birth, but say that experience indicates that "interruption of pregnancy, always dangerous, is much more so for lupus patients, no matter how it is performed and no matter at what stage of gestation. The end of the pregnancy, whether premature or at term, can itself precipitate a crisis. It is preferable, therefore, and less traumatic, to manage the patient with increasing doses of steroids and allow the pregnancy to progress with the possibility of producing a living child." It is felt that saline abortion is particularly objectionable for lupus patients because of the heavy salt load that must be sustained in the face of circulatory and excretory mechanisms already seriously compromised.[125]

Other experiences such as this have led several specialists to list renal disease and/or hypertension as contraindications to saline abortion. [127, 128]

VERY EARLY ABORTIONS

The earlier, the safer, they say, but even very early abortions have been known to kill women.

Nancy,* just 16 years old and days away from cheerleader tryouts, was five weeks pregnant when her doctor inserted a rubber catheter into her uterus and packed it into place. She went home and returned the next day for removal and completion of abortion by sharp curettage. Two days later, complaining of chills, fever and severe pelvic pain, Nancy went to a hospital emergency room. Her blood pressure was low and her temperature slightly elevated; she had a thick, black-bloody discharge. Her condition was diagnosed as sepsis (infection—the thing that legal abortions are supposed to prevent) and endometritis. She was given antibiotics and discharged with instructions to seek followup help later. But within six hours she returned with severe chills, a higher fever, and a lowered heart rate. This time she was admitted and lab tests were made.

Nancy's temperature went up to 104.6°; four hours later she had no blood pressure and was sent to intensive care. After receiving six different antibiotics in less than 24 hours, the infection stopped—but pulmonary edema developed and her heart stopped; efforts to save her failed. Nancy died.

Her doctors now warn that there are disadvantages to catheter-placement abortion: the time until completion can vary from 16 hours to 15 days (giving infection ample opportunity to develop) and a second procedure is often necessary.[221] For a pretty cheerleader some might also consider untimely death a "disadvantage."

TEENAGERS
Teenage girls fall victim to the most alarming diversity of dangers and some of the most catastrophic complications of legal abortions.

MATERNAL MORTALITY AND MORBIDITY
WITH LEGAL ABORTION AXIOM:
The younger the patient
The greater the gestation
The higher the complication rate

E. T., age 19, died of a pulmonary air embolism after an instrumental intrauterine abortion at 20 weeks gestation.[126]

Fourteen-year-old Kelly* underwent saline abortion of a mid-term pregnancy. Because her uterus was incompletely emptied, she continued to bleed heavily after delivery and multiple sharp curettages had to be performed during which her uterus was perforated and the bowel torn. Despite repairs, Kelly died of peritonitis and septicemia twenty-two pain-filled days after her legal abortion.[51]

46

Mindy*, 18 and in the 14th week of pregnancy, had a saline abortion and despite a fever, was discharged from the hospital two days later. She was readmitted to a local hospital in four days, in shock and with a fever of 106°. Ten days after the abortion she was dead.[119]

Frances*, 16 years old, had a saline abortion at four months' pregnancy in a California hospital; delivery was delayed for 30 hours. Fever, blood poisoning and meningitis subsequently developed. She died of severe congestive heart failure and extensive bronchopneumonia.[119]

At age 18, H. McM. was fourteen weeks pregnant when she underwent a hospital D & C; she died following perforation of her uterus, peritonitis, hysterectomy and removal of both ovaries and fallopian tubes.[126]

Nineteen year old Holly* bled so briskly following suction curettage of a 10 week pregnancy that deep sutures were used through four quadrants of the cervix. When severe bleeding continued, a second curettage was done. Resuturing was necessary, as was uterine packing; six units of blood were given. The bleeding persisted and a hysterectomy was decided on but as the packing was being removed, Holly's heart stopped beating; external massage got it going again. Exploratory surgery was performed to discover the extent of the damage—a uterine artery had been cut. Her uterus was removed, but Holly suffered recurrent convulsions and died.[120]

Lynn*, age 19, went to her family doctor for severe abdominal pain and nausea the day after a legal suction abortion. Because her condition worsened, she was hospitalized the next day and found to be markedly anemic. As a result, exploratory abdominal surgery was performed and six pints of blood were found in her abdominal cavity along with a fully formed preborn three inches long, and a uterine perforation. Following surgery she stopped breathing and required surgical insertion of an airway through her throat. Other complications set in: collapsed lungs, consumption coagulopathy (a bleeding disorder) and a stroke. Even removal of her womb failed to stop the bleeding and 19 days after her "safe legal abortion" she died.[272]

According to documented reports, many teenage girls

47

undergo abortion needlessly as they were never pregnant to begin with. One such casualty was 18-year-old Vita* who underwent suction curettage for a suspected pregnancy of 8 weeks duration. Overwhelmed with guilt, believing she had killed her baby, she committed suicide three days later. The pathology report came too late; by laboratory findings, only her own body tissues had been removed. Vita never knew she hadn't been pregnant. She died for nothing.[51]

ECTOPIC PREGNANCIES

Unnatural termination of pregnancy can effect and affect ectopic pregnancy. First, it can cause the next preborn to implant outside of his/her natural habitat by making the womb unsuitable, or impossible to get to. Second, it can interfere with a diagnosis of ectopic pregnancy if the preborn to be removed isn't in the womb; after the procedure, this woman goes home still pregnant. Believing any pain or strangeness to be from the abortion, she goes about her business until the preborn, if in the fallopian tube, grows to such a size that the tube bursts, causing lethal hemorrhage.

While science may not yet have arrived at a complete understanding of how abortion effects ectopic pregnancies, it is sure of this: paralleling the rise in abortions in the past ten years has been a rise in the numbers of ectopic pregnancies, and the inevitable increase in the importance of ectopic pregnancy as a cause of death.[133] In one part of the country, an increase from one ectopic in 111 pregnancies to one in 76 took place between pre-legal-abortion days and the present. In another part of the country the rate increased from one in 222 to one in 88 in the same time span.[236]

It has further been suggested that large doses of estrogen, such as that contained in the morning-after pill, may increase the incidence of ectopic pregnancy. In reports of 29 pregnancies continuing as failures of the morning-after pill, there were 3 ectopic pregnancies—a tenfold increase over the expected rate.[230]

On June 2, 1975 the Commissioner of Health of New York City issued a letter to physicians that began, "Fatalities due to ruptured ectopic pregnancies have occurred . . . The possibility of an extrauterine pregnancy should always be considered when first trimester pregnancies are to be terminated."[270] In the average abortion clinic, where the waiting-room-treatment-room-recovery-room routine cranks out dozens of aborted women by the hour, and where people believe safety is achieved through legality, how many people are considering the possibility of extrauterine (outside of the womb) pregnancy?

The prompt and correct diagnosis of ectopic pregnancy is frequently difficult and abortion can compound this difficulty. Having had an abortion can create a hazard by delaying a woman from seeking medical care and by impeding a correct diagnosis of her condition.[133]

Kristin*, a 19-year-old mother of two whose last period had been nine weeks earlier, underwent a suction curettage abortion. Pelvic examination while under general anesthesia revealed her womb to be about eight weeks in size and no abnormalities were noticed; the abortion was uneventful. Kristin left the hospital the next day but returned that evening complaining of increasing weakness, shortness of breath, nausea and vomiting. She was examined in the emergency room, given medication, and sent away. About two hours after leaving she became agitated and complained of being unable to breathe. She died several minutes later. The pathology report on the abortion specimen revealed uterine changes consistent with pregnancy, but there were no fetal or placental parts. An autopsy revealed she had died of internal bleeding from a ruptured ectopic pregnancy.[133]

Twenty-six-year-old Sherry Emry died from massive internal bleeding resulting from a ruptured tubal pregnancy. She was found dead in her apartment following treatment at a Chicago abortion clinic. Had it not been for the corners cut in health care at that clinic, Sherry might be alive today.

That clinic is one of many that saves money on lab fees by throwing away tissue that should be sent for analysis. Pathological examination must be performed to determine whether fetal parts or other signs of pregnancy are present; if none appear, the doctor must conclude one of three things:

1. the woman was not, in fact, pregnant and has undergone an unnecessary operation
2. the abortion was incomplete and fetal parts are beginning to rot in her womb
3. the woman is suffering a life-threatening ectopic pregnancy and must be contacted immediately for observation and treatment.

An ectopic pregnancy occurs when the embryo settles down

in the fallopian tube (or some other unlikely spot) instead of in the womb; it can be fatal if undetected because as the little one grows, the tube bursts and the woman's abdominal area fills with blood. Victims of such abnormal pregnancies can quickly bleed to death.

In seven months of working at the clinic where Sherry's abortion was performed, an undercover investigator did not see any aborted tissue sent to pathologists. Medical experts say a pathological report that shows no evidence of pregnancy must be treated as a medical emergency; the woman must be tracked down and watched because of the danger of ectopic pregnancy. "It would be the grossest kind of malpractice," claims one director of surgical pathology, "to miss one ectopic pregnancy and one woman went home and bled to death . . . " One woman like Sherry Emry, a young, vibrant, independent business-woman from Indiana.

Sherry went to the clinic December 28, 1977 for an early abortion; she was back at a friend's apartment in time to catch the noon news. Three days later the pain began. The clinic had given her its standard sheet of instructions for postoperative care. Yes, it said, expect some cramps. It's OK, she told her friends. Just cramps; maybe a touch of flu. It was New Year's Eve, but Sherry went to bed early.

By January 2, she couldn't walk. Friends tried to persuade her to see a doctor, but she believed she'd get better. She slept fitfully, sweating one minute, shivering the next. Her knees ached, her stomach ached, every part of her hurt. On the second day of 1978, tough, proud Sherry Emry died. [112, 253]

Women are not powerless to improve their chances of surviving an ectopic pregnancy complicated by a legal abortion; the following demonstrates the need for cooperation and communication between woman and doctor:

Malissa* was 24, her pregnancy test was positive, and physical examination showed her uterus to be about ten weeks pregnant in size. She had a suction curettage abortion and went home. But the pathology report, returned after her discharge, revealed only parts of her own body had been removed—the abortion had failed. An attempt was made to contact her, but her phone had been disconnected. Five days later she died at home; her right fallopian tube had ruptured. [133]

Could her death have been prevented? Probably. The presence of fetal tissue should be confirmed after each abortion;

a woman must know this finding has been made, otherwise the likelihood is that the attempted abortion failed to disturb the preborn, or s/he wasn't in the womb and remains somewhere inside the woman.

CONCURRENT INTRAUTERINE AND ECTOPIC PREGNANCY

Sometimes a woman may have both an intrauterine and an ectopic pregnancy at the same time. After an abortion, a woman in this position may be fooled into believing that she is no longer pregnant. Pain, nausea, difficulty in breathing or other distress and signs of pregnancy after an abortion may be signals that something is very wrong.[133] In such cases there should be no delay in seeking medical attention. Make them listen to you; don't placidly accept their polite prescription (as a previously mentioned victim did) when your body is crying for help.

THE RISING DEATH RATE

In America it's common knowledge that more women died annually from illegal abortions than from legal abortions before the 1973 Supreme Court decisions legalizing abortion throughout pregnancy. But the decline in illegal abortion deaths has been offset by a *persistent rise* in deaths associated with *legal* termination of pregnancy. There appears to be current evidence of at least as many fatalities after legal as illegal abortions.[118] According to the Center For Disease Control, in every year since abortion was legalized, more women have been killed by legal abortions than by illegal—as many as seven times more known deaths have been caused by legal abortions, and the true total may be even higher! The known total is kept low, says CDC, by selective underreporting of legal abortion deaths in the most recent years.[116]

THE VALIDITY OF COMPARISONS TO CHILDBIRTH

You may have heard that "abortion is safer than childbirth." This is a highly effective advertising slogan, but a poor representation of fact. While there are certain maladies associated with pregnancy, and the natural termination of pregnancy, these are the results of some disease process. The pregnant woman carrying to term in a natural state has the advantage of being seen at regular intervals by a doctor who is looking for problems. The pregnant woman who opts for forced

51

termination, on the other hand, places herself into an unnatural situation; she is seen briefly by non-professionals, and a doctor who does not know her and who is not looking for problems.

What concerns *you* is, what are *your* chances of dying from a legal abortion (or childbirth)? The distinction between these two unpleasant possibilities is clear, striking, and significant: the overwhelming majority of women who die from a legal abortion are perfectly healthy before their lethal surgery; in carrying their pregnancies to term few—if any—would die. But most maternal childbirth deaths occur within a very small group of high-risk patients.[306] Those women who died in childbirth died from a disease process—an abnormality in the pregnancy/childbirth experience which for some reason could not be adequately treated. *No valid comparison can be made between two so entirely different classes of pregnant women: one group healthy and the other group diseased.* The death of a healthy woman from a legal abortion is totally preventable simply by not aborting; furthermore, as shown in the section on Conditions Complicating Pregnancy, this also holds true for very many women with health problems.

Unfortunately, the death from childbearing of that woman with a disorder is mostly unpreventable because of medical inability to understand or control the disease process which takes her life. What this means to *you* is that allowing *your pregnancy* to follow its *natural course* is probably more healthful and *more free of risk* than unnatural, forceful, surgical intrusion into your body and its natural processes.

CONCLUSIONS

In an attempt to learn how pervasive the problem of serious abortion complications is, an American obstetrician surveyed 486 of his colleagues regarding their experience with abortion patients. 87% revealed they had hospitalized women with complications following legal abortions; 91% had treated patients for complications. Twenty-nine of the doctors reported patients of theirs dying from legally-induced abortions.[103]

This problem is world wide. In England and Wales abortion remains the most common cause of death associated with pregnancy.[118]

"There has been no major impact on the number of women dying from abortion in the United States since liberalized abortion was introduced . . . Legal abortion is now the leading cause of abortion-related maternal deaths in the United States."[261]

Protection of the health of women is an interest of the highest individual and social priority. Emergency wards and cemeteries bear dismal testimony to the fact that adverse reactions to routine procedures may arise from any individual case.

4

EARLY COMPLICATIONS

These particular consequences occur or begin during the abortion or immediately afterward, while the woman is still under medical supervision.

ABDOMINAL CRAMPS are experienced in degrees varying from mild to unbearably severe; in one study six women complained of cramps sufficiently painful to require treatment.[134] In a group of suction curettage abortions four women reported cramping and bleeding lasting longer than two weeks after the abortion.[277] Painful uterine cramping, severe enough for the patient to request pain killers for relief, was seen in 10% of both prostaglandin-treated groups (20 women in each group received PGF2α or PGE2 suppositories prior to suction abortions).[297]

ABDOMINAL SURGERY may be necessary to detect the cause of hemorrhage[8, 113, 120, 122, 219] or to remove a laminaria tent (seaweed used to dilate the cervix).[42] Laminaria become soft as they take up moisture and they sometimes fail to dilate the cervix properly, although they may swell up around it. In an hourglass shape, with the cervix in the middle, removal of the tent is quite difficult.[285] (See Unintended Major Surgery)

ABORTION OF ONLY ONE TWIN: the surviving baby is born normally months later.[15, 16]

ALLERGY: In one study three women had drug rash reactions following suction abortions.[134]

AMNESIA classified as a major complication has occurred following legal abortion.[65]

ANESTHESIA COMPLICATIONS: The use of anesthesia for any operation increases the risk of complications from that procedure. A recent randomized clinical trial demonstrated that local cervical anesthesia was associated with complication rates resembling those of general anesthesia. Similarly, another recent study observed that major complication rates associated with suction curettage under general—or local—anesthesia were not significantly different.[271]

These symptoms and signs have been reported following syringe and needle injections of paracervical blocks: generalized convulsions with and without respiratory arrest, athetoid movements (slow, irregular, twisting, snakelike movements of the upper extremities, especially hands and fingers), shaking, muscle fibrillation, respiratory distress, hypotension, hypertension, collapse, palpitations, pallor, flushing, faintness, feelings of apprehension, headache, dizziness and disturbances of vision.[155] Anesthesia complications were experienced by 132 women undergoing all types of abortions in a one year study.[64]

ANTIBIOTIC RISKS: A number of experienced abortionists advocate antibiotic administration routinely after abortions.[134] But according to an article in the *New England Journal of Medicine,* "Overuse of antibiotics drives up medical costs, increases the number of drug-resistant bacteria and adds to the amount of negative reactions to medication."[299] Still other experts "think that antibiotics tend to increase the incidence of vaginal infection and other minor complications secondary to drug therapy and help to build immunity against antibiotic effectiveness when they are specifically needed."[167]

ASPIRATION PNEUMONIA can result from an anesthetic accident.[5]

ATELECTASIS: a collapsed or airless condition of the lung; sometimes a complication following abdominal operations such as hysterotomy or hysterectomy abortions or emergency exploratory surgery (laparotomy) which may be necessary to deal with certain complications and which may or may not include removal of the reproductive organs. In one case it followed surgery which revealed a rip in the womb of a woman who had undergone a prostaglandin abortion in the 14th week of pregnancy.[259]

BACTERIAL INVASION OF THE URINARY SYSTEM can mar all types of abortions; in one study urinary tract infections were reported in 109 women after suction abortion, in 6 following D&C, in 103 after hysterectomy, 84 after saline, and 44 from hysterotomy.[63]

BIRTH OF A LIVING CHILD DURING AN ABORTION: Leela* was 28 and in good health, before her abortion. The suction bypassed her womb and attacked her internally, inducing indescribable injuries. She was rushed to a hospital where doctors worked feverishly to repair their ravaged patient. Subsequently, the womb was opened and then reclosed after removing the preborn, who was alive.[6]

According to doctors at the Center For Disease Control, the infant aborted alive "has become one of the most difficult medical, legal and ethical problems associated with midtrimester abortion." The dilemma stems from the fact that abortion merely intends to remove the infant from its rejecting mother; forced termination does *not* invariably result in the death of the aborted baby and long-term survivors are not unknown.[271]

Saline and prostaglandin abortions, particularly in pregnancies of more than 18 weeks duration, have resulted in the premature births of living infants.[267]

"It is not too unusual that a pregnancy turns out to be four weeks more advanced than would be determined by the given dates. A number of 28 week gestations have been salted-out, resulting in the birth of living children. The emotional distress engendered is horrendous."[230] Living infants have been discharged from hospitals having to be classified as live births rather than as abortions.[82]

This occurred at least 86 times in New York City alone within only two years [83, 84] and there were 1,802 more babies delivered alive by hysterotomy who subsequently died of exposure.[85] The birth of a living child has been known to occur from a saline abortion even when her twin was "successfully aborted" (killed).[214]

In a single locale, scrupulous records kept over a five month period revealed 27 births-by-abortion—not a single month went by without at least one; and as many as *three babies a day*

57

weighing up to 3 lbs. 6 oz. were delivered alive from legal abortions.[136]

Of 36 live births following induced abortions in upstate New York, 9 followed hysterotomy and 27 saline or urea. "Viable infants with iatrogenic (physician-caused) central nervous system damage from salt poisoning are a possible consequence of improperly planned saline-induced abortions." [135, 271] Preborns delivered by hysterotomy or aborted by prostaglandin are more likely to be alive and to have a better chance of long-term survival.[271]

Under the Court rulings legalizing abortion, a woman has a legal right to become unpregnant; however, her rights may not avert motherhood. "The Supreme Court offered no guidance on how to treat the fetus once out of the womb."[292] Granting even the most broad interpretation of Roe and Doe, explains one expert, a woman's "new-found constitutional right of privacy is fulfilled" when the preborn is out of her body. "If an infant survives the abortion, there is hardly an additional right of privacy to then have him or her killed or harmed in any way . . . "[291]

On the very day their 1973 opinion was handed down, a baby was living in California who had been born at only five and one half months gestation, weighing just one pound and 13 ounces. He had been born 21 days earlier, so young their decision held that a preborn of that age would not have even "the potentiality of human life." The Court's arbitrary assessment of viability was at variance with the facts of life—Aldies Patterson III's life.

A number of states have adopted laws requiring proper medical attention for abortion survivors. Once the baby is out of her body, he or she is out of the mother's control—legally, a live born person with rights of her/his own, including the right to be resuscitated, to be fed, and to live his own life. From Massachusetts to California legal abortionists have been brought to trial for murder charged with killing babies in these circumstances; not many doctors today are going to risk their careers over this! The only way a woman can be assured her baby will be legally dead to her is by placing him or her for adoption. State-licensed agencies have professional counsellors who can help a woman discover if this decision is right for her. Thorough consideration should be given to this option.

Nola and Anders had no qualms about abortion; on the other hand, they hadn't experienced it. They were on equal footing in their marriage and made decisions together, so Anders was supportive when Nola's boss told her to abort the pregnancy or quit her job. Neither could have imagined at that time that Nola would eventually lose the job because of abortion-related illness.

In a doctor's office two rubber catheters were inserted into her womb and Nola was told to go home and get into bed; within twelve hours she should start feeling some pain and then she should sit on the toilet and flush the discharge. "Nothing to it, right?" Nola says, lighting another of the cigarettes she chainsmokes. "Only it didn't work out that way."

She alternates between firing her words off in a rapid staccato and long, drawn-out, dewy-eyed pauses. "I was lying down on the sofa, trying to relax. The kids were here, sitting on the floor, watching TV. All of a sudden, blarp! This huge gush, blood all over the place. I tried to move, but I couldn't. Right there, right there in front of me—in front of the kids, for God's sake—this little baby. Alive. I could see his heart beating. A little boy baby.

"Anders didn't know which way to go. The kids were screaming, I was screaming. I think he shut them up in the powder room. I couldn't touch it, but I couldn't stop looking at it. Its heart was beating until, slowly, it stopped. I didn't know it would be like that. Nobody told me it was a baby."

Nola was taken by ambulance to a nearby hospital where doctors worked feverishly to stop the hemorrhaging. Surgery, although indicated, was impossible due to shock. A month of bed-rest followed her lengthy hospitalization. Today Nola has recovered physically, but emotionally the entire family remains affected. All are involved in a counseling program and Nola, who never returned to her job, works part time as a volunteer at an emergency pregnancy service, sharing her story with women who are trying to sort out their fears from their knowledge and arrive at a decision they can live with.

BLADDER DAMAGE: Helen*, 27, had a suction abortion in the twelfth week of her pregnancy. Although the abortionist had a very difficult time, she was taken to the recovery room in satisfactory condition. But before long Helen went into shock; a foley catheter released grossly bloody urine. Exploratory surgery showed her bladder had three holes in it and her uterus had been damaged beyond repair. The bladder lacerations were closed and the womb removed. It's likely that the uterus was perforated at the time of dilatation; then when the suction curette was inserted, it passed through the uterus and into the bladder. Thinking back, the abortionist recalled a sudden rush of clear yellow fluid during suction—he had emptied the contents, not of the uterus, but of the bladder![137]

Forty-one-year-old Gail's* hysterotomy abortion was complicated by gashes of her uterus and bladder. The damage was so great her womb had to be removed and the bladder reconstructed; it ended up less than half its original size.[265]

BLEEDING: A certain amount of bleeding is to be expected from any type of forced intervention in pregnancy. An analysis of 71 abortions by PGE2 suppositories showed that "vaginal bleeding occurred" and blood clots had to be removed prior to each insertion of the drug (at 2 hour intervals). Ten women suffered blood loss in excess of 250 ml. and "in five cases vaginal bleeding became so profuse that the . . . suppository was washed out of the vagina."[296]

BLOOD PRESSURE DECREASE always occurs in hemorrhage and is a problem in itself. A sudden fall in blood pressure can considerably complicate a legal abortion.[215]

BLOOD TRANSFUSIONS: The need to have blood transfusions is classified as a major complication which affected 277 women during a one year study,[64] exposing them to the dangers of serum hepatitis, allergic reactions, virus infections or postoperative kidney or lung complications.

Blood is sometimes given even when it's not necessary. One group of abortionists who made this a routine practice following their procedures said, "It occurred to us that we were using blood transfusion as a prophylactic method in some cases to prevent a low hemoglobin level upon discharge and were risking all the inherent problems associated with transfusion." They have abandoned this practice and now give iron supplements which "provide a healthier outcome with fewer possible complications."[167]

BOWEL MAY BE SUCKED OUT: "The ribs and spinal column develop from cartilage cells, which begin to be replaced by bone cells at about the ninth week." When the preborn is twelve

60

weeks old, "the substitution of bone for cartilage in the long bones of the arms and legs is well under way."[35] When suction abortion is attempted after 12 weeks gestation firm fetal parts may block the tube and accidental perforation of the uterus may not be readily recognized.[37]

"When the New York State law on abortion was liberalized in July 1970, Women's Lib movements claimed that suction abortion was so safe and so easy that even paramedical personnel could perform it in a minute. This, of course, is a dangerous untruth," says a doctor whose elation at the legalization soon plummeted to deep concern. "In the event of unsuspected uterine perforation, the operator may readily advance the suction tube into the peritoneal cavity. The heavy attached suction cord prevents good tactile sensation and the high negative pressure immediately sucks delicate bowel into the tube. This is not a rare syndrome," he emphasizes. "If the operator does not recognize the bowel in the specimen and does not do an immediate laparotomy, the patient may shortly be near death."[230]

BOWEL OBSTRUCTION complicated the abortions of 29 women in one group studied.[64]

BRAIN DAMAGE: Cases of permanent brain damage have been reported following the use of intra-amniotic hypertonic saline.[34] This is due to seepage of the deadly saline into the bloodstream where it is carried to the brain and does to the woman what should have been done only to the preborn.

BREAST ENGORGEMENT: This uncomfortable reminder of pregnancy can last for days or weeks after an abortion. [141, 277] The body's natural offering at the end of pregnancy, breast milk, may flow for some period of time.[218]

BURNS: A woman undergoing suction curettage and having her tubes tied at the same time, suffered second-degree skin burns from the wound disinfectant used on her.[143]

CARDIOVASCULAR EFFECTS: 30 of 71 women (42%) who had abortions by prostaglandin E2 suppositories experienced heart rate increases of "30 beats per minute or higher, and 7 patients had a heart rate of 120 b.p.m. There was in general a mean (average) decrease in systolic and diastolic blood pressure of 10 mm. Hg. In 9 patients the diastolic blood pressure dropped more than 20 mm. Hg and in 7 of these patients the diastolic pressure dropped to 40 mm. Hg."[296]

CERVICAL ADHESIONS and STENOSIS (constriction or narrowing of the opening of the cervix) are potential complications of vaginal abortions because the cervix resists being opened; its nature is to remain tightly closed until the natural termination of pregnancy. In artificially ending the pregnancy, force must be used to gain entry to the womb. Some instruments used in dilatation require greater force than others; this, and a lack of control "may account, in part, for incidences of cervical injury reported as high as 4.8 per 100 abortions."[271]

CERVICAL DETACHMENT: Not a cut or laceration, but actual separation and eventual loss of the cervix can occur. Twenty-six-year-old Emily*, mother of one child, was 18 weeks pregnant when she chose to be injected with urea in dextrose and water plus PGF2α; 24 hours later oxytocin was also given. After 31 hours of labor she delivered; curettage with local anesthesia was performed after two hours to remove the afterbirth.

Two weeks later, with a fever and having had cramps for two days, Emily went for an examination which revealed endometritis and partial detachment of the cervix. The amazed doctor gave her antibiotics but did nothing for the condition of the cervix; he discharged her four days later. However, due to a recurrence of fever, she was readmitted in three days for more antibiotics and a repeat curettage. At this time the lip of the cervix had sloughed off. Emily's third hospitalization lasted five days. An examination six weeks after the original procedure revealed the absence of most of the cervix.[222]

"Future childbearing may be impaired following such injuries." It is known that preborns of women with this problem who are not taken by cesarean section, deliver prematurely and die.[222]

CERVICAL LACERATION: Dilatation of the cervix (forcing open the passage to the womb) is difficult because it's unnatural. Cervical muscle keeps this passage tightly closed, protecting the womb and its inhabitant.

To gain access to the preborn's natural environment a series of gradually larger rods is pushed through the cervix which is sometimes held fast by a hooklike, toothed grasping instrument called a tenaculum. The intensity of this assault may result in the tearing of muscle fibers by the dilators; or the tenaculum counter-traction necessitated by the force required for dilatation may cause laceration of the cervix.[297] One team of doctors observed, "The single-toothed tenaculum *frequently* pulled through the cervix during dilatation and evacuation."[305]

15% of women in one study, and 20% of women who had received PGE2 suppositories to ease cervical dilatation, suffered tenaculum tears. One of the women in the former group was sutured because of persistent bleeding.[297]

Tenacula tears require direct pressure or suturing to control bleeding. Dilators tend to cause more serious lacerations which may extend into the blood supply of the womb causing heavy bleeding; occasionally removal of the womb may be necessary.[271]

"Cervical laceration is probably the most worrisome complication. Despite immediate repair, breakdown is not uncommon."[267] These injuries are reported in virtually every group of abortions: one study shows 533 women affected—495 from suction, 26 from D&C, and 12 from saline[64]; another indicates 39 out of 812 vacuum or D&C abortions and "in a further 3 damage occurred during expulsion of a mid-trimester fetus." Two vaginal terminations causing lacerations of the cervix also caused severe hemorrhage necessitating hysterectomy. For a single girl or a young married woman pregnant for the first time, damage making removal of the womb necessary would be a major catastrophe.[21]

Other studies report damage in 17 women after first trimester abortions,[28] in 87 women[139] and in one of every eight girls aborting a first pregnancy.[30]

Analysis showed 73% of the cervical lacerations occurred in *women pregnant for the first time* suggesting that more force is used to dilate the cervix in these patients[134]; they are at the greatest risk for spontaneous miscarriage or premature delivery of their next pregnancies. Further investigation has shown laceration of the cervix the most frequent complication, affecting 22% of aborters.[144]

"The rate of cervical laceration in the urea-prostaglandin group is certainly of some concern. Five of the six lacerations" occurred in women who had never had a child before; one 5 cm laceration was "noted to be broken down three days after abortion, when the patient was readmitted with endometritis. At

---

5 cm

---

subsequent followup, some healing had occurred, though a significant amount of scarring remained . . . Unfortunately many reported series have not included routine cervical inspection . . . In our series, despite routine examination, one case of cervical laceration went undetected until followup . . . These findings madate careful routine speculum and digital exploration of the lower genital tract after mid-trimester abortion . . . "[141]

This type of injury is most damaging because: it may go unrecognized until the woman becomes suddenly shocked from blood loss,[308] it's a prime cause of subsequent cervical incompetence, it can impair reproductive capabilities, and may bring about premature delivery and low birthweight in babies conceived subsequently.

211 women who had had vaginal abortions of their first pregnancies "and were pregnant again were investigated. . . . Among 11 women whose cervices had been lacerated at the time of legal termination the fetal loss in subsequent pregnancy was 45.5% and only one pregnancy went beyond 36 weeks . . . and only 5 infants survived." When compared to another group of pregnant women whose first pregnancies had ended in spontaneous abortion (miscarriage), there were "significantly more" first and second trimester miscarriages and premature deliveries "in the termination group than in the spontaneous abortion group."[281]

CERVICAL LESION: In a comparison study between a group of women who had aborted their first pregnancies and women who had carried first pregnancies to term, a trend was noticed "toward earlier spontaneous onset of labor" in the second pregnancy of the women who had previously aborted. "If a cervical lesion (caused by that abortion) is the factor responsible for this trend and for the increased frequency of late spontaneous abortion (miscarriage) and premature delivery, one would expect a higher rate of primary as well as premature rupture of the membranes. Primary rupture of the membranes, defined as an interval of six hours or more between this event

64

and the onset of labor pains, *was more frequent* in the study group than in the other group . . . the difference was highly significant."[260]

CERVICOVAGINAL FISTULA: One of the disadvantages of laminaria tents has been "the formation of false cervical passages."[297] But they aren't the only cause of this damage. Saline and prostaglandin-induced midtrimester abortions can produce serious cervical trauma, as manifested by formation of cervicovaginal fistulas.[275]

When the cervix fails to open simultaneously with the development of strong uterine contractions, and these powerful contractions are forcing the preborn's head against an unopened cervix, she may be pushed out of her mother through the back or side of the cervix.

In one study four women undergoing saline abortions manifested this complication.[275] Cervicovaginal fistula has been reported as frequently as 1 in 100 cases[146]; another hospital noted a tenfold increase following prostaglandin abortion compared to saline.[271]

Leslie,* seventeen years old, was 16 weeks pregnant; she had saline instillation and immediate oxytocin after two laminaria tents had been inserted to facilitate opening the cervix. Cramping began after 9 hours and delivery occurred 21½ hours after infusion; the placenta came two hours later. Leslie subsequently developed a fever of 101° and a pelvic exam 7 hours later revealed the fistula. Although laminaria tents effectively dilated her cervix, the dilatation was inadequate in not preventing the formation of the fistula. Her doctors now recommend mandatory cervical inspection after midtrimester abortion.[217]

In numerous instances this problem goes unrecognized: 3 out of 4 have not been detected at the first pelvic examination after abortion. Some bleed and need repair at the time of abortion but most recur immediately or during subsequent pregnancy. Since many *are* small and undetected, women who have had midtrimester abortions "should be carefully followed" during subsequent pregnancy. Women in whom this condition goes unnoticed "are predisposed to future obstetric difficulty. Other complications include pain, bleeding, painful sexual intercourse and permanent fistulas despite multiple surgical repairs." [146, 217]

CHILLS: In a group of 71 women "five patients complained of shaking and chills during the administration of vaginal PGE2 suppositories."[296]

CLOSTRIDIAL ENDOMYOMETRITIS AND SEPSIS: Twenty-year-old Monica* experienced a particularly severe infection following forced delivery of her third pregnancy at 16 weeks.

December 28, 6:00 p.m.—A needle is inserted into Monica's womb; a catheter is passed through the needle which is then withdrawn, and PGF2α is infused. Two medium thick laminaria tents are inserted into her cervical canal.

8:00 p.m.—Monica reports she is in labor.

8:50 p.m.—The amniotic sac ruptures; all is well, or so it seems. Bacteria have begun to multiply.

December 29, 6:00 a.m.—Monica's nurse notes she has a temperature of 102°F and is complaining of severe lower abdominal pain. Blood and cervical cultures are taken.

8:00 a.m.—The preborn comes out.

10:00 a.m.—Because the afterbirth has not come out, Monica is taken to a treatment room for surgical removal and a scraping of her now empty uterus.

11:00 a.m.—She receives a dose of antibiotic.

Later that afternoon—Nurses note blood in her urine and a provisional diagnosis of clostridial sepsis is made. A new antibiotic is given intravenously, to be continued at six hour intervals.

December 30, shortly after midnight—At age 20, in the cold chill of night, Monica loses the sexual organs that provided her body's female hormones; because the infection has rotted her womb and cooked her tissues into a foul-smelling jelly, the womb, both fallopian tubes and both ovaries have to be removed. Before and during the surgery she receives 3 units of whole blood and other assorted medications to stave off further infection and to correct hypovolemia (diminished blood volume).

Daytime—Monica is one sick girl. Still battling the virulent infections that rack her body and struggling to recover from major surgery, she now develops kidney disease (nephropathy) and is hemodialyzed.

For the next 2 weeks—Monica receives antibiotics every six hours and intermittent hemodialysis.

January 22—On the fourth anniversary of the Supreme Court decision that supposedly made abortion safe, after nearly a month in the hospital (did she have insurance?), Monica has recovered sufficient renal function to be released. There is little doubt she was unaware, before her abortion, that rates of pelvic infections range from 5.2% to 12.1% among women aborted in midtrimester with intraamniotic PGF2α augmented by intracervical laminaria tents.[304]

COAGULOPATHY: Coagulation defects are another potentially life-threatening complication of legal abortions. Intraamniotic instillation of PGF2α appears to have less impact on the clotting mechanism (although it does affect it to some degree) while there is a greater risk of coagulation defects from instillation of saline and urea. Oxytocin use has been shown to increase fivefold the risk of coagulopathy during saline abortion and recent reports of coagulopathies after late D&E procedures indicate this problem may not result solely from labor-inducing agents. In one group of women, six suffered this gravely serious complication. [140, 227, 267, 271]

COMA has resulted from the effects on the central nervous system and/or kidneys of hypertonic salt solution entering the bloodstream directly or via the peritoneal cavity.[5] It has been associated with salt poisoning, rupture of the uterus, and death. [24, 115, 122, 125, 126, 227]

CONVULSIONS: In one study 5 women—and in another, 6 women—suffered major convulsions during second trimester abortions by intra-amniotic prostaglandin F2α. [142] In 14 women convulsions were attributed as often to suction abortions as to saline[64]; local anesthesia can cause convulsions. [75, 155]

Peggy*, a 23-year-old mother without any history of epilepsy, convulsed 30 minutes after injection with PGF2α and urea; the convulsion was grand mal in nature and lasted one minute, after which her condition was "depressed."[224]

CORNUAL CONTRACTION RING WITH RETAINED PLACENTA: Fifteen-year-old Maurine* was 20 weeks pregnant at the time of saline abortion. Nine hours after instillation the bag of water broke and contractions began. Oxytocin was given then and for the next 13 hours. 22 hours after instillation the preborn aborted but the placenta had not yet delivered three hours later. Curettage produced nothing; with general anesthesia, manual exploration could not obtain it. After a blood loss of 1500 cc, exploratory surgery was performed. A cornual contraction ring was found with the placenta held in a thin-walled bulge of the uterine wall. An incision was made through the bulge and the placenta was separated and removed. Maurine needed to receive 4 units of blood and was hospitalized for 7 days.[219]

Jackie* was 18 weeks pregnant when she underwent a saline abortion. Fourteen hours later regular contractions began and oxytocin was given; it was another six hours until delivery. Two hours later doctors attempted to remove the placenta with forceps, curettage and then suction curettage; the attempts were unsuccessful. Blood loss was estimated at 800 cc. Exploratory surgery revealed the afterbirth implanted in a cornual contraction ring; it was removed through an incision. In addition to this unplanned surgery, Jackie suffered persistent endometritis and was hospitalized for 11 days.[219]

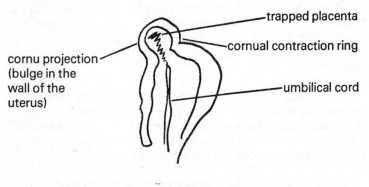

FIGURE 1
[219]

DAMAGE TO A URETER: Leela*, 28, was admitted to the hospital in shock after an attempt to interrupt a 3-month pregnancy by suction. A ureter, 22 cm long, was found completely detached.[6]

Eight days after her D&C abortion, 21-year-old Heather*
underwent a second D&C for continued bleeding; pieces of the
placenta were removed and a rip in her womb was discovered.
Ten days later doctors thought her well enough to be released
from the hospital; but in a week she returned, in pain and with a
high fever, leaking urine from her vagina. Exploratory surgery
revealed a damaged ureter and a ureterouterine fistula.

Heather was drawn to abortion by the lenis lure; she believed
a "safe, legal abortion" would enable her to have a baby when
she wanted. Instead she experienced pain, infection, damage, a
second surgery, more pain, extensive diagnostic testing, a third
surgery, removal of her reproductive organs and loss of her
fertility.[264]

DIARRHEA was observed in 45% of women receiving
PGF2α suppositories and in 15% of those receiving PGE2 sup-
positories for cervical dilatation prior to suction abortion.[297]
(See Gastrointestinal Disturbances and Particular Problems of
Prostaglandins)

DISSEMINATED INTRAVASCULAR COAGULATION:
a common, calamitous condition of altered blood coagulation,
when the delicate balance between factors favoring clotting and
factors opposing it becomes deranged, and inappropriate coagulation occurs. This "severe state" can be induced by infusion
of hypertonic saline[183] as can other, similarly dangerous, disturbances in the coagulability of the mother's blood.[9]

One report noted 3 women with serious coagulation defects
resulting in hemorrhage, and found evidence of subclinical DIC
in 25 others undergoing saline abortion.[39] Reports from the
Communicable Disease Center state that disseminated intravascular coagulation occurred in 0.3% of women undergoing
saline instillation, *which is a significant risk factor when considered in light of the large numbers of saline procedures performed each year.*[305] According to some sources, coagulation in
the veins is suffered by almost every woman undergoing saline
abortion.[102]

DURATION DIFFICULTIES: The length of time between
the beginning of an abortion and its completion takes its toll of
women in discomfort, exhaustion, hunger when food is not permitted, and emotional stress. Moreover, the duration may have
a direct bearing on complications: induction-to-abortion time

69

for saline averages about 30 hours; one study showed a complication rate from saline-induced abortion directly related to the interval between instillation and delivery. [275, 296]

Different doctors determine different times within which they consider an abortion successful if completed; for one group of women, successful abortions were those in which abortion was achieved within 72 hours. [215]

In a series of 72 abortions by PGE2 suppositories, some women didn't deliver for 24 hours; the average time was more than 11 hours. "One patient had an abortion time of more than 24 hours"—36 to be exact! She required surgery under general anesthesia for completion. [296]

Even some of the newer methods of abortion, introduced to "reduce potential trauma" by dilating the cervix, work so slowly that prolonged hospitalization results. [267] In his search for safety, one doctor inserts laminarias and moistened gauze into the cervical canal on the first day; 24 hours later the gauze is removed and more laminarias are inserted. Not until the third day is the abortion begun surgically, and the woman is not released before one or two hours after completion at the earliest. [276] "The use of laminari . . . may not reduce the need for either hospitalization or frequent patient visits over a 24 to 48 hour time period."[267]

ECTOPIC PREGNANCY COMPLICATIONS: When the developing embryo situates him/herself somewhere other than in the uterus, the pregnancy is termed "ectopic" or abnormally positioned. An attempt to abort an out-of-place pregnancy may produce a significant amount of tissue without disturbing the preborn. [53] In one series there were 7 ectopic pregnancies present at the time of early suction abortion; 6 of the women developed painful symptoms after the abortion attempt and were hospitalized; their fallopian tubes were removed. In the seventh case, the tube ruptured while the woman was still in the recovery room; after immediate transfer to a hospital, exploratory surgery revealed damage sufficient to warrant total hysterectomy. [134]

Of 11 women found to have ectopic gestations, 3 had rupture of tubal pregnancy immediately following suction curettage, 6 had rupture of the tube from 1 day to 19 days after the suction curettage. Only 2 ectopic gestations could be diagnosed prior to the danger point. [270]

Nov. 8—Mariellen*, a 24-year-old married woman who had

been using a brand name IUD for a year, went to a Planned Parenthood center for a pregnancy test. Her uterus showed some increase in size but the test was negative; she was told to come back.

Nov. 27—When she returned for another test, it was positive. The device was removed and a suction abortion was done under local anesthesia. Another IUD was inserted.

Dec. 4—Mariellen went to the emergency room of her local hospital with lower abdominal pain. Her IUD was removed and she was sent home.

Dec. 5—She returned to the hospital and was admitted with pain which was now abdominal and in her shoulder and chest, making breathing painful. Various tests and examinations were performed; they were normal.

Dec. 6—A chest x-ray was normal.

Dec. 8—More tests showed nothing.

Dec. 11—A pelvic examination revealed a definite mass. When the Planned Parenthood clinic was contacted, it was discovered their pathology report on the tissue obtained at suction curettage had been received belatedly on December 8. Planned Parenthood had not contacted the woman or her family to notify them that this report showed the pregnancy had not been aborted. Exploratory surgery was performed—blood was found and an ectopic gestation; the tube was removed.

Dec. 17—Mariellen was finally released from the hospital. Her doctor believes delays of 12 days in receiving pathology reports are unacceptable; they should be available in two or three days at most. And the laboratory should contact the clinic immediately any time confirmation cannot be made. Women who become pregnant with an intrauterine device in place are at greater risk of ectopic pregnancy.[270]

Andrea*, 34, also went to a Planned Parenthood clinic for a pregnancy test five weeks after her last normal period. The result was negative and she was told to return, which she did a week later, and the test was then positive. Suction curettage performed under local anesthesia yielded a small amount of tissue and the pathology report showed the abortion had been ef-

71

fective. But the abortion did nothing to relieve her discomfort, which intensified so greatly she underwent a series of gall bladder tests; they turned out negative.

Three weeks after the abortion, Andrea returned to the clinic complaining of nausea and vomiting, and incessant abdominal pain. An examination and pregnancy test showed she was still pregnant. A second abortion was performed and again only a very small amount of tissue was removed. Immediately afterward, Andrea complained of severe pain and her blood pressure dropped dramatically. She was rushed to a hospital where a ruptured ectopic pregnancy was discovered and the tube removed. Her doctor now cautions that microscopic examination should be mandatory if the amount of tissue is small or if fetal parts are not readily visible. This includes all early, menstrual extraction-type abortions.[270]

ELECTROENCEPHALOGRAPHIC CHANGES were induced in 4 women aborting by prostaglandin, in 5 of 21 women aborting by saline, and in 5 of 16 women receiving prostaglandin in a separate study; two of the latter showed spike activity, similar to epilepsy, after infusion. It would seem prudent, therefore, to avoid using intraamniotic prostaglandin for midtrimester abortion in women with a history of epilepsy.[142] Beyond this, there appears to be a threat to *every woman* considering second trimester abortion, as evidence suggests that regardless of the method used, EEG changes are relatively common following midtrimester abortions.[142] Can abortion be the act of a woman controlling her body if her mind gets messed up in the process?

EMBOLISM: This is a pathological condition in which some substance—a blood clot, fat, tissue or air—gets into the bloodstream, circulates, and eventually becomes jammed in some vital area where it may cause serious trouble or even death.[5] There have been several air embolism tragedies when suction tubing was inadvertently attached to the exhaust port of a machine.[21, 64, 123]

Amniotic fluid embolism causes hemorrhage, respiratory distress, cardio-vascular collapse, cyanosis and coma; its symptoms are anxiety, sweating, coughing, chills, swelling in the lungs and convulsions. Over 40% who survive the initial episode develop coagulation defects.[271]

72

ERYTHEMA NODOSUM: Painful red nodules erupt on the skin after some abortions.[123]

EXPULSION OF FETAL PARTS INTO THE ABDOMEN: "This case is reported to emphasize the importance of recognizing uterine perforation after suction abortion and to alert others to an unusual complication of perforation, namely, expulsion of fetal parts into the abdomen."

Jeanette*, a mother of five children, was 25 years old when she chose suction abortion to terminate a 12-week pregnancy. The next day she had abdominal pain, nausea and a fever and was admitted to a hospital for two weeks during which she received penicillin for a presumed infection. The doctors treating her there didn't know and never found out that during her abortion, a hole had been torn in her uterus and a three inch preborn was forced through it into her pelvis.

In the days before her second admission to the hospital (a month after the abortion) Jeanette's nausea and vomiting worsened, making her thin and dehydrated. Doctors belatedly decided on exploratory surgery. They found the perforated uterus, abscess of several loops of the small bowel, and something blocking the intestine—a skeleton. It was removed along with the uterus, one fallopian tube and portions of the bowel. Jeanette received two units of whole blood during the operation and spent two more weeks in the hospital; 57 days later she was readmitted with acute hepatitis (possibly caused by the transfused blood). In all this one supposedly simple suction abortion cost Jeanette four hospital stays, the aggravation of leaving her young children during the confinements, and several body parts she had not intended to lose.[268]

EXTRAPERITONEAL BLEEDING: major bleeding into and around the lower abdominal cavity; a potentially fatal complication which may lead to significant maternal morbidity; chiefly affecting women undergoing saline abortion.[147]

FAILED ABORTION: A persistent problem of midtrimester abortion has been failure of the initiating method. Women with this problem are allowed to linger in labor 24, 36, even 48 hours or longer before undergoing repeat intraamniotic injection or receiving oxytocic agents. Risks include infection, fluid electrolyte abnormality and uterine rupture. Furthermore, there are a number of women for whom the second attempt also fails and surgical management is required. The surgery is frequently hysterotomy which causes complications resulting in prolonged hospitalization.

Fifty-eight women aged 14 to 40, who were 13 to 23 weeks pregnant, suffered failed primary abortions and required surgical completion. Ten of them underwent uterine evacuation due to persistent fever. Nine were hospitalized up to five days for treatment with parenteral antibiotics. Wanda* developed an infection so severe, which didn't respond to vaginal evacuation and high-dose antibiotics, that she needed to have her entire reproductive system taken out. She remained in the hospital for 15 days and required three units of whole blood.[269]

Of the methods used for aborting first trimester pregnancies there appears to be a much greater rate of failures associated with menstrual extraction techniques: the earlier it is performed, the greater the possibility the pregnancy will not be disturbed. Menstrual extraction done shortly after the first missed period meets with a high incidence of continued pregnancy.[149]

A "technical operative error" may sometimes be responsible for the failure of an attempted abortion to disturb the preborn.[149] Michigan doctor W. G., subject of a civil suit charging negligence arising from an unsuccessful abortion he performed, declared, "These things happen—not regularly, but frequently." His patient gave birth to an 8 pound son despite the abortifacient procedure.[148]

Eighteen such failures resulted from punctures of the uterus being noticed immediately by the doctor, who was then forced to stop the abortion to repair the damaged womb.[57]

One study reveals 46 women with unintentional continued pregnancies following attempted first trimester abortions; one cause is likely to be examination of uterine contents not being carried out routinely in 4 out of 5 clinics. All 46 of these women returned for post-abortion followup and half of them told the doctor they still "felt pregnant" but their impressions were ignored. Two miscarried at 14 to 20 weeks gestational age and most of the remaining preborns were sufficiently disturbed that they might have met a similar fate had not their mothers jumped the gun by aborting them. One infant managed to survive both the attempted abortion and her mother's mood fluctuations, and was born whole and well.[149]

"Care should be taken to ascertain histologic confirmation that evacuation of the pregnancy has, in fact, been performed."[151] Some clinics, in an attempt to keep costs down, may not offer the analysis necessary to obtain this confirmation.[253] The average woman probably won't shop around for an abortionist who routinely performs this vital testing—she's likely to be unaware of its importance—and it's unlikely that a clinic could be persuaded to have the tests done if it's not their custom to do so.

Besides error on the part of the abortionist, failed abortion can be caused by an abnormality of the uterus, particularly where a double uterine cavity is present. A pregnancy may occur in one, while the other remains normal, as in the case of 30-year-old Brenda* who underwent two unsuccessful abortions due to curettage of the non-pregnant separate uterus.[150]

Colleen* took PGE2 suppositories to end her pregnancy of 18 weeks. Because her preborn had nestled down in the "blind horn" of a duplex uterus, she endured hours of unproductive labor pains before surgical intervention.[296]

As 27-year-old Lorena* discovered, a woman can have a pregnancy in both sections of a double uterus. Three days after a suction abortion Lorena developed pelvic pain severe enough to send her searching for medical help. Again and again she had pregnancy tests; they were persistently positive—the abortion had failed to destroy one of the two pregnancies.[151]

FEVER: Elevation of body temperature to an abnormal level, sometimes called pyrexia, complicated 15% of early abortions in one series.[38] In a study of hysterotomy abortions, 16 women had fevers of unknown origin, suspected to be genital tract infection.[123]

In 1182 legal abortions performed by various methods 312 women developed fevers of 100.4° or more, lasting longer than 24 hours. In a comparable series, a similar number—27%—developed fevers lasting three days or longer.[21]

Of 606 women undergoing suction curettage abortions, 17 developed fevers; in another group, 16 did.[143] 2,700 women in a one year study were reported having fevers from legal abortions.[64] Some may be of undetermined origin and antibiotics may be given (putting the woman at risk for both adverse drug reaction and subsequent immunity to the drug). Fever always accompanies infections and some other complications.

It was "the most frequently encountered side effect" among 71 women aborting by PGE2 suppositories; "all patients developed temperature elevation." In 50 women (70.4%) it went up 2° or higher. Twenty-one patients had an oral temperature of 102° or higher and four patients spiked at 104°F. Their temperatures remained abnormally high until "a few hours" after the last dose of the drug was given. This effect was also found by other researchers who noted "temperature elevation of 100°F in 60.9% of their patients."[296]

Two out of three women with ectopic pregnancy following an induced abortion of their first pregnancy, had had fevers without local symptoms on the first day after their legal abortions. "This indicates that fever without local symptoms might be of more importance than is generally considered."[260] (See Traumatic Intrauterine Adhesions)

GASTROINTESTINAL DISTURBANCES: Prostaglandins are infamous for causing gastrointestinal disturbance, chiefly nausea, vomiting and diarrhea; in one study 62% of women who received PGF2α became sick.[303] It's nearly impossible to find a report of this drug inducing abortions in which there is no mention of such problems developing.

Among 71 women aged 14 to 42, these disturbances were *common* despite a low initial dose of PGE2 and premedication with antiemetic and antidiarrheal agents which were begun an hour before the first dose was given, and were continued throughout the abortion process. "Although the initial dose of PGE2 was reduced (from 20 mg.) to 10 mg. and all patients were premedicated . . . gastrointestinal side effects could not be eliminated." Forty women (56%) had to endure these miseries and in no case was the process discontinued because of discomfort.[296]

In a study of abortions by PGF2α suppositories "there was such a high incidence of vomiting and diarrhea that the clinical usefulness of this method was felt to be severely limited."[296]

GENERAL COMPLICATIONS: "An unfortunate aspect of abortion is the vast number of complications."[153] "Complications associated with elective termination of pregnancy are numerous."[151] "The later the abortion, the higher the risk of complications such as bleeding, infection and uterine damage."[172]

76

GENERAL DANGERS OF D & E: "This University (of Alabama Medical Center in Birmingham) has had an inordinate number of referrals of patients with complications from evacuation abortions performed after 14 weeks of pregnancy. Retained products of conception, infection, and hemorrhage are complications that are prevalent throughout the country and explain the reason this technique has not achieved . . . popularity . . . There are inherent risks and problems associated with this procedure..."[263] not the least of which were two perforations of the uterus and a maternal death! According to this doctor, even though some physicians "can perform midtrimester abortions above 14 weeks safely by dilatation and evacuation . . . when the average physician in the United States starts performing midtrimester abortions above 14 weeks by dilatation and evacuation, the country will experience a sizeable increase in maternal deaths and morbidity."[298]

GENERAL HAZARDS OF INTRA-AMNIOTIC UREA & PGF2α: "There are persisting problems with this method. Failure to abort and incomplete abortions with their need for surgical management continue as problems. The complications of hemorrhage, infection and cervical laceration have not been eliminated and gastro-intestinal side effects during the abortion process persist."[141]

GENITAL TRACT INFECTION is a well-known complication. In one study 228 women developed infections and 81 required hospitalization, 20 of them for more than five days. Five of the women underwent long-term antibiotic therapy (a health hazard for women with drug sensitivities). So severe was one woman's infection that she required both a hysterectomy and hemodialysis for treatment of renal failure.[154] Immediate acute inflammatory complications occur in about 5% of women.[89]

HEADACHE: Severe headache has been recorded as a result of accidental intravascular injection of hypersomolar urea[141] and also following an accident with saline.[103]

HEMORRHAGE: Bleeding serious enough to require transfusion considerably outweighs the expense and adverse effects of transfusion.[271] One possible source of serious hemorrhage is hypertonic saline creating disruption of the maternal-fetal barrier allowing release of thromboplastic materials into the maternal circulation.[39]

In two groups five and six women bled quite profusely following termination. [215, 232] 23 women lost 250 ml of blood or more in one series of early suction abortions and 41 more suffered loss of an indeterminate amount of blood—39% required an additional surgical procedure for relief.[134] 17% of 812 women undergoing first trimester abortions (94.5% done by suction) hemorrhaged.[38] In a one year study, hemorrhage was the second most frequent complication; 97 women bled severely.[139]

Twenty-three-year-old Amber* was rushed out of the recovery area of an abortion clinic and had just boarded a bus when she began hemorrhaging. Leaving a puddle of blood on the seat, she stumbled off at the next stop and went into a public library where two librarians called an ambulance for her. Amber lost two pints of blood and went into shock; that night, in emergency surgery, her womb was removed.[248]

The risk of hemorrhage increases with advancing gestation and approximately doubles with selected periods of gestation.[153] Separation and retention of the placenta and failure of the uterus to contract account for much of the heavy bleeding from instillation abortions.[271]

In a series of saline abortions, hemorrhage accounted for over half of all complications[76]; 901 women in a single year study suffered this debilitating complication and 66% of them required repeated curettage.[64]

In one study "the most frequently encountered complication associated with second trimester D&C was hemorrhage," periling the life and health of 30 women. One hemorrhaged after the operation because of "an undetected external cervical laceration." Nine women needed to receive one unit of blood, 17 needed two units, 3 needed three and one woman needed four units of blood.[167] In each instance the woman was exposed to the multiple additional risks inherent with transfusions. [38, 167]

HEPATITIS: Some percentage of women in any group receiving blood transfusions may die from hepatitis contracted through the blood; for each woman who dies, others will have milder cases resulting in lengthy illness and some degree of loss of health. [4, 268]

78

HYPERNATREMIA: an excessive amount of sodium in the blood—salt poisoning; causes headache, thirst, numbness and tingling of the fingers, and the sensation of being overheated. This is the "most feared," potentially fatal complication of saline abortion; symptoms develop while the procedure is being performed and may be mistaken by the doctor as "due to upper respiratory infection and nervousness."[180] Mild cases may go undetected.[271]

HYPERSOMOLAR UREA HAZARDS: when used to terminate a second trimester pregnancy it "requires physicians and other personnel who are *well* trained in recognizing and managing its associated side effects and complications."

It may be 24 hours before delivery and the labor can be expected to be difficult and painful. Its disadvantages include frequent need for repeated doses, vomiting and diarrhea, cost and a higher proportion of babies delivered with signs of life than with the hypertonic saline method.

Significant complications include hemorrhage, infection, gastrointestinal side effects, occasional intravascular spill and cervical laceration. These lacerations are difficult to repair and even with immediate, careful repair after debridement, breakdown is not uncommon; the scars may affect future childbearing.[175]

HYPOKALEMIA: Extreme potassium depletion in the circulating blood has been reported in association with cardiac arrhythmia (irregularity in or the absence of rhythmic heart beating) following second trimester abortion by PGF2α.

Rosalind H.*, 23, sought abortion of her first pregnancy 18 weeks after conception. Shortly after admission to the hospital a laminaria tent was inserted into her cervical canal; PGF2α was injected intraamniotically without difficulty. About one hour later she felt weak and faint; her pulse became irregular; she was nauseated and vomited. After an ECG she was transferred to the Cardiac Intensive Care Unit. Luckily, her condition stabilized after delivery of her three pound baby. Doctors determined the increased cardiac irritability was due to hypokalemia which was attributable to the prostaglandin; they suggest that prior to prostaglandin administration, serum potassium levels should be determined and monitored.[182]

HYSTERECTOMY: In one group of second-trimester abortions, two women each underwent a total abdominal hysterectomy and blood was given during both procedures. One was necessary because the womb was torn during the abortion. "The other hysterectomy was necessary when an anemic patient with two previous cesarean sections started to bleed from the scar tissue of the lower uterine segment. At the same time, her uterus failed to contract."[167]

2 of 812 women choosing vacuum aspiration abortions needed to have their wombs removed because they ruptured during suction. The report of these catastrophic losses does not indicate whether the women had known beforehand that their sexual organs might be aborted during the surgery.[21]

Throughout this book there are numerous instances of women's wombs being surgically removed as a result of other complications.

INCOMPLETE ABORTION: After waiting five hours to see a doctor, Kara's* abortion went very fast; the doctor spent just five minutes. His manner seemed rude and he allowed no time for the anesthetic to take effect. More than a week later Kara was still bleeding heavily and suffering from severe cramps. She had to undergo another scraping to remove tissue left behind during the quickie abortion.[245]

Even in a clinic with an experienced and well-trained staff the incidence of this complication remains high—32% of total complications in one study; 83 women undergoing first trimester suction abortions suffered severe bleeding and cramping because of it. Their doctors say that in any group of abortions this particular problem is to be expected because complete removal of the products of conception has always been difficult in artificial pregnancy termination.[134]

Three factors influencing this difficulty are the size of the preborn, his firm hold onto the wall of the uterus, and "progesterone block" which during early pregnancy influences uterine motility and may operate as a survival mechanism for the developing fetus. The function of progesterone is to prevent premature expulsion of the newly conceived life. So inhibitory is the effect of progesterone that it "may be great enough to prevent expulsion of retained uterine contents, even following attempted induced abortion in women less than 7½ weeks pregnant." Thus, for one group of women, "incomplete abortion was the most frequently recorded complication."[153]

80

	weeks into pregnancy	
- - -conception		

rate of incomplete abortion 4 times higher	7 ½ to 9 ½ weeks	rate of incomplete abortion 11 times higher

Figure 2 shows the increased risk of incomplete
abortion compared to women 7 ½ to 9 ½
weeks pregnant

"The incidence of incomplete abortion in pharmacologically induced pregnancy terminations is high, varying in most series from 40 to 55 per cent."[267] Abortions were incomplete in 20 women in one group[143]; 811 in another[267]; and 86 (44%) in a third.[21] One explanation: the prolonged, sustained contractions achieved with the PGF2α /hypersomolar urea method may lead to placental entrapment.[141] "The fact does remain, however, that *a high percentage* of women undergoing pharmacologically induced second-trimester pregnancy terminations will continue to require completion of the process as part of their after-care."[267]

INCOMPLETE SEPARATION OF THE PLACENTA may lead to curettage in some 8% of women, and blood transfusions for excessive bleeding at the time of separation in a smaller percent.[180]

INFECTION may be localized in the lining of the womb, fallopian tubes or in the structures immediately adjacent to the uterus; may be more regionally located resulting in pelvic thrombophlebitis, cellulitis, or peritonitis; may be distant as in pneumonia, endocarditis or septic emboli to the lungs; may be generalized as in septicemia; is usually the direct result of instrumentation; is a frequent cause of subsequent sterility, as infection blocks the fallopian tubes which lead from the ovaries to the womb making pregnancy impossible.[172]

Tube infection and subsequent blockage may also lead to an ectopic pregnancy in which the new life grows in the tube instead of in the uterus. "Considering the unquestionable risk of infection connected with induced abortion, it is no wonder that an ectopic pregnancy occasionally may be caused by this operation."[172,260]

81

A study covering only one-seventh of one year's abortions reported 747 women suffering pelvic infections.[64] A study of 1182 abortions revealed septicemia in 6 women, extragenital infection in 66, urinary tract infection in 32, chest infection in 21, abdominal wound infection in 13, and "a pelvic abscess or vault infection after hysterectomy developed in 10 of 106 patients treated in this way." Of 255 women with pyrexia due to genital-tract infection "142 had undergone sterilization either by tubal ligation or abdominal hysterectomy. This left 113 patients who had not been sterilized but developed genital-tract infection. Their subsequent fertility may be jeopardized . . . It is disquieting that postabortal infection, which is one of the common causes of death after criminal abortion, should have occurred in 27% of this series."[21]

Infection may be resistant to antibiotics or so severe that removal of the uterus becomes necessary.[267]

Laminaria tents may also be a source of infection, as their power to expand the cervix is limited, making several hours necessary for effectiveness. This gives bacteria ample opportunity to multiply. When 48 hours or more pass between instillation of an abortifacient and delivery, the risk of infection is greatly increased.[271]

INJECTION OF SALT SOLUTION INTO A VEIN during a saline abortion causes dehydration resulting in fever and hemorrhagic cerebral infarctions (bleeding in the brain) which can be fatal.[37, 215]

INJECTION OF UREA INTO A VEIN: "Intravascular injection or spill characterized by flushing, dizziness, and intense abdominal cramping of up to 30 minutes was experienced" by one woman in a group having urea-oxytocin abortions and by 2 women undergoing urea-PGF2α abortions.[267]

INJURY TO THE CERVIX: "Cervical trauma is a common and potentially serious complication which can occur during curettage or instillation abortions."[271]

"Cervical injury sustained during dilatation of the cervix for abortion has been linked to later pregnancy wastage."[277]

"Women who have had transverse cervical lacerations should automatically be identified as high-risk pregnancy patients when they subsequently conceive and intend to carry the pregnancy."[267]

INJURY TO THE INTESTINES harmed 11 women undergoing early suction abortions in one 12 month study.[64]

INTRA-ABDOMINAL UTERINE RUPTURE has been caused by a high dose of oxytocin administered in prostaglandin abortion when rupture of the membranes (the breaking of the preborn's bag of water) is not followed by delivery within a few hours. This is a prime concern in older women who have had previous pregnancies.

Phoebie* was 37 and pregnant for the sixth time when admitted for elective abortion at 18 weeks gestation. A laminaria tent was inserted into her cervix to soften and open it (this peculiar application of seaweed is supposed to reduce the likelihood of cervical rupture). The laminaria was removed the next morning when PGF2α was given. Fifteen hours later the amniotic sac broke and an hour after that oxytocin was begun by intravenous infusion pump. At 27 hours the pump was stopped for a rest. Two hours later Phoebie began having trouble breathing, shoulder pain and extreme abdominal pain. Exploratory surgery was performed, revealing that the preborn and his placenta had been ejected through the wall of the uterus. A total abdominal hysterectomy was performed.

Sylvia*, a 34-year-old mother of four, underwent the same procedure for prostaglandin abortion at 18 weeks. 25 hours later her baby's sac broke and contractions stopped. Three hours after that oxytocin was given and this continued for 10 hours until the pump was stopped for the traditional two hour rest. *Eight hours later* it was realized that the oxytocin should have been restarted six hours previously; so the artificially-induced painful contractions began again for Sylvia 46 hours after the beginning of her abortion. Four hours later her temperature was 101°; an antibiotic was given. Delivery began two hours later. Curettage (under general anesthesia) was necessary to control the bleeding, but when that failed, her torn uterus and one fallopian tube and an ovary had to be removed.[156]

INTRAUTERINE LOSS OF THE CURET TIP: Seventeen-year-old Donna* had a suction abortion at 10 weeks gestation. "When the suction curet was removed, the tip of the curet was missing. After a thorough search . . . we concluded that the curet must have broken off within the uterus."

Numerous scouting expeditions through her uterus attempting to blindly locate the fragment were unsuccessful. An x-ray taken on the operating table didn't show it. Ultrasound examination the next day was equally futile. Donna was sent home "with careful instructions to search the perineal pads for possible spontaneous expulsion of the curet tip."

She had to return to the medical center three more times in the next three weeks; "on the first two visits, attempts to remove the curet tip blindly were unsuccessful." Nearly two months after the abortion, Donna was anesthetized for yet another surgical intrusion into her body; the broken tip was finally found imbedded in the wall of her womb.

Her doctors now caution that "the curet tip should be inspected at the end of a procedure to ensure that it is still intact."[262] Failure to do so could be disastrous.

ISOIMMUNIZATION: For centuries, women with Rh negative blood carrying Rh positive babies suffered terrible threats to their own lives and the lives of their children. Now, thanks to a special serum called RhoGam, these women can deliver, or abort, their babies without risking sensitization "against the blood of an individual" (the next baby they conceive). *But they have to get that shot.*

"I've known for years I'm Rh negative, but at the abortion clinic they said I was O positive," recalls one abortion patient. "I insisted they test me again. After giving me a hard time, they finally found out I was right! Without that injection my future children's lives would have been endangered."

When another client at the same clinic reminded a lab technician she had paid for a RhoGam shot and hadn't gotten it, he snarled, "We're too busy to remember everything."

In a study of women who had aborted their first pregnancies (compared with women who delivered first pregnancies) "two cases of isoimmunization occurred in the study group, none in the other group."[260]

"Abortion by curettage seems to provoke isoimmunization in almost every pregnancy (nearly one in four in some areas) where ABO incompatibility exists."[28]

When the blood of mother and preborn mingles before the abortion (as it often does),[73] the danger is not from abortion-caused sensitization, but from the mother's belief that abortion prevented motherhood, that there was in effect no baby, that

84

she's the same as though she hadn't been pregnant at all, and of course this isn't true. There *was* a baby and the sensitizing effect on her body was the same as if the pregnancy had terminated naturally. Again the lenis lure draws a curtain around the reality of abortion by allowing the mother to delude herself. She may blithely go about her business, never realizing she now harbors within her body the seeds of destruction, the tiny weapons which can attack her next, perhaps wanted, baby.

KARMAN CANNULA COMPLICATION: Dr. Harvey Karman of Los Angeles has supposedly invented a cannula technique which eliminates the problem of dilating the cervix. The staff of at least one hospital has found "limitations with this, related to the problem of completely evacuating" the uterus. The head abortionist says, "We don't see how total evacuation can be done in advanced first trimester gestations without dilating the cervix, which immediately eliminates the primary advantages of the Karman Cannula."

With adolescent girls, where dilating the immature cervix is a great concern, "the best one can hope for is to disrupt the pregnancy, creating an 'iatrogenic' (physician-caused) incomplete abortion leading to the potential hazards of infection, delayed hemorrhage, the need for rehospitalization and a second D&C."[105]

KIDNEY DAMAGE AND LOSS: 23-year-old Gerri* was thought to be in the 12th week of pregnancy when she had a D&C abortion. But the abortionist had made a mistake and the preborn was much older and bigger than he had expected; large sharp curetters and ring forceps were necessary.

Gerri did poorly after the operation; four days later a mass could be felt in her abdomen and her number of red blood cells had dropped dangerously low. Five days after the D&C another operation was performed. Surgeons found a cyst and damage so severe that her right kidney had to be removed; the right ureter (tube carrying urine) was already missing! It was found—all 17 centimeters of it—amid the abortion specimen labeled "products of conception." Thinking back, the abortionist remembered removing an elongated tube, but he thought it was part of the umbilical cord. [103, 104]

Leela* was also at that stage of pregnancy—three months—when she chose to undergo a suction abortion. Few women

85

realize that a preborn of this gestational age is perfectly formed—a miniature baby compared to a newborn, but a *big* four inches long and proportionately three dimensional compared to a slender, tightly closed cervix through which s/he must pass (see Appendix).

The delusion that any pregnancy can be terminated by a simple suction procedure at any time during the first trimester stems from ignorance of fetal physiology. The vacuum aspiration technique is designed to, in a manner of speaking, liquify soft tissues; what it can do to an embryo it cannot do to a fetus, and this differentation takes place midway through the first trimester.

Before the 12 week mark the preborn's head, shoulders, rib cage, arms and legs are bone under the skin! Attempting suction abortion is comparable to trying to clean a floor by vacuuming up toy cars; what works well on small bits of dust and dirt doesn't work at all on larger, solid objects.

28-year-old Leela learned this lesson the hard way, and she paid a dear price for it—rupture of her cervix, bladder and parametrium (connective tissue around the womb) and loss of her right ureter, ovary and kidney.[6]

The pain that she endured will not have been in vain if through it other women can learn that *it is not possible to make a free choice about a pregnancy in ignorance;* a woman must know how well formed and how large her preborn is and what the advantages of natural termination are compared to the treacherous consequences of the brute force method.

LABOR PAINS: In some of the methods used to cause a pregnancy to end prematurely, the abortion process imitates labor and delivery. These methods include catheter-insertion and instillation of urea, saline, or prostaglandin.

In natural labor contractions begin weakly and increase in strength and proximity gradually. But the artificial labor brought on by abortifacients, particularly prostaglandins, begins with a bang and gets worse fast.

"Prostaglandin administered via the intramuscular or extraovular route" is characterized by a "sharp and immediate increase in uterine activity." In a series of PGE2 suppository abortions, the frequency of contractions rose within one hour to an average of one minute apart and "varied between 7 and 10 contractions per 10 minutes throughout the treatment period" which lasted an average of 10 hours for women with other children and 13 hours for women who had never given birth before. 69 of 70 women in this particular group were in labor as long as 24 hours, and one woman didn't deliver for 36 hours[296] which is a dreadfully long time to be having labor pains every minute. The average time until delivery for extraovular administration of PGF2α was 16.21 hours and 15.98 hours with serial intramuscular injections of 15-me-PGF2α.[296]

LAMINARIA TENTS, "although apparently effective, can be inserted only by trained personnel and require several hours for completion of their mechanical activity. The patient would either have a prolonged clinical stay or require a separate preoperative visit for insertion of intracervical laminaria tents. The additional disadvantages of laminaria tents have been the formation of false cervical passages and, on occasion, the inability to insert even a small laminaria tent into some patients with small cervical openings."[297]

LOSS OF SLEEP: For nights after their abortions, women may be awakened at night by chills and fever, uncontrolled bleeding and painfully incapacitating cramps. Investigations have found women with dead tissue still inside them, infections, damaged organs and other unsettling physical and emotional conditions causing restlessness and insomnia.

METABOLIC COMPLICATIONS affected three women in one series of legal abortions.[139]

MISCELLANEOUS HAZARDS: The incidence of complications reported at one major facility was 12.8%; the three most frequently encountered were cervical laceration, hemorrhage and infection.

The incidence of complications at one hospital was more than 16% during its first quarter of performing abortions; as the doctors gained experience, complications decreased. Apparently, one of the crucial factors affecting safety is the novice abortionist; but can every woman be sure *her* doctor will have ample expertise? And if he does, can that guarantee safety? Another survey reported, "It is significant that some of the more serious complications occurred with the most senior and experienced operators. This emphasizes that termination of pregnancy is neither as simple nor as safe as some advocates of abortion-on-demand would have the public believe."[21]

"Although all risks of abortion are reduced when it is performed in the early weeks of pregnancy, as confirmed by many reports, including those of Loung, Beric, and Sood, these authors record *the same pattern of serious complications,* including perforation which sometimes necessitates hysterectomy." (emphasis added)[21]

The major complications of hemorrhage, uterine perforation, metabolic disorders and related sequelae comprise 25.4% of all dangers. Complication rates in one group remained about the same throughout the first 12 weeks of gestation but more than *tripled* after the 12th week.[139] "It should be evident that as pregnancy progresses terminations become increasingly more difficult, different procedures must be employed, and complications are more common, with an inevitable increased mortality rate."[113]

The complication rates associated with the late-pregnancy termination methods of hysterotomy and hysterectomy are always so much higher than the rates for other procedures that it is distressing to realize that hysterotomy and hysterectomy must sometimes be used as a treatment for abortion complications,[144] thereby exposing the woman to the possibility of still more complications.

MULTIPLE ORGAN REMOVAL: Rosa T. endured an exceptionally painful abortion. Within a week she was suffering an infection so severe and so pervasive doctors had to remove her spleen and colon and all her reproductive organs; a trachetomy was performed when breathing problems developed. Permanent damage was done to her heart, lungs and kidneys and she needed to relearn simple functions like talking and walking. It was a full year before she was able to return to her job. Virtually every part of her body was affected. A lawsuit against the legal abortionist was settled out of court for $600,000, but Rosa discovered that money could never replace what she lost by choosing abortion.[246]

MYOCARDIAL INFARCTION, a potentially fatal heart problem, has been documented following suction abortion.[143]

MYOMETRIAL NECROSIS, the death of the muscular wall of the uterus, can be (indeed, has been) caused by saline abortion.[138]

OVARY LOSS: Attempting to end Leela's* three month pregnancy by suction, her doctor passed the suction device through her cervix (which he had perforated while trying to open) and into her abdomen, rupturing the bladder and dislodging her right ureter. Major abdominal surgery was required to repair the mutilation; doctors found it necessary to remove one of her ovaries.[6]

Other case histories, elsewhere in this book, further document the loss of one or both ovaries.

PAIN: Although most studies do not report pain as a complication it would be inaccurate to describe any legal abortion as painless. Moreover, each complication encountered is painful to some degree.

"Intense and prolonged pain that requires large amounts of analgesics is not unusual" with both saline and prostaglandin abortions.[276] Pain during saline instillation was recorded for 5 women in one study[215]; in another, pain from cramps was listed as a complication affecting 145 women. "Considerable pain" was a reality for 12 women undergoing rivanol instillations.[215]

"During the induction of abortion by intra-amniotic administration of PGF2α, most women experience pain." In one series of abortions *every* woman asked for and received meperidine for relief of "severe" pain.[220]

Individual experiences of painful abortions are plentiful. "I expected to be completely unconscious," Gretchen readily relates. "They told me I wouldn't feel a thing. Take it from me—I felt *everything*. I nearly fell off the table it was so bad!"

Abortionists claim early vacuum curettage isn't necessarily painful, but women suctioned without anesthetics disagree. "My doctor never uses anesthesia," Connie growls through clenched teeth. "Of course he's a man; he's never been through it. It was so awful, so overwhelming, I couldn't help crying. It was much worse than they led me to expect."

In some clinics if a woman screams she's told to shut up. Aides may be called on to hold down thrashing patients. Often doctors will not delay abortions by giving in to pleas for additional pain-killers. A secretary who paid $50 extra for an injection of Valium got it just seconds before the doctor came in. "He would not wait, he would not do another woman first, he just wouldn't listen to me. I begged him to stop because I couldn't hold still." Her screams were ignored. The medication finally took effect—in the recovery room.

89

Karen T., 23, had a similar experience. "They told me the local would be less dangerous and that general anesthetics would give me cramps and make me throw up and have to stay there for hours recovering from it. The local, they said, was just a shot in the cervix, which has no nerve endings, and that I'd be out in 45 minutes. And like an ass I believed them . . . instead of shaving my crotch, they spray-painted it with some orange disinfectant. It was like graffiti. Then I saw a long syringe and nearly died. But it didn't hurt, just like they said. The doctor said he'd have to dilate me three times with rods to open me up enough. So when he starts to work, the nurse starts asking me dumb questions like what religion I am and who the father was. God, the pain. I was screaming and the doctor was getting worried. 'Hang on,' he kept saying, 'It'll be all over in a minute.' I kept screaming back, 'You said there'd be no pain and you lied!' Then they made me sit up and I didn't know if I was going to faint or throw up. The nurse gave me some smelling salts and led me over to a cot . . . the cramping got so bad I had to stay there five hours."[278]

When a woman goes to a clinic for an abortion, it's unlikely she'll find out before it's too late whether the doctor is guilty of such surgical brutality. One former clinic worker describes the scene she left as one of total chaos where the agonized voices of many women could be heard. "That's because this one doctor doesn't give anything for pain before the abortion," she explained. "The pain is so bad it makes them vomit."

Years later some women still live with the pain. Rosa T. remembers her abortion as incredibly painful. She will never forget having a tampon shoved into her mouth to keep her quiet. A week later, complications set in. Rosa signed herself into a hospital where she spent eight painfilled months, three of them in intensive care.[246]

Pain can be responsible for a woman losing more in an abortion than just one pregnancy—she can be coerced into giving up all future chances of bearing children. Oleta* was writhing, grimacing, and groaning throughout her suction abortion. She clenched the hand of a nurse's aide; her fingernails dug into the other woman's skin. "You don't ever have to go through this again, you know," the helpful doctor said evenly as he continued the abortion, deaf to her cries of protest. "You could have your tubes tied and that would be the end of it." "Okay, okay, anything you say," Oleta cried. The doctor, wasting no time, ordered the aide to leave the room and get a pen and a form, so the sterilization could be arranged.

PARALYTIC ILEUS: Paralysis of the wall of the intestine, marked by swelling, acute pain and collapse—a potentially fatal complication—may occur after any abdominal surgery (e.g. hysterotomy, hysterectomy abortion or emergency exploratory surgery). The risk of death increases if there is a delay in the diagnosis and the woman has been discharged from the hospital.[86] A 42-year-old mother suffered this debilitating complication in addition to uterine rupture, emergency removal of her reproductive organs and a collapsed lung following a midterm abortion by PGF2α and saline.[259] In a series of fewer than 1200 legal abortions, 7 women developed paralytic ileus.[21]

PARTICULAR PROBLEMS OF PROSTAGLANDINS: Prostaglandins are a large family of naturally-occurring compounds which affect many body processes; they have the ability to contract isolated smooth muscle (the uterus, for example). Unlike other methods of abortion, taking this drug will not directly kill the preborn—it just makes labor begin. Because the baby may be born alive, and because of the many serious side effects, this drug is recommended for use only in hospitals. It can be given in many different ways; labor can last 50 hours; in 20 out of 100 women it fails to cause birth. It does affect the autonomic nervous system[160] and causes: [36, 41, 129]

shock	hypotension
nausea	tachycardia
erythema	bronchospasm
diarrhea	skin flushing
migraine	cervical rupture
shivering	intense uterine pain
headaches	prolonged contraction
bradycardia	fall in cardiac output
hot flashes	inflammatory reactions
grand mal seizures	cervicovaginal fistula
cramps	vaginal burning sensation
pyrexia	superficial thrombophlebitis
vomiting	gastrointestinal disturbance
dizziness	electroencephalographic changes
hemorrhage	

Of 102 women undergoing legal first trimester abortion by PGF2α, 93 experienced bleeding, usually starting within four hours. In 12 women this bleeding lasted over 3 *weeks*. Other adverse effects in this group included one case of postabortal endometritis, 38 cases of diarrhea and 24 women with nausea and vomiting.[159]

A study done by two medical doctors has revealed that 42.6% of women undergoing PGF2α abortions had some sort of medical complication, including decrease in hematocrit (posing the danger of anemia), blood loss in excess of 1000 ml, infections, cervical lacerations and rupture of the uterus necessitating total abdominal hysterectomy.[163]

Another doctor reports seeing gasping babies brought to his hospital's nursery after they survived prostaglandin abortions. In one week this happened twice, he said, with the dying babies "fighting valiantly for breaths they cannot keep and for a life they cannot have . . . Each time it happened the hospital had to deal with a near-hysterical mother; none of these mothers had known the 'thing' they were aborting was really a baby. They were always surprised to find this out."[158]

The use of oxytocin after prostaglandin for midtrimester abortion mimics the situation at term in the womb and therefore the woman who has had previous pregnancies "must be considered at significant risk" if this treatment is used. "Two classes of patients appear to be in jeopardy when abortion is induced by intra-amniotic PGF2α and high dose oxytocin—the young woman pregnant for the first time is at risk for cervical rupture and the older woman with past pregnancies is at risk for uterine rupture."[156]

In a group of 122 women undergoing PGF2α abortions, 52 had complications: 16 suffered severe bleeding, 16 endured prolonged abortion time, 18 became infected, 4 had cervical lacerations and the uterus of one woman ruptured and had to be removed.[163] (See Rupture of the Cervix)

After studying prostaglandin abortions, the World Health Organization concluded "a high frequency of gastrointestinal side effects has been encountered with the intramuscular use of prostaglandins; it is also associated with disturbing local reactions: the amount of pain and erythema (diffused redness over the skin) makes this method unacceptable." Shivering and fever, vomiting and diarrhea are not uncommon; cervical lacerations, flushing, chest pain, difficulty breathing and uterine pain are also noted as well as readmission to the hospital for bleeding and infection. Repeated painful injections were necessary and cervical damage was found in 20 women examined vaginally immediately after the abortion.[223]

15-methyl-prostaglandin F2α vaginal suppositories have been offered as a method of early pregnancy termination, but unpleasant gastro-intestinal side effects are relatively common with it; the abortion process is often slow; and the pain is so severe that 32 women in one group required parenteral analgesics.

A gel containing 3 mg of prostaglandin F2α was instilled by catheter into the uterine cavities of 197 women in an attempt to achieve dilatation of the cervix. The doctors were seeking two improvements: 1) to avoid the use of rigid metal rods to force open the cervix, and 2) to avoid the risk of cervical-vaginal fistulae.

Their plan was unsuccessful. Two-thirds of all the women still required forceful dilatation. The method was least effective in women whose first pregnancies were being terminated prematurely—96.6% of them required subsequent cervical dilation by metal rods (these women, as previously noted, are at the highest risk of permanent cervical damage which can make it impossible for them to carry a future pregnancy to term).

There were a number of complications in this group of abortions. Pain and abdominal cramps were experienced by over 70% of the women even though they had received a pain-killer. Nausea occurred in 33.5% and vomiting in 19.2% despite the prior administration of anti-emetics. Four women needed blood transfusions.[286]

Thirty-one women received vaginal prostaglandin suppositories to induce mid-trimester abortions. This study was performed "in collaboration with the World Health Organization Task Force on Prostaglandins." Among the findings:[287]

1. Three women failed to abort; two needed a D&C after 24 to 30 hours. In the third woman 'ballooning' of the lower uterine segment was observed.
2. Eight women suffered incomplete abortion and surgery was necessary to remove the placenta.
3. One woman required a blood transfusion.

4. A number of women experienced a copious flow of breast milk. "Postabortion lactorrhea is a seldom mentioned but real side effect of prostaglandin-induced abortion."

5. Gastro-intestinal disturbances including vomiting and diarrhea afflicted many women despite their having received medication to prevent this.

6. One of the most frequently encountered side effects was sleepiness. "Some slept almost continuously, only waking briefly to vomit."

7. "Any objective insight into the degree of painfulness is difficult to assess. Some of those who had complained most loudly during the process said afterwards that things had not been too bad; conversely, some patients who behaved stoically, complained bitterly when everything was over."

8. "Induction with prostaglandins during the second trimester is a time-consuming, laborious and complicated procedure . . . The disadvantages are that not all the patients responded favorably . . . the method is unsuitable for mentally labile (unsteady) women and for those who cannot be motivated to collaborate in such a prolonged procedure."

PELVIC INFECTIONS were among "the most frequently encountered complications associated with second-trimester D&C."[167] One cause of this nasty problem is tissue or blood clots retained within the uterus providing a medium for the infection to grow in. It's also a problem after other early and late methods of abortion.[143]

PERFORATION OF THE BLADDER: Twenty-year-old Luci* underwent suction curettage and tubal ligation in the eleventh week of her first pregnancy. Inadvertently, an incision was made into her bladder which required suturing. The abortion was further complicated by chest pains, abdominal bleeding, the need for exploratory surgery, nausea, vomiting, chills and respiratory arrest.[113]

PERFORATION OF THE BOWEL can occur during suction and other first trimester abortions [57, 134] and during curettage for completion of instillation procedures. [51, 227]

PERFORATION OF THE UTERUS: "The two principal dangers of uterine perforation are bleeding and trauma to the

94

abdominal contents."[271] This "ever present hazard" and "major concern requiring emergency care and frequently major surgical intervention" damaged 34 women in one group (one-third were girls pregnant for the first time). Eight of them required emergency hospitalization and removal of their wombs (one woman in this group also had to have her damaged bowel repaired).[134] When injury to the womb can be mended by stitching it closed, a woman may have to stay five additional days in the hospital.[167]

Of 812 suction abortions of pregnancies not exceeding 14 weeks' duration, 14 women were known to have experienced perforation of their wombs, and in still more women "perforation may have remained undiagnosed. This observation is based on the fact that in 3 of the 14 cases perforation was recognized only after opening the abdomen for tubal ligation. This comment would apply equally to other published series." Six of these women required emergency surgery and "hysterectomy was twice necessary to save life . . . because of hemorrhage and shock resulting from severe cervical laceration."[21]

In another group of women having abortions "28 definite uterine perforations occurred." Seventeen women were hospitalized immediately and in 15 cases immediate surgery was carried out—6 women had their wombs removed (2 of them had never had a child before and never will again); another woman was released from the hospital, but had to return a month later for a hysterectomy "because of uterine hemorrhage." Three of the 28 women suffered bowel damage as well.[57]

Perforation can occur during dilatation of the cervix or while the preborn or his placenta is being scraped from the womb. "Suspected uterine perforation with the dilator occurred in one patient . . . during passage of the No. 31 Pratt dilator" even though the cervix had been premedicated with a PGF2α suppository to reduce resistance.[297]

Perforation can be expected during scraping because there is no loophole to the abortionist's dilemma: ABRADING BLINDLY, by touch alone, the abortionist must exert a pressure which is hard enough to forcibly remove the firmly rooted placenta from its natural environment, yet be delicate enough not to damage the soft tissues of the uterus. Perforation frequently causes major hemorrhage and up to 65% require exploratory abdominal surgery; many women unexpectedly lose their sexual organs this way. [8, 51, 107, 108, 109, 117, 120, 126, 227, 231.] Such was the case for 19 of 215 women who suffered perforations during routine abortions.[64] Besides coping physically with the trauma of a second major surgery, these women must overcome the loss which leaves them forever unable to "have a wanted child."

Drawn to an abortion counseling and referral service by a clever newspaper ad, Leita* learned she was about 21 weeks pregnant. For a $75 fee she was sent out of town for an abortion by a doctor supposedly specializing in borderline cases; they never suggested she go to a local hospital. The out-of-town location was nothing but a doctor's office. After a cursory examination the doctor began her abortion; moments later he began to swear, saying part of the skull was stuck. Leita was keenly aware of a stabbing sensation; she had to be hospitalized later for repair of her punctured uterus.[255]

In other groups studied, uterine perforation including associated abdominal or pelvic pathology maimed 8 women,[144] 3 women having suction abortions,[28] and 23 out of 7833 women undergoing D&C abortions.[28]

At the trial of a chiropractor convicted for performing an illegal abortion, a referral service owner testified she had referred a 16-year-old girl there, unaware that the "doctor" could not legally perform abortions. The girl suffered a perforated uterus and was so badly damaged by the abortion she had to undergo a total hysterectomy.[251]

A New Hampshire abortionist was sued for $600,000 as the result of a carelessly handled abortion; his patient required emergency surgery to remove her perforated uterus, and according to papers filed with the court, the doctor left a sponge in her as well![157]

Uterine perforation occurs more frequently and with more serious consequences in women aborted after 12 weeks gestation. Perforation may be precipitated by a thin uterine wall, a condition common among women who have had several children.[308] Such women will want to take the likelihood of this complication into consideration when making a choice about pregnancy termination. Even a woman with minor damage must be "followed carefully." Undetected perforations "may lead to hemorrhage, bowel obstruction, infection and death.[268] "Only time can tell whether these perforations will have any effect on the future happiness and safety of these women."[21]

PERITONITIS occurred as often after suction abortion as after all other types *combined* in a study of 73,000 legal abortions.[64] It can be part of a painfully larger picture, as in the case of 21-year-old Laura* who was treated for peritonitis following a D&C abortion.[264]

PERMANENT BRAIN DAMAGE can be, and has been, caused by saline abortion.[34, 106]

PNEUMONIA affected 25 women in one group having legal abortions.[64]

POSTABORTAL SYNDROME or PAS is a particularly nasty complication now recognized by most physicians who perform suction abortions—the mouth of the cervix "apparently contracts tightly or the cervical canal is blocked by a clot, and the uterus fills with clotted blood. In the recovery room the patient complains of intense uterine cramping that is not relived by the usual analgesics. When intrauterine suction is repeated, 200 to 500 ml of clotted blood are removed and the patient is dramatically relieved of her symptoms." In one series, 11 women developed PAS.[134]

POSTERIOR CERVICAL RUPTURE: a risk of primary concern to women pregnant for the first time. The pressure of the contractions rips open the side of the cervix ejecting the preborn into the abdomen. This may occur as a result of failure of the inelastic lower portion of the cervix to stretch open while forceful pressure of the contractions has dilated the upper portion; three women in one group suffered cervical rupture and it has been noted in up to 10% of prostaglandin abortions particularly when oxytocin is also given.[156, 216, 232]

PULMONARY COMPLICATIONS are four times more likely to follow abdominal than other surgical procedures. Abdominal surgery in general reduces pulmonary function and puts women with compromised lung function at high risk for postoperative pulmonary complications. Hysterotomy and hysterectomy abortions probably expose a woman to greater risk of pulmonary complications than does chest surgery.[162]

COMPARING FOR SAFETY
PGF2α and SALINE

" . . . the incidence of coagulation changes was minimal with prostaglandin-induced abortion as compared to saline-induced abortion.[296] PGF2α abortions required less time but had a significantly higher rate of major complications: there were nearly 100 ranging from vaginitis to death. Not only did PGF2α cause more major complications, but it also required treatment of complications significantly more often than saline.[161]

The largest randomized clinical trial and the largest observational study of these two agents found women given PGF2α had significantly higher rates of hemorrhage; blood transfusion rates were also higher for PGF2α.[271]

Documented deaths and major complications will be found elsewhere in this book.

Figure 3

PULMONARY EMBOLISM was suffered by 16 women in a single year study;[64] by 13 women in another study;[123] and by 7 in a third.[21]

PUNCTURED VAGINA: Victoria* suffered a puncture of her vagina during a legal clinic abortion. The doctor began the operation without giving her any anesthetic. When Victoria began screaming in pain she was told to lean back and shut up; afterward she and the table were covered with blood. Doubled over with cramps, she asked for an ambulance but apparently her right to choose didn't extend to hospitalization—her request was denied and she was told to get dressed. Later that evening Victoria was so pale and still in such pain that a friend took her to the hospital, where emergency surgery was performed to complete the abortion and repair her damaged vagina.[245]

RENAL FAILURE: Becky*, 16, was 18 weeks pregnant when she submitted to a saline abortion; a severe headache began shortly after they started. Six hours later she was discharging bloody urine; she labored 32 hours before delivery. Afterward nosebleeds and hematomas developed; acute renal failure was diagnosed. Medication was given to clot the blood and renal dialysis was begun. Becky's "safe legal abortion" triggered a kidney failure that kept her in the hospital for 28 days.[103]

Ann Marie* and Kia*, aged 19 and 22, also had saline abortions. Hemolytic anemia, hemorrhage, blood in the urine and acute renal failure ensued. Only after prolonged hospitalization and peritoneal dialysis did normal kidney function return.[266]

RESPIRATORY INFECTION was a problem for 38 women following hysterotomy abortions in one group studied.[123]

RETAINED PLACENTA: one of the most common complications of saline abortion[76]; in one such group 34 were removed without surgery and an additional 34 had to be removed by surgery[214]; affects up to 73% of women aborting by prostaglandins.[41] Retention longer than four hours increases the complications "significantly."[40]

RETAINED TISSUE was a complication affecting 84 women aborted by various methods in a 21 month study;[139] its symptoms are severe bleeding and cramps that are not relieved by oral medication. Repeated surgery is necessary.[134] Retained decidual or placental tissue was reported in 2,730 women in one group.[63] The need for surgical removal was as high as 41.3 per 100 PGF2α abortions and 32.8 per 100 saline abortions; if this is not done within 2 hours of delivery, infection may set in.[271]

RISKS: "Few risks in obstetrics are more certain than that which occurs to a pregnant woman undergoing abortion after the 14th week of pregnancy."[163]

RUPTURE OF THE BLADDER: The attempted suction abortion of a three month pregnancy caused Leela* extensive damage and multiple complications including rupture of her bladder and cervix.[6]

RUPTURE OF THE CERVIX: This is an example of a serious complication, with lifelong repercussions, which was virtually unknown before the legalization of abortion. Because of it doctors are now raising serious questions about the safety of prostaglandin abortion.[216]

"Transverse cervical rupture is a potentially serious complication" which "may adversely influence future reproductive performance with an increased chance of premature delivery or even uterine rupture in a subsequent term delivery." How does this disastrous deviation develop? The artificially-induced uterine contractions are intensely strong, but the cervix doesn't stretch open rapidly enough; the part of the cervix near the uterus stretches so thinly it bursts open. "Not enough attention has been paid to the effects of PGF2α upon the mechanism of cervical dilatation. IF PGF2α DOES INDEED CAUSE EVEN A MINIMAL DEGREE OF CERVICAL CONTRACTION, THIS AGENT MAY NOT BE IDEAL FOR INDUCTION OF MID-TRIMESTER ABORTION BECAUSE OF AN INABILITY TO CONTROL THE FORCE OF UTERINE CONTRACTIONS IN THE PRESENCE OF A CERVIX RESISTANT TO DILATATION." (emphasis added)[216]

Francine* was 16 years old and 21 weeks pregnant when her prostaglandin-prodded baby aborted through a rupture of her cervix. The rupture "was detected after delivery when fresh vaginal bleeding was observed."

Nineteen-year-old Mandy* delivered twins in a 20-week abortion through a cervical laceration which bled so "briskly" she needed two units of whole blood.

The doctors who treated these girls suggest that "all prostaglandin-induced abortions have a vaginal examination so that such lacerations may be immediately detected and repaired." Tragically, these needed repairs will not be made on many unlucky women if the pharmaceutical drug pushers are successful at inveigling approval of the do-it-yourself prostaglandin suppository currently being touted for home abortion; women deprived of proper medical supervision will suffer this and other deadly complications more frequently and with frightening consequences.

RUPTURE OF THE UTERUS: Alison*, 22, was 8 weeks into her first pregnancy. During her suction curettage abortion at a clinic, she went into shock and was immediately transferred to a nearby hospital where they found her uterus had ruptured. She was operated on to repair 16 inches of torn intestines and a rip in her womb. She remained hospitalized for six weeks.

At 46, Nicole* leaves a large family of children at home to go to a university hospital for abortion of a 17 week pregnancy. Until now she has been in good health.

hour 0— removal of some amniotic fluid is followed by injection of hypertonic saline

hour 8— oxytocin is given "over a 4 hour period and repeated every 4 hours for a total of 12 hours"

hour 9— membranes rupture and contractions begin

day 2— the same infusion is repeated

hour 30— labor pains continue "without evidence of cervical dilatation;" Nicole's body will not cooperate in the attempt to prematurely end the pregnancy

hour 40— She complains of pain and is having trouble breathing; her blood pressure drops sharply. The uterus has ruptured! Nicole is whisked to an operating room where emergency surgery reveals "a massive hematoma," blood loss of approximately 2500 cc; "the entire right lower segment of the uterus had ruptured."

Nicole's entire reproductive system had to be removed; six units of blood were given and she was unable to leave the hospital for seven more days. Her doctor now recommends that women having saline abortions who have had several pregnancies, NOT be given oxytocin to shorten the length of labor.

Shayna's* uterus ruptured from a prostaglandin abortion. After laboring for 48 hours, with contractions strong enough to burst the side of the womb itself, her 14 week preborn plowed into her peritoneal cavity; emergency surgery was necessary. The damage was so severe her doctors had to take out her female organs. Shayna's recovery was delayed by a collapsed lung and paralytic ileus.[259]

"Prostaglandins increase intrauterine pressure to levels far beyond that of normal labor. The increased risk of uterine rupture after previous cesarean section is well recognized. This case . . . of spontaneous rupture of the uterus following induction of labor for midtrimester termination of pregnancy by intravaginal PGE2 suppositories . . . raises questions about the presently unlimited use of vaginal PGE2 suppositories with previously scarred uteri."

Joan* was a 23-year-old diabetic, the mother of a child born by cesarean section; her doctors wanted to end this pregnancy prematurely due to her physical condition. "A first vaginal suppository . . . was inserted and within 90 minutes regular contractions were noted sufficiently severe to require sedation . . . [however] despite continuous reinsertion of vaginal suppositories at 4 hourly intervals, a decrease in uterine activity was reported over the following 12 hours . . . In retrospect it must be assumed that uterine rupture occurred within the first 12 hours of labor . . . "

After over 13 hours of painful labor, with her uterus burst and shredded, Joan faced an additional 24 hours of useless abortifacient drug treatment and surgery. Oxytocin was given to coax her womb to stronger contractions. "Over the ensuing 24 hours six additional PGE2 suppositories were inserted with no change in the cervical dilatation or effacement." A D&E, attempted under general anesthesia, was unsuccessful because the uterus was empty. The only thing doctors "recognized" was the rip in the wall of the womb through which the preborn had been thrust. A total abdominal hysterectomy was performed.

"If PGE2 suppositories are to be used in previously scarred

uteri," her doctors emphasize, "utmost caution must be taken in order to recognize early signs of uterine rupture. The vaginal route of prostaglandin administration may carry the same risk for uterine rupture as has been reported for the intra-amniotic instillation."[295]

SALINE ABORTION COMPLICATIONS: Outlawed in Japan because of its lethal effect on women, saline abortion is still permitted in most American states. Others, with good laws regulating abortions to protect the health of women, have condemned it. The average time until delivery in one group of women was 35.6 hours; overall (for several groups) it was 31.7 hours from instillation until delivery.[214]

"The procedure of repeat saline instillation has been discontinued because it was felt that this method was potentially hazardous."[214]

SALPINGITIS: Inflammation of the fallopian tubes affected 225 women in one study of legal abortions.[64]

SEPTIC INCOMPLETE ABORTION: This prime spectre of illegal abortion affected 607 women in a single year's study of legal abortions.[64] There is a "statistically significant association between gestational age at termination and the incidence of septic incomplete abortion."[153]

SEPTICEMIA: Blood poisoning was suffered by 24 women in one year in one study.[64]

SEVERE REACTION TO PROSTAGLANDIN with hypotension, bradycardia, shivering, and difficulty breathing affected two women in one series. Of the others in this group, Angela D.* ruptured her uterus and Tanya M.* developed blood in her urine from an accidental intravenous injection of hypertonic urea. She required extensive treatment for this condition in addition to the fact that she did not abort within 14 hours; an oxytocin infusion was begun, and it was 12 more hours before the small stillborn body was delivered.[166]

SHOCK-COLLAPSE: In a series of first trimester abortions 9 women collapsed during suction and 17 during D&C.[28]

STERILITY: One of the most severely harmful injuries occurring from legal abortion is uterine perforation necessitating major exploratory abdominal surgery and hysterectomy. In a typical case[56] 17-year-old Marcy* had a suction curettage at 10 weeks gestation. Due to poor anesthesia, she made a sudden move resulting in perforation of the uterus by the curette. This made exploratory surgery necessary; because a uterine artery was found lacerated and bleeding profusely, she had to have her womb removed.

Such permanent impairment is a most unfortunate consequence for the young woman who wants to have a family some day, but chooses abortion because she feels now is just not the right time for her. There will be scant consolation in the empty years that lie ahead for the woman alone with the knowledge that she voluntarily terminated her only pregnancy.

SUBACUTE BACTERIAL ENDOCARDITIS: an inflammation in the heart caused by infection has been known to result from urea-oxytocin abortion.[267]

TEENAGE TROUBLES: "Girls are still victims of a double standard, under great social pressure to have dates, and the media has made them feel it is not 'normal' to refrain from sex . . . They are too young to recognize the tragic consequences."[172]

It is typical that an adolescent cannot accept the fact that she's pregnant and thus will delay—for as long as four months[283]—confiding in anyone about it. If denied the opportunity of obtaining supportive help, she will arrive at the doctor seeking abortion in the second trimester, putting her immediately in a high-risk category.

Even early abortions can damage a young girl's sensitive reproductive organs. Both suction and D&C frequently involve dilating an immature cervix and therefore risk a difficult and potentially traumatic dilatation, often resulting in an incomplete abortion, infection, delayed hemorrhage, the need for rehospitalization and surgical evacuation. One adolescent clinic found a very high rate of complications: 26% following suction curettage and 47% following intra-amniotic saline; 10 girls undergoing suction had immediate complications and 7 required readmittance for delayed complications. One girl was readmitted in septic shock with a temperature of 106⁰. Twelve girls having saline had immediate complications and 7 required readmission; 3 didn't go into labor following saline injection.[105]

PROSTAGLANDINS COMPARING FOR SIDE EFFECTS AND COMPLICATIONS

Sixty women, scheduled for abortions by suction curettage, were divided into 3 groups of 20 each. Three hours before cervical dilatation, 20 women (Group B) received a 50 mg. PGF2α triglyceride vaginal suppository; 20 women (Group C) received a 20 mg. PGE2 suppository; 20 women (Group A) received no suppository. The test was designed to see if the suppositories would reduce the amount of force necessary to pry open the cervix. Although the suppositories did their job, they were responsible for almost all of the complications that occurred.[297]

ADVERSE EFFECTS	Control group	F2α group	E2 group
Women	20	20	20
Vomiting:			
number	0	8	12
percent	0	40	60
Diarrhea:			
number	0	9	3
percent	0	45	15
Pain:			
number	0	2	2
percent	0	10	10
Cervical trauma:			
number	3	0	4
percent	15	0	20
Uterine perforation:			
number	0	1	0
percent	0	3	0
Vertigo:			
number	0	1	3
percent	0	3	15

Figure 4

THROMBOEMBOLISM: A blood clot blocking a blood vessel affected 21 women in one study of hysterotomy abortions; the addition of sterilization to the operation increased the risk of this fourfold.[123]

THROMBOPHLEBITIS: inflammation of a vein developing before the formation of a blood clot obstructing the vein; affected 35 women in one group;[64] occurred as often from suction as from saline abortion in another series—64 women had to be readmitted to the hospital for from 14 to 18 days.[65]

THROMBOSIS: "Symptoms and signs of deep-vein thrombosis developed in 12 patients—after vaginal termination in 8 out of 812 cases and after hysterectomy in 4 out of 106. All these patients required anticoagulant therapy."[21]

TRANSPLACENTAL HEMORRHAGE sensitizes 3 to 10% of Rh negative mothers.[13] 48.7% of women known to be Rh negative are untreated and therefore unprotected from the danger to their future babies who could develop Rh hemolytic disease.[14, 73]

TRAUMA OF THE REPRODUCTIVE TRACT is thought to be responsible for a highly significant increased rate of late miscarriages in women who have aborted a first pregnancy.[260]

TRAUMATIC BIRTH: A team of reporters investigating abortion abuses found that referral services rarely explain the methods and risks of mid-trimester abortions and doctors' reasons for wanting them performed in hospitals rather than in clinics. As explained elsewhere in this book, beyond the 12th week of pregnancy the interior of the uterus is very soft and easily damaged by the instruments commonly used for early suction abortions. For this reason mid-trimester implementation of these instruments and procedures poses special dangers:

Lorraine* had been pregnant for quite some time when her mother took her to a clinic for the kind of abortion that only works in early pregnancy (because in the eighth and ninth weeks of life, the cartilage in the preborn's legs and arms begins to turn to hard bone and it can't be sucked into the tiny opening of the suction device). The abortionist had already begun suctioning Lorraine's womb when she began hemorrhaging. She was sent by car to a nearby hospital where doctors determined she was seven months pregnant.

A few days later she was released from the hospital but she returned, in labor, within 48 hours. Less than a week after the attempted legal abortion, Lorraine gave birth to a baby girl normal in every way except that she was missing a piece of her scalp about the size of a fifty-cent piece, which had been torn off by the suction abortion machine.[255]

UNINTENDED MAJOR SURGERY: In locales where abortion is unregulated, women may be put on tables in clinics and doctors' offices which are not equipped for emergencies. Yet when an emergency does occur, it can pose *the* most treacherous threat to a woman's life and well-being, for this is the most delicate part of her body. The loss of a minute in administering oxygen or blood may mean the loss of a life; still, unregulated abortions may be performed miles away from hospitals, hours away from surgeons. Even in a hospital, the specialist needed to repair an organ or save a life may be unavailable when needed.

Few if any women place themselves on abortion tables unless they feel it's what they need most in their lives at that moment. Yet with a shift of her hips, or a flash of the curette, her most pressing need suddenly may become general anesthesia, an operating room staffed with surgical nurses, exploratory surgery, hysterotomy or hysterectomy, a surgeon more experienced in urology than in emptying wombs. The unexpected need for unintended major surgery may be the worst complication of legal abortion.

Unanticipated laparotomy—surgical opening of the abdomen—was needed by 120 unsuspecting women in one study.[64] In another, it was required following injury to the uterus in 6 of 812 aspiration or curettage patients. Re-evacuation was necessary in 130 (11%) in one series; also in 11% following hysterotomy and in 9.5% after vaginal termination in another.[21]

"Re-evacuation of the postabortal and post-partum uterus carries increased hazards which are not recognized as widely as they should be. Within a few days of delivery or abortion the uterus is soft, edematous [swollen], and often infected, particularly if fetal products are retained. In this state it is so easily perforated that it may be ruptured even by the gentle opening of ovum forceps within the cavity. Moreover, curettage under these circumstances is particularly liable to remove the

107

deeper layers of endometrium and lead to the formation of synechiae [adhesions, fibrous bands]."[21] (See Traumatic Intrauterine Adhesions)

UNINTENDED MINOR SURGERY including suturing of cervical lacerations was among the "most frequently encountered complications associated with second trimester D&C . . . In two cases, repeat D&C was used in the treatment of post-abortion pelvic infection."[167]

Additional curettage may also be necessary to control severe bleeding[120] or to empty the womb[227]; 30 out of 64 women undergoing prostaglandin abortions required surgical completion.[296]

UNNECESSARY SURGERY: Menstrual extraction, and menstrual regulation, are the euphemisms given to a technique of early suction curettage performed when the only presumptive sign of pregnancy is a late period; it is usually performed on an out-patient basis, without the use of anesthetics or pain-killing drugs, and the cervix is not dilated.

"A limitation to performing early abortion is that pregnancy tests are usually unreliable until after 44 days of amenorrhea (absence of menstruation). Most physicians are understandably reluctant to expose a woman to the risks of abortion until the suspected pregnancy can be *reliably* diagnosed."[238] When the pregnancy test is indefinite or negative, or performed so early as to be unreliable, the chances of the surgery being unnecessary may be more than 60%.[239]

Major complications reported following early vacuum aspiration include retention of tissue, perforation of the uterus, cervical laceration requiring stitches, substantial blood loss, shock, apnea (transient cessation of breathing), pelvic infection, pain, nausea, vomiting, dizziness, fainting and, inevitably, followup examination showed some women were still pregnant.[239]

The total complication rate for menstrual extraction may be lower than the complication rates for D&C and regular suction abortion, but this apparent safety is deceptive, because when you don't know for sure if there is a pregnancy, you don't know if the woman is being subjected *needlessly* to a procedure known to cause dangerous complications.

COMPARING FOR SAFETY

SALINE   and   D&E

more frequent cases of fever, endometritis, hemorrhage, retained tissue, urinary tract infections	more cervical injuries
	more uterine perforations
minor, occasionally operative, treatments of complications were required significantly more often	complication rates increase with gestational age
antibiotic therapy required 2.5 times more often	suturing of the cervix was 2.3 times more frequent
blood transfusions were necessary 4.7 times more often	
rates of curettage or manual evacuation 34.7 times higher	

SUCTION CURETTAGE   and   D&E

less dangerous	more dangerous
	more frequent and more severe complications, most commonly infection and hemorrhage
similar complications	damage to the internal opening of the cervix, caused by the greater dilatation required, is a major concern; spontaneous abortion and low birthweight of future babies are related to the degree to which the cervix must be forced open

273, 275

Figure 5

109

URETEROUTERINE FISTULA: an abnormal, tube-like passage between the ureter (tube carrying urine from the kidney to the bladder) and the uterus:

Beverly's* legal abortion was the first chapter in a most unpleasant story. Only 16 years old, she had a curettage abortion in a hospital at 12 weeks gestation. Following her release, she was hospitalized a second time, at a different hospital, for chills, fever and a vile vaginal discharge. Retained products of conception of 12 weeks size were found.

Days later she came into still another hospital emergency room, again complaining of chills, fever and a heavy malodorous discharge. This time the presence of a "macerated fetus of about 14 weeks gestation" was confirmed by x-ray examination. After treatment for infection and stabilization of her condition, she was taken to the operating room where the small body was removed through her dilated cervix.

Before and during this surgery, clear fluid was seen flowing from the uterine cavity. Postoperative evaluation revealed a ureterouterine fistula—urine was flowing freely from the kidneys through the uterus and out of the cervix and vagina. Doctors inserted a catheter (diverting the urine and allowing the ureter to heal itself) and left it there eight days; at the time it was removed the fistula was better, but still there. No further treatment was given.

"With the vast number of uterine curettages performed for elective first trimester abortion, surgeons should be aware of this rare but important complication of the procedure.[168] (See Damage to a Ureter)

URINARY TRACT INFECTIONS were seen in 2 women after suction curettage and in 8 women following suction and sterilization[143]; it also appeared in 68 women undergoing hysterotomy abortions in one study.[123]

UTERINE ATONY: Failure of the uterus to contract may occur after saline abortion[64] and may make removal of the womb necessary.[167]

VERTIGO: 4 out of 20 women who received prostaglandin suppositories to reduce cervical resistance before dilatation for suction abortions "complained of transient vertigo" which lasted for 15 minutes.[297]

VOMITING: 70% of women undergoing urea-prostaglandin abortions had episodes of vomiting; this was reported in each of two series.[141] 40% of women treated with PGF2α suppositories and 60% of those treated with PGE2 suppositories for cervical dilatation prior to suction curettage experienced vomiting.[297] (See Gastrointestinal Disturbances)

WATER INTOXICATION: a potential danger for women undergoing instillation abortions, particularly saline[214]; may cause headache, dizziness, vomiting, convulsions, coma, and death.

"The risks of water intoxication with high dose continuous intravenous oxytocin infusion are well known."[48]

"Water intoxication during abortion is an entirely preventable iatrogenic (physician-caused) complication."[271]

WHITE BLOOD CELL COUNT RISE: In a study of women undergoing delivery abortions by PGE2 suppositories "the white blood cell count significantly rose from a mean of 8.34 at control to 13.58 at 6 hours and 13.94 at the time of abortion . . . This rise in white blood cell count was not associated with any clinical sign of endometritis or infection"[296] but it may be a sign that the body rejects the prostaglandin, sees it as an invader and attempts to destroy it; the elevation of temperature in every patient in this study, and in over 60% of women in another study, supports this theory.

WOUND DEHISCENCE: bursting open of the wound made in the major abdominal surgery of hysterotomy (which is a miniature cesarean section) happened to 12 women in one group.[123]

WOUND INFECTION was a problem for 2 women having their tubes tied at the time of suction abortion[143] and for 20 women aborting by hysterotomy.[123]

"There probably has not been developed and probably never will be identified an 'ideal' method of bringing about interruption of second-trimester pregnancy. It continues to be a cumbersome, time-consuming, somewhat unpredictable, and never completely safe process which demands that only highly skilled, trained practitioners should be responsible for initiating these procedures...

"Most of the complications of second-trimester abortions are inherent in the biologic challenge of the interference with a normal second-trimester pregnancy ..."[267]

5

LATE
COMPLICATIONS

Late complications are those which are detected or develop after the abortion, after the woman has been released from medical supervision, or which are connected with a subsequent pregnancy, or with future attempts to conceive.

ADHERENT PLACENTA: Normally a placenta (the after-birth) is firmly rooted to the wall of the womb. In some women who have had induced abortions, the placenta becomes adherent to the wall of the uterus—it may not separate completely and surgical removal may be necessary. [78, 89]

AMENORRHEA: A decrease or absence of menstruation is often attributable to intrauterine adhesions caused by scraping the womb during an induced abortion; 27 out of 28 women who underwent elective first trimester abortions developed amenorrhea compared to only 3 of 22 women who had a D&C completion of a spontaneous miscarriage. This "significantly higher incidence of secondary amenorrhea" may be due to the difficulty of disturbing "the 'intactness' of the pregnancy, or to peculiarities of suction curettage in elective abortion." [169]

AMPUTATION OF THE CERVIX may be the treatment of choice when dealing with a cervical pregnancy which can result from the curettage termination of a prior pregnancy. [226] (See Cervical Pregnancy)

BIRTH OF A DEAD CHILD: The lenis lure and the pressure of family and acquaintances can combine to induce a woman to relinquish control of her body and submit to an unnecessary abortion with frightening consequences.

Marjie* describes her suction curettage as "a real bummer, the worst down of my life." The slim mother of three was abandoned by her husband shortly after she learned she was pregnant. Although she knew how well-formed her baby was at 12 weeks, and despite having friends to help her through her pregnancy, she allowed another "friend" to talk her into a late-first-trimester abortion she didn't really want.

"I wasn't examined; they didn't take my temperature or blood pressure. I didn't even see the doctor's face until I was on the table and he was doing the abortion. It was terrible, terrible," she sobbed.

She was kept in the recovery area for three hours as the bleeding became more profuse. "They gave me three shots, but it just wouldn't stop," she explained. Marjie says that while she was in the recovery area, a girl carrying a plastic bag "came right past me; I was sitting beside the door to the doctor's office. She told him she'd had an abortion there the day before, but just a couple of hours ago this baby came out. On the forms they give you it says to come back if you have trouble and that's why she came back, and brought this baby in this plastic bag." Marjie was horrified. She did not realize then, that that scene would be repeated with herself in the leading role.

Because the cartilage in the preborn's collarbone, arms, legs and rib cage begins to turn to bone around the ninth week, these parts of the body can't be liquified by the suction abortion machine. By the 12th week of gestation a suction abortion can't produce much more than trouble.

The day after her "abortion," Marjie gave birth at home to a tiny son. "I couldn't believe it was happening. First I saw this hand, then a foot . . . He was almost as big as my hand; I held him. I touched him. I was alone with him for an hour and a half before Pat* (a family member) came to take me to the hospital. I counted ten little fingers and ten little toes. He was perfect. I couldn't believe it."

Marjie had to have a D&C; she was hospitalized for two days. She wishes she had allowed the pregnancy to continue. "I didn't realize until now that I could have let it go on. It was going to come out one way or the other; I wish I hadn't given up." For emphasis she adds, "I'd have ten kids before I went

114

through another abortion," but she knows she'll never conceive again. Marjie needed extensive psychiatric therapy to recover emotionally.

BIRTH OF A LIVING CHILD: In 70 women pregnancy remained undisturbed by suction abortion and the preborn "continued to develop normally." [134, 139] (See Failed Abortion)

The following case illustrates not only a pregnancy continuing to term and resulting in the delivery of a live infant after exposure to three abortifacient doses of intra-amniotic PGF2α, but also how a young girl may be railroaded into an abortion against her will.

Sara Jean* was 15, mildly retarded, and pregnant for the first time. On April 16, 1975 at 15 to 16 weeks of pregnancy, she was admitted for an abortion. PGF2α was injected through a catheter. The day passed uneventfully; that night she experienced some vomiting, but no contractions or cramps.

The following morning pitocin was infused; the second day brought no contractions, no bleeding. On April 18, still in the same bed, still with the catheter lodged in her abdomen, Sara Jean underwent a second attempt—a reinjection of PGF2α; "this procedure was unsuccessful [according to the medical journal] due to the dislodging of the catheter. The patient refused further treatment and was discharged with plans to be readmitted." Reading between the lines of this sterile report, we can see a young girl, probably terrified, confined against her will, who for three days tolerates the intolerable before "dislodging" the thing that has been sticking out of her stomach. She refuses further invasion of her body; she leaves—subject, no doubt, to her mother's steely determination to terminate the pregnancy.

Three weeks later, on May 8, she was returned to the hospital and again injected without incident. Again, no contractions. The next day she was started on the pitocin drip; May 9 passed uneventfully. With the dawn May 10, rose Sara Jean from her bed. For no less than four days her preborn had been subjected to lethal doses and now she had had enough; her ire matched the preborn's will to live. Against medical advice she signed herself out of the hospital. She sought the help of a high-risk obstetric clinic and went there faithfully every two weeks; no problems developed.

115

On September 9 she was admitted to the hospital at 36 weeks gestation with premature rupture of the membranes; after six hours of labor her son was born, healthy at 5 lb. 6 oz., with an Apgar score of 8/9 and no congenital abnormalities. During his infancy he was examined three times by a private pediatrician who found him to be physically well, developing normally, with no abnormal neurologic signs. Wanting the best for him, as she had all along, Sara Jean courageously placed her son for adoption.[170]

BLEEDING BEFORE 28 WEEKS OF GESTATION in the pregnancy following an induced abortion occurs more often than in pregnancy following a normal delivery. This finding supports the theory held by medical experts that forced pregnancy termination increases the risk of bleeding in a subsequent pregnancy.[309]

CERVICAL CANAL DIAMETER INCREASE: "Women who have had abortions have greater cervical canal diameters and a tenfold increase in the incidence of second-trimester miscarriages"; the overall loss of wanted children conceived after an abortion was 17.5% of 211 women, compared with only 7.5% in women who miscarried following a natural miscarriage.[171]

CERVICAL INCOMPETENCE: Sometimes called cervical insufficiency, this is the unhappy state in which the cervix has been damaged during an abortion to the degree that it is unable to perform its function (See Premature Delivery). Its risk is influenced by the age, and consequently the size, of the preborn and the way the cervix is forced open. In a study in which nearly three-fourths of the women had suction abortions, 10% were apparently suffering from cervical insufficiency two years later.[232]

A team of investigators comparing second pregnancies and their outcome, reported that following legally induced abortion women tended to have shorter pregnancies than other women who previously had a spontaneous abortion. The statistically significant differences strongly suggest cervical incompetence is responsible for the loss of a great many wanted babies conceived after legal abortions. Lending weight to this suggestion is the fact that poor reproductive performance resulted when it was known that the cervix had, in fact, been damaged during the abortion.[281]

Cervical incompetence causes a 30% to 40% increase in spontaneous miscarriages of wanted babies following suction done at less than 12 weeks gestation[61] and a tenfold to 40% increase in spontaneous mid-term miscarriages. [72, 89] It is a prime contributory factor in premature delivery of a wanted child conceived after a legal abortion.[101] (It should be noted that cervical incompetence may be caused by other factors than forced abortion, although here we are looking only at cervical incompetence specifically caused by an induced, legal abortion.)

CERVICAL PREGNANCY: In cervical pregnancy, the newly-conceived takes up residence in the mucous membrane of the cervix instead of in the lining of the womb. The mechanism by which this occurs is unknown, but all evidence points to an earlier curettage as the prime cause. "The reported incidence has been rising in the past decade" (the liberal abortion era). The highest incidence is reported in Japan where abortion has been legal for over 25 years.[226]

Doctors report cervical pregnancy in 3 women, all of whom had had curettage previously, 2 of these for elective abortion. In all 3 cases removal of the womb and cervix was necessary to control excessive, persistent bleeding.[226]

In 13 of 19 cases the immediately preceding pregnancy had been surgically aborted; a review of 31 cases of cervical pregnancy revealed 25 of the women had undergone an earlier curettage.[226]

This is another of those tragic, unanticipated results of a perfectly legal abortion that will cheat a woman out of the satisfaction she sought in the abortion: the ability to have a baby when she wants to. Virtually all victims of this complication lose the last baby they'll ever have as a direct result of choosing to abort the older sibling. The grief and loneliness these women bear as a result cannot be measured, it can only be endured. And yet, they may be the lucky ones. "Hemorrhage in cervical pregnancy can be most alarming and sometimes fatal." Death is usually due to shock from persistent bleeding or delayed hysterectomy.[226]

117

CHORIOCARCINOMA, a form of cancer, has been mentioned in medical literature as a possible complication of induced abortion.[308]

COMPLICATED LABORS: prolonged; adherent placenta; placenta previa[28]; excessive bleeding at delivery[29]; an increased need for cesarean section with subsequent births.[77]

DAMAGE TO THE MYOMETRIUM: Induced abortion damages the muscular wall of the womb leading to second trimester miscarriages, premature births and still-births.[97]

Yvonne* lived in Orange County, California. She had two abortions prior to a pregnancy she hoped to carry to full term, but "the top of the uterus blew off as if from a hand grenade . . . labor had not begun, but pressure of the growing infant against the weakened wall of the womb caused rupture. The child was thrust into the abdominal cavity and its umbilical lifeline to oxygen was lost as the placenta separated. The beautiful, full-sized baby was dead." Yvonne nearly lost her own life as well. And a hysterectomy had to be performed. Now she can never have another baby.[172]

DAMAGING INFLUENCE: "Our own studies—as well as those reported by other authors in medical literature—confirm the damaging influence of induced abortion, especially induced abortion of the first pregnancy."
Comparison of the second pregnancies of women who had aborted their first pregnancy—with other women who had not—showed a significant difference in these areas: the women who had previously aborted had more premature deliveries, had more cases of early separation of the placenta, had longer labors, had more complications of delivery, had more lacerations of the cervix, lost more blood at the time of delivery and had more severe bleeding episodes, and had babies with an average lower Apgar score.
The doctors conclude that physicians and counsellors who are "giving advice for the interruption of a first pregnancy (have) a duty of scrupulous explanation to the women of all the consequences."[225]

DANGER TO A LATER PREGNANCY: One relation between induced abortion and subsequent abnormal outcome of pregnancy is shown in the "increasing evidence that aborting a first pregnancy yields a considerable increase in the births of prematures in subsequent pregnancies."[68]

DECREASED REPRODUCTIVE CAPABILITY: Your chances of having a baby "when you want to" after an abortion are significantly decreased by that abortion. A review of world literature[61] shows that induced abortion increases:
sterility
menstrual and other disorders
pelvic inflammatory conditions
premature birth by at least 40%
extrauterine pregnancies 100% to 150%
spontaneous miscarriages by at least 30% to 40%
subsequent perinatal mortality after one abortion 50%

Miscarriages were observed more than twice as often, and twice as many premature deliveries were recorded, among women with previous abortions as compared to women without; 143 women suffered significantly higher rates of pre-delivery hemorrhagina and blood loss, longer and more painful labor and post-delivery complications from retained or adherent placentae than women who had never aborted a pregnancy. Life-threatening ectopic pregnancies were also twice as frequent in women with past abortions and one clinic recorded a 130% increase, since the legalization of abortion.

During later pregnancies, abortion related complications, especially prematurity, greatly increase the number of children born handicapped; illustrating this is the fact that in the six years following liberalization of abortion laws in Japan the *birth rate decreased* 37% but the number of malformed infants who *died increased* 43%.[183]

In a review of 45 women who between them had 53 pregnancies after hysterotomy abortions, evidence was found of substantial risk of rupture of the uterus and a high incidence of small-for-dates infants.[123]

"Abortion? It's nothing!" Lainie used to say. But a first-hand experience changed her mind—and her life. Jake and Lainie had been going together for three years when she became pregnant. She had just begun working as a law clerk and Jake urged her to abort the pregnancy. She agreed.

"The clinic was much different than I expected," Lainie recalls. Assailed by sounds and odors as unpleasant as they were

119

unfamiliar, she became frightened. Jake handed over the money—nearly two hundred dollars—then they were separated and Lainie waited, alone, for two hours, in a tiny room before being put on a table and given an injection to relax her.

She has no recollection of the abortion itself, but vividly remembers waking in severe pain and crying for some time before a nurse told her she could dress and go home.

"A couple of days later I had to go back for an Rh shot," Lainie grimaces, "which I know now was like locking the barn door after the horse got out because that shot has to be given within 24 hours of when the baby comes out. Of course, I didn't know that then. But anyway, while I was getting it, in comes this secretary and says I owe her $135 more because the, you know, the preborn—that's what you call it, right?—was bigger than they thought so they had to do a D&E. Now, this was the first I'd heard of that, so I didn't have the money and she sort of gave me a hard time.

"I pulled as much overtime as I dared; just being new on the job, it wasn't easy, but I needed the money to pay what I owed. But then I started getting so sick I couldn't work, not nervous sick, but the pain. So I went to this doctor that was up a couple flights in our building. He could hardly get near me because it was still so soon and I was so sore, but he said he could see this string hanging and I should come back in a few days, which I did. At that time he told me I'd been cut inside during the abortion and the doctor stitched me up but didn't clip the suture.

"All this was a little more than a year ago and I'm still seeing this doctor regularly. He says he doesn't think I'll ever be able to get pregnant again or avoid a miscarriage if I do. I hope other women don't have to go through what I've been through to learn what abortion is really like!"

DELAYED ABORTION: "Three patients did not go into labor following saline injection. One was readmitted for an elective D&C after her uterus regressed in size. Two finally aborted spontaneously three weeks later."[189] Such delays between the initial procedure and eventual abortion/delivery are bound to take their toll in anxiety and depression as well as in possible physical effects. (See Late Termination of Pregnancy)

DISRUPTION or INFECTION of the WOUND: 117 women who'd had suction, D&C, hysterotomy and hysterectomy abortions needed to be readmitted to the hospital for from five to eleven days because of this frightening and painful complication.[64]

DYSMENORRHEA: Difficult or painful menstruation can be caused by endometriosis, a complication of induced abortion. [19, 174]

ECTOPIC PREGNANCY in a gestation following a pregnancy terminated by induced abortion, is mainly caused by tubal malfunction due to infarction or scarring; furthermore, "a post-abortion infection may predispose to an increased risk of subsequent extrauterine pregnancies in future conceptions."[271]

An ectopic pregnancy causes death from rupture and bleeding[27]; one study found a 100 to 150% increase after abortion[96]; another major government survey reported a 400% increase[78] and a third indicates an 800% increase following legal abortion.[77] A study in Japan revealed a "markedly increased risk for cervical pregnancies in women with histories of previous induced abortion."[271]

"Three cases of ectopic pregnancy were recorded in the second pregnancy of a legal abortion group, none in the other (comparison) group (who had carried first pregnancies to term). The delivery group showed the best reproductive performance."

One of the three women, Erica*, had an induced abortion which was "uncomplicated except for fever-without-local-symptoms on the first postoperative day." She married three years later and proved to be infertile because of blockages of both fallopian tubes. A plastic operation was performed on the tubes and after five years she finally did become pregnant, but it was an ectopic pregnancy. "In this case the induced abortion was probably the primary cause of the events leading to this complication."

One other woman who aborted a first pregnancy and had an ectopic second pregnancy in this series, also had fever without local symptoms on the first day after her abortion. The fever of undetermined origin is implicated in the subsequent ectopic pregnancy.

An association between induced abortion and ectopic pregnancy has been suggested in several reports and confirmed in a case-control approach. [89, 260]

121

ENDOMETRIOSIS is a serious problem known to be caused by hysterotomy abortions. One reputable abortionist "has been opposed to hysterotomy, either abdominal or vaginal, because of extensive Scandinavian experience demonstrating a high incidence of implantation endometriosis, and because of personal experience of this complication." It can cause "monthly distress" and sometimes necessitates hysterectomy which will leave the woman unable to have future wanted children. [19, 21]

ENDOMETRITIS, an inflammation of the mucous membrane lining the womb, strikes up to 10.7% of women after curettage. One researcher says, "Of all the late complications listed, endometritis is the most important."[61]

This pelvic infection was seen in 6 women in one group[232]; in 7 women following suction abortions[143]; in 114 women after first trimester elective abortions[233]; in 9 women aborting by urea-prostaglandin and urea-oxytocin[141]; in 29 women after saline abortions[214]; in 114 women after second trimester procedures[233]; and in 826 women after various types of abortions.[64] In a study of 73,000 abortions "endometritis was by far the most frequently reported form of pelvic infection."[74]

"The vast majority of patients with postabortal endometritis presented with symptoms five or more days after the abortion procedures . . . 20 patients were hospitalized for more than 5 days; five of these underwent long-term antibiotic therapy (up to six weeks)."[233]

FALLOPIAN TUBE DAMAGE: a "disconcerting" problem of "serious importance"; in a study done 2 years after legal abortion, 17 women "had some abnormality" of the fallopian tubes leading to involuntary infertility.[232]

FRIGIDITY after abortion was reported by several women in one study.[18] (See Sexual Coldness)

GENERAL BAD EFFECTS: legally-induced abortion results in an overall complication rate to women which is "horrendous": 35% of all women aborted in Germany suffer long-term ill effects; in Japan, 29%; in Canada, 39% among teenagers; in Czechoslovakia, 20% to 30%. In Australia, two studies show 20% and 70%—the latter in a public hospital. The death rate in numerous countries is twice as high for first trimester abortion as it is for pregnancy and childbirth. Logic alone should verify this point: which is more dangerous for women: the natural process, or the abrupt and forceful interruption of it?[52]

45% of Japanese women responding to questions about their health since an abortion said it was "not as good as before the operation."[18] In analyzing 27,435 abortions in Denmark, three gynecologists said, "It is clearly apparent that all methods involve a risk of more or less serious complications."[93]

"The prevalence of morbidity following induced abortion depends on how long the women concerned are kept under surveillance after the operation. The longer the surveillance, the higher the morbidity reported," state two research teams whose meticulous followups disclosed 35.6% and 36% of women suffering from long-term complications.[94]

Complaints also rise with the number of abortions: 22% after two, 40% after three, 51% after four[23]; another report shows 59% were either "severely troubled with adverse after-effects" or in less than good health following legal abortions.[99]

A doctor with 25 years experience in legal abortion charges that the sudden, unexpected change from pregnancy causes in the body an imbalance of the sympathetic nervous system and many other ill effects including dysmenorrhea, sterility, habitual spontaneous miscarriage, extrauterine pregnancies, cramps, headaches, vertigo, exhaustion, sleeplessness, lumbago, neuralgia, debility, and psychosomatic illness.[174]

20% to 30% of women reported abdominal pain, headaches, dizziness, and other irregularities in one follow-up[78]; in another, 145 women reported cramps and pain and 48 suffered from shock, syncope (a transient loss of consciousness) or hypotension.[64]

"Permanent complications such as chronic inflammatory conditions of the genital organs, sterility, and ectopic pregnancy are registered in about 20% to 30% of all women who had pregnancy interruption. These consequences are definitely higher in primigravidas (women pregnant for the first time) than in multigravidas (women who have been pregnant before). Especially striking is an increased incidence of ectopic pregnancy. Furthermore, as noticed recently, a high incidence of cervical incompetence results from interruption of pregnancy that raises the number of spontaneous abortions from 30% to 40%. *These legal abortions affect subsequent pregnancies and births.* We rather often observe complications such as rigidity of the cervical os, placenta adherens, placenta accreta (adhesions), and atony of the uterus."[89]

"Most of these physical effects are not apparent to the patient just after the operation (dilation of the cervix and curettage), and the statistics of consequences immediately following an abortion give a false picture of the actual long-term physical effects."[101]

In one series of legal abortions, 5 women developed parametritis; two of them had to be hospitalized.[134] Adnexitis, parametritis (inflammation of tissue adjacent to the uterus), endomyometritis or damage to pelvic organs is sometimes apparent soon after the operation, but more often much later. "Intermittent or chronic ill-health may result. Many cases of such ill-health may be brought to an end by hysterectomy, but this means is available (of course) only to those women who do not wish to remain progenitive."[61]

GROSS IRREGULARITY OF THE MENSTRUAL PERIOD: "The number of patients with postabortal amenorrhea, dysmenorrhea, or infertility due to [synechiae] is certain to increase with escalation in the number of legal abortions."[21] Indeed, increased incidences of irregular periods have been noted following legal abortions[77]; 17% of the women in one follow-up reported menstrual irregularities.[78]

This may reflect a physiological change in the uterus caused by induced abortion, or a psychic component may be present by which women with prior abortion perceive their menses differently than other women.[173]

IMPLANTATION OF FETAL REMNANTS can give rise to growth of the dead preborn's brain tissue, bone or cartilage inside the womb, eventually causing heavy, persistent and painful menstruation[46, 91]; 2,730 women in one series of legal abortions were affected.[64]

INCAPACITY: In any given group of women who have had legal abortions, there are women with greater post-operative intervals before resumption of full activities. In a group of 168 women for example, 7% were inactive 8 to 14 days; 3% were incapacitated for 15 days to one month; 4% were disabled longer than a month.[176]

COMPARING FOR SAFETY

OBJECTIONS TO SALINE	OBJECTIONS TO PROSTAGLANDINS	OBJECTIONS TO HYSTEROTOMY
death of the woman	infection	transfusions
hospitalization "sometimes for several days"	cervical tears	4 or 5 days in a hospital
"often a D&C and/or transfusions are required"	uterine rupture	as dangerous as saline and prostaglandin
"occasionally a hysterotomy is necessary"	fistula formation	"the infection rate is high"
disseminated intravascular coagulation	unpleasant side reactions	future pregnancies require termination by cesarean section
hemorrhage	"significant percentage of failure"	30% major complication rate
infection	"patients often have to be 'pitted' out (pitressin) over many hours or even days"	
uterine rupture	retained placenta necessitating surgical removal	
cervical tears	"transfusions for hemorrhage are not rare"	
fistula formation	"hysterotomy occasionally becomes necessary"	
20% major complication rate	40% rate of major complications	

Figure 6

276

125

INFERTILITY: Infertility is on the rise and one reason is legal abortion. Several studies covering more than 10 years *all indicate* that a large proportion of women undergoing abortions will become unable to have children.[177]

To test these findings the role of induced abortion as a cause of infertility was evaluated. The medical histories of 100 infertile women were compared with those of healthy women; they were matched as far as age, number of pregnancies and level of education were concerned. It was discovered that the relative risk of infertility among women who had had an induced abortion was 3.4 times greater than among women who never had an abortion.[177]

Researchers doing this study found a cause-and-effect relationship between forced abortion and the inability to have a baby afterwards: nationally, 45% of infertile women are probably suffering the effects of elective abortion.

"Anyone who treats patients for infertility must be alarmed at the marked increase over the last five years in salpingitis and tubal adhesions."[178] In one study "26 of the patients tried to initiate a new, wished-for pregnancy [after legal abortion] without succeeding . . . (they) found themselves involuntarily infertile."[232]

"There has to be post-abortal infection. We're all very casual about this; a woman has her abortion and in two hours she's home. La-dee-da." But according to prominent experts, invasion of the preborn's natural environment can cause tubal infection which in turn causes infertility. [179, 308]

The proportion of women suffering permanent tubal damage due to genital-tract infection is unknown, however "gynecologists interested in tubal surgery are all too familiar with the syndrome of the infertile wife complaining of primary infertility but confessing in confidence that she had an abortion many years before. It was expensive, was performed by 'a very clever specialist' in an excellent clinic, and was apparently uneventful. The silently damaged tubes are the only physical evidence of what appeared to be a successful and skillfully performed operation."[21]

When fertility—the ability to have a baby—is unwittingly and unwillingly relinquished in abortion, it raises the question of what sort of control over their bodies women are able to achieve by aborting.

Tasha and J. T. had been together for a year when she learned she was pregnant. Both were in college and wanted to continue their schooling. It might be assumed from this point that an abortion was inevitable, but such simplistic reasoning rarely coincides with reality. These students were disturbed by the prospect of pregnancy, but didn't act impulsively. They wanted information and erroneously believed the "reproductive health clinic" would give it; they were told a three-month preborn was just a formless mass of tissue. Had their studies included basic embryology they would have known instantly they were being misled. Relying on the "counsellor's" description they saw no need to delve further and went ahead with the abortion.

Two semesters later their curriculum included a course on embryology. Tasha rushed from the classroom in tears upon seeing pictures of preborns in various stages of development and realizing, for the first time, that the three-month "mass of tissue" had a face and form, arms and legs, and was in fact a perfectly formed little baby. The abortion that was intended to protect her studies ended up disrupting them substantially, as Tasha found herself unable to continue the course.

"J. T. and I grew apart. I'm married to someone else now and I'd like to postpone my career and have a family, but I can't seem to get pregnant again. It could be a hormone problem, but my doctor thinks it's more likely an abortion-related blockage.

"I resent the fact that they lied to me about the baby. I would have waited and thought about it more and I probably would have had the baby, although I don't think I would have kept it.

"The abortion has affected my freedom to choose what to do with my life now. I want to start a family and I can't. I thought, then, I was being very liberated but now it feels more like bondage. It turned out all wrong."

INFLAMMATION OF THE VAGINA, before the first postoperative menstrual period, frequently follows D&C and suction abortions; in one study 120 women were affected after suction abortions and 130 after D&C.[28] On the average, this complication can be expected by 13,900 women per year.

LATE TERMINATION OF PREGNANCY: Two days following an outpatient saline abortion, Shirlee* delivered her dead infant at home; she cut the cord herself without realizing that the afterbirth should also have been delivered. For eight weeks she had a bloody discharge until the placenta finally came out.[180]

MILK SECRETION: When pregnancy ends, a change occurs in the body's hormone balance causing milk to come from the breasts. Because the body only knows that the baby came out, and not what was done with it, milk flows after forced as well as natural delivery. In one study 3 out of 10 women experienced milk secretion after saline abortion and 7 out of 10 after prostaglandin abortion.[218] The flow can last for several days.

MISCARRIAGE: One study reports "a tenfold increase in the number of second trimester miscarriages in pregnancies which followed a vaginal abortion"[72]; another found 14% subsequent habitual spontaneous miscarriage[78]; a third shows the rate of miscarriage 30-40% higher in women with a history of legal abortion.[89]

OSSIFICATION IN THE ENDOMETRIUM: The one common feature in most cases of this unusual, disquieting condition is a history of previous abortion. In one woman, endometrial bone formation was discovered exactly 8 weeks following an induced abortion. Calcification and ossification can develop in old, healed inflammatory tissue or in the area of an old hemorrhage.[181]

PELVIC INFECTION: Fevers begin several days after release from the hospital or clinic and last at least a few days. In one group, 7 women returned to the abortionist for treatment; 3 more sought help from private physicians (it's not known how many more women in this group may have had pelvic infections which weren't reported). 2 of these 10 women appeared to have had incomplete abortions and required additional surgery—a repeat D&C. All the rest were hospitalized from one to three days and treated with antibiotics.[167]

PERSISTENT BLEEDING: Five women in one group undergoing urea-prostaglandin abortions needed to receive medication in an attempt to control persistent bleeding.[141] Prolonged hemorrhage was reported in 73 women following suction abortions and in 44 women after legal D&C abortions.[28]

PELVIC INFLAMMATORY DISEASE or PID: low-grade, smoldering, postabortive pelvic problem; the most common complication found among teenagers and the one most worrysome to the doctor because it can make girls subfertile or infertile in later life.[189]

PLEURAL EFFUSION: fluid in the membrane that enfolds the lungs; one woman who developed this problem had to be readmitted to the hospital for 13 days.[64]

PREGNANCY POTENTIAL INCREASE: If pregnancy is something you don't want, you should be aware that abortion may increase your opportunities for conceiving: a pregnancy carried to term provides you with 12 months of infertility (adoption will make the child legally dead to you and is thought by many to be more humane). Aborting, on the other hand, shortens the time during which conception is impossible to only 5, 4 or even 3 months (depending on how early the abortion is performed). This means leaving yourself open to pregnancy 4 times longer—increasing by four times your chances of becoming pregnant! These chances are further increased by the fact that after an abortion you are more likely to return to the same situation that caused the pregnancy—while your situation will undoubtedly be different after the 12 month infertile period afforded by carrying the pregnancy to term.

PROLONGED HOSPITALIZATION: "Prolonged hospitalization and/or readmission because of major problems brought on by midtrimester abortion requires serious consideration. Second procedures frequently are necessary. The threat to life and health is a reality."[276]
In one study of second trimester D&C abortions, 36 women remained hospitalized longer than 48 hours: 27 for observation and 9 for abortion-related complications. One woman stayed five days following repair of a rip in her uterus. Two longer stays were 10 and 11 days for women who were so badly damaged all their reproductive organs had to be removed.[167]
A woman whose second trimester abortion took 33 hours to complete returned to the hospital two weeks later with pains and a fever; she spent four days in the hospital. When the fever

129

returned she was readmitted for antibiotic therapy and a second surgical scraping. This third hospitalization lasted five days.[222]

An Illinois woman spent eight months in the hospital fighting for her life after a botched legal abortion.[246]

There are numerous other instances in this book of prolonged hospitalization for treatment of abortion-related complications.

PROLONGED LABOR: "Women who had passed 28 weeks of pregnancy" before natural termination of their first pregnancy "had a highly significant shorter duration of labor" in the next pregnancy than women who had terminated their first pregnancy by force.[260]

RECURRENT PREGNANCY despite ready access to contraception is regarded by some as a complication.[105] "The adolescent girl who has once been pregnant is a much greater risk for a repeat performance . . . very likely to be sexually active again within three months."[189]

211 women who'd had vaginal abortions and were pregnant again were investigated; despite good contraceptive advice "43.2% had become pregnant within one year of termination."[281]

RETAINED TISSUE: Neither suction abortion nor D&C is perfectly successful in removing the "products of conception"—the preborn's head, torso, arms, legs, umbilical cord, amniotic sac, and placenta. In one group of first trimester abortions, 320 women were found to have retained tissue.[28]

A woman terminating her second pregnancy by childbirth has a greater chance of experiencing retained placenta or retention of placental tissue if her first pregnancy was terminated by legal abortion rather than by childbirth.[309]

RUPTURE OF THE UTERUS: "Overt rupture of the pregnant uterus can be one of the most devastating events seen by the modern obstetrician. The scar from the previous cesarean section [or hysterotomy abortion] is the largest predisposing factor leading to rupture . . . Spontaneous rupture of a cesarean scar can happen at *any* stage in the gestation [not solely before or during labor]."[164]

During observation of 45 women who together had 53

130

pregnancies after hysterotomy abortions, evidence was found of substantial risk of rupture of the uterus and a high incidence of births of babies who were much smaller than they should have been.[123]

SEXUAL COLDNESS may be related to the psychotraumatic experience of the abortion and emotional weakness following[17]; it affected 33% within nine months after legal abortion and an additional 14% four to five years later in two groups studied. [17, 59]

Robin T., 30, an attractive travel agent in San Francisco, had a disastrous abortion "after which she continued living with the man for four years without ever having intercourse with him again."[278]

Jessica W., now 27, had an abortion four years ago and was happy about it, at that time. "I felt so relieved in recovery. I just wanted to get back to my life." But it didn't work out that way; she found her warm sexual nature changed. "My sex life didn't pick up. The whole time I was pregnant, which ran almost 10 weeks, I had felt very cold . . . Six months after the abortion I finally felt turned on by a guy . . . I got pain . . . For five months afterward I didn't sleep with anyone. I thought maybe I was a lesbian, but I didn't feel anything sexual about women. Mostly I felt dead a lot of the time. I was afraid. Then I started again, but it wasn't like it used to be. And it never has been again."[278]

At four months of pregnancy, Missy B. underwent a difficult saline abortion. It took her over four years to reestablish a satisfying relationship with a man.[278]

Three years after his wife's abortion, Robert F. has never forgiven her or himself for letting it happen. "I didn't start making love to her for a long time . . . I felt that this child had been sacrificed to her work and I resented her work from then on . . . From then on our sex life was a real strain . . . The abortion killed a part of our life together."[278]

SHOCK: After having one abortion each year for three years, Vanessa T. relates, "Now I've been through three years of a whole new awareness. If I had been in touch then the way I am now, I would have understood that my body was involved in a little bit of survival. That's what a child is. It's continuance. The body is striving to protect it, so the body is shocked by such an action (an abortion). The body is offended and shocked and reeling and insulted. It's exactly like throwing a monkey wrench into the works . . . it's not allowing things to flow their natural way . . . I'll never have another abortion."[278]

SMALL BOWEL OBSTRUCTION has occurred, or been discovered, after hysterotomy abortion, requiring readmission to the hospital—in Debbra's* case, for 17 days.[65]

STERILITY is a tragic disorder which may not be discovered until five years or so after an abortion. It's a problem of greater magnitude because unlike an infection that can be controlled by antibiotics, or blood loss which can be replaced, sterility is irreversible.[68] In one group, 50 women admitted for early abortions left permanently unable to have another baby.[74] Each complication that results in the removal of ovaries, or fallopian tubes, or the womb inflicts sterility.
"Kolstad's Norwegian investigation shows that 3%-4% of women become childless subsequent to a legal abortion. Recent statistics from several countries show no improvement on this percentage. Childlessness is a big burden, even for the best of marriages."[101]

SUICIDE ATTEMPTS: Research has revealed nine times as many women who tried to kill themselves have had abortions (compared to other women in the general population).[165]

SYNECHIA: Scarring of the inner walls of the uterus results from attempting to remove the placenta before the body is ready to let it go.[78]

TRAUMATIC INTRAUTERINE ADHESIONS: fibrous bands which take the form of bridgelike connections between the uterine walls or ledgelike projections from the side wall of the uterus; adhesions usually develop from vigorous curettage which destroys the walls of the womb. Adhesions cause a decrease or disappearance of menstrual flow and repeated miscarriages or sterility.
"Traumatic intrauterine adhesions follow instrumental abortion because the uterine walls during pregnancy are extremely softened . . . Mechanical evacuation of the uterine con-

132

tents risks removal of the myometrium (the muscular wall of the uterus) as well as the basal layer of the endometrium *even with* gentle manipulation." Of 192 women presenting with this condition, *all* had a history of intrauterine manipulation and 63 had had fevers as well.[184]

"Intrauterine adhesions pose significant diagnostic and therapeutic problems"—they can be removed by hysteroscopy but in two women this treatment caused further damage by perforating the uterus. Of 28 women whose elective first trimester abortions (24 by suction curettage and 4 by D&C) caused adhesions, one had required a second curettage for persistent bleeding.[169] This raises the tragic possibility of a domino-principle chain of misfortune befalling an unsuspecting woman who, choosing abortion, could require a second scraping to complete the abortion and suffer a puncture of the womb during that, making a third surgery necessary. for repair. She could develop intrauterine adhesions, the removal of which would require a fourth procedure; another perforation could occur at that time which would require a fifth surgery to detect and repair. Each surgery, in turn, exposes her to the multiple risks of infection, to the need for and complications of blood transfusion, possibly more severe lacerations of the cervix and internal organs and arteries which could lead to removal of the womb.

WANDERING LAMINARIA: Laminaria tents, used to dilate the cervix, are a natural product in short supply. For this reason some doctors may sterilize them after an abortion for use on another woman. This may not be safe because they tend to change shape and fragment. A fragmented piece could travel about in a woman's reproductive tract and become lost, inviting infection.[285]

133

"The worse the psychiatric state demanding an abortion, the worse the psychiatric problems after the legal abortion . . . Abortion . . . is a bad way of treating true psychiatric disease . . . Investigation shows that there is less psychological trauma associated with normal birth than there is with a legal abortion."[101]

6

PSYCHOLOGICAL COMPLICATIONS

Our emotions, the subconscious underpinnings of our intellectual faculties, always seem to be the last passengers on the train of progress; abortion's psychological problems increase as the legal barriers decrease. Shortly after their abortions a number of women were interviewed by a team of doctors studying the psychological effects of abortion. Their unexpected findings: 67 women said they were upset, 23 were quite saddened at the experience, and a full 60% indicated they would have chosen natural termination if induced abortion had not been legalized.[176]

"The ability of mothers to accept infants after they are born is underrated and underestimated."[185]

One researcher states that "abortion is a serious assault on the integrity of the body and is a tremendous threat to the integrity of the ego structure." He believes loss of the preborn reactivates castration fears, causing guilt and subsequent depression; if the guilt is unmanageable, it can lead to pathological projection.[186]

Another expert believes that "in all cases, regardless of the reason for loss of the preborn, there is danger of a depressive reaction of a severe degree." One very important point that has, he says, been overlooked, and which could well be the cause of much domestic unhappiness, is the change in attitude toward the sexual partner.[187] (See Sexual Coldness)

135

ADVERSE REACTION was seen in 18.1% of women surveyed by psychiatrists; they felt no relief or just a bit. They were overwhelmed by negative feelings. Even those women who were strongly supportive of the right to abort reacted to their own abortions with regret, anger, embarrassment, fear of disapproval and even shame.[198]

Women who were less emotionally disturbed about their abortions were interviewed four months afterward; 4 in 10 continued to be troubled or regarded their abortions as too upsetting to think about; "other emotional responses including anger, disappointment, and nervousness were indicated by about 17% of those who had wanted and those who had not wanted the pregnancy, while these emotions were expressed by 31% who had not thought about it (wantedness)."[152]

This study also showed that in *every* relationship in which the abortion was unwanted by the infant's father, the woman reported that the abortion experience was "extremely upsetting."[152]

"Negative emotional response (to abortion) involving guilt, sadness or regret" is seen by some psychiatrists as a "part of the normal spectrum of response to abortion."[283]

ANGUISH was the feeling reported by 384 women (73.1% of those questioned) who had undergone a legal abortion.[18]

ANXIETY, which if present after an abortion is felt very keenly, was reported by 43.1% of women in one group.[198]

One doctor reports, "Since abortion was legalized I have seen hundreds of patients who have had the operation. Approximately 10% expressed very little or no concern . . . Among the other 90% there were all shades of distress, anxiety, heartache and remorse."[274]

DEPRESSION: "The significance of abortions may not be revealed until later periods of emotional depression. During depressions occurring in the fifth or sixth decades of the patient's life, the psychiatrist frequently hears expressions of remorse and guilt concerning abortions that occurred twenty or more years earlier."[234]

"The prenatal detection of many genetic defects is now available and has begun to influence the way parents make decisions about childbearing. There may, however, be a psychiatric

136

price that the family pays for this newly available knowledge . . . Since this practice is becoming more widespread, it is pertinent to study the psychological sequelae of selective abortion."[282]

There is a significant risk of emotional and psychological trauma to the family who has experienced amniocentisis specifically for the prenatal detection of a genetic abnormality. Depression after the mid-term abortion of a fully-formed handicapped preborn, whose active movements have been felt by his or her mother, is likely to be more intense than depression following abortion for other reasons. In a study of families who had amniocentesis, and aborted a disabled preborn, "feelings of guilt, doubt and ambivalence were common . . . The incidence of depression following selective abortion may be as high as 92% among the women and as high as 82% among the men and was greater than that usually associated with . . . delivery of a stillborn."[282]

Depression frequently appears as an immediate response to selective abortion. Only 2 of the 13 women and 4 of the 11 men in this study failed to mention depression in describing their emotional reaction to abortion *but* their personal profiles indicate a tendency in each of them to deny emotional problems; "therefore, the actual incidence of depression following selective abortion may be as high as 12 of 13 (92%) among the women and as high as 9 of 11 (82%) among the men studied . . . Certainly these patients exhibited more depression than that described in the literature for women undergoing abortion on psychosocial grounds."[282]

One woman in the study had "previously experienced an 'abortion of convenience' and the depression which ensued lasted less than one week . . . In contrast, she described selective abortion as 'the worst thing that ever happened to me' and is uncomfortable about the procedure even three months later."[282]

Mrs. G. maintained that a delivery by abortion produced "much more depression" in her than the previous delivery of a stillborn child. "Certainly," her doctors assert, "the stillbirth of a wanted child is associated with the disappointment, regret, and sense of loss which are also experienced after selective abortion." But it's the cause of the preborn's death that makes the difference. "A stillbirth is usually regarded as an unfortunate accident, while the etiology (cause) of fetal loss in selective abortion is much more clearly comprehended"; the infant's death by abortion is a premeditated choice. This "role of decision-making," the doctors continue, "and the responsibility associated with selective abortion explains the more serious depression following . . . The responsibility of making the decision to abort may prove to be an uncomfortable burden for the parents."

It's not difficult to see the "relationship between this perception of responsibility and the sense of guilt sometimes associated with abortion . . . Even more important is the woman's realization that she is responsible for a decision which must sacrifice some important goals and values (motherhood and the value of life) in order to sustain or attain other beliefs or achievements (career, self-determination, independence)." Thus, as society has increasingly accepted abortion as permissible, the guilt coming from that source (society) has been lessened, only to be "at least partially replaced by an intrinsic awareness of responsibility" which increases self-accusation and self-guilt.[282]

DEPRESSIVE REACTION or POSTABORTAL PSYCHOSIS with hospitalization and/or suicidal attempt (including two deaths) befell 66 women in one study.[64] 15% to 25% of women will show mild psychological damage lasting several weeks.[193] Depression, one of the emotions likely to be felt with more than moderate strength, was reported by 31.9% of women surveyed.[198]

DISTRESS: "Abortion tore at the fabric of our relationship," said Charles A. five years after his girlfriend's abortion. Both were students when she became pregnant and both favored abortion, although Charles was deeply troubled at night by thoughts of the child. He never spoke about his concern, but instead supported Marge* who was very depressed. After the abortion he admitted his feelings to her and they agreed that abortion was much more of a moral dilemma than they had previously thought. A year later Charles became impotent with her and they broke up. Five years later he was still disturbed about the abortion and has never resolved his feelings about it.[278]

EMOTIONAL DISORDERS: Women who undergo legal abortion may develop, even years later, all sorts of emotional disorders which reach a climax with the menopause.[188] 84 women who had had legal abortions were visited in their homes about two years later; 4 were still embarrassed and distressed

138

and didn't like to talk about it. 9 were classified as consciously repressing guilt. 22 had open feelings of guilt. 10 were classified as having suffered impairment of their mental health.[185]

EMOTIONAL SEQUELAE OF HYSTERECTOMY will affect every woman who unexpectedly loses her womb during an abortion; concrete changes in functioning, attitudes and behavior result.

FAMILY FETICIDAL SYNDROME: People learn by experience and tend to apply as adults behavior they encountered as children. While for the most part, this aspect of child development is beneficial, it may nurture the roots of destructive behavior. A young girl may learn at home from observation that the range of response to pregnancy includes the decision to abort. The woman whose mother chose abortion as a means of dealing with a problem pregnancy may abort even though her own situation could be handled in another, safer, even better way. The decision to abort may be less a response to medical or economic exigency than an aspect of family feticidal syndrome, the three or more generational pattern of artificial pregnancy termination. The feticidal woman's mother may have had a desire to abort her and may have, in fact, aborted one or more pregnancies. Generations of marital disharmony may have played a role in the grandmother, or possibly even the great-grandmother beginning this family feticidal tradition. Proper counseling and supportive help throughout pregnancy can aid in breaking this pattern of misery.

FEAR: "Cowboy boots. That's it. He must have been wearing cowboy boots." Tessa examines her fingernails closely when talking about the suction abortion she experienced two years ago. Her most vivid memory is the fear she felt while waiting on the operating table, a fear that continues to haunt her. "I could hear the doctor's footsteps echoing in the hall as he went from room to room doing the abortions. Those heavy footsteps booming and reverberating until they stopped near me." Tessa's voice drops off, and her long pause suggests she will say no more until, with a strangled laugh she says, "He was like Santa Claus—you know, spoke not a word but went straight to his work? Only I didn't get no present. No present at all."

139

GENERAL NEGATIVE REACTIONS: Of 742 women questioned after abortion, 64 were sad; 23 expressed great sadness. 36 cried and felt somewhat guilty; 37 mothers cried very much and claimed considerable guilt. 50 would have responded to offers of positive help with their problem situations. Most could not justify having induced abortion and nearly two-thirds of all those questioned said they would have given birth if abortion were still illegal.[176]

There is evidence to suggest that women with a negative self-image would benefit from accepting the supportive assistance of, for example, an emergency pregnancy service center rather than trying to escape from their situations by means of abortion; in this way they would receive both practical assistance to improve their status and help in coping with their feelings.[152]

GRIEF: 109 girls between the ages of 14 and 18 underwent abortions at a special adolescent clinic during a 12 month period. Careful follow-up revealed "all of the girls had some sort of grief reaction"; 3 of them required psychotherapy.[189]

GUILT and DEPRESSION are the "most frequent emotional reactions" in patients who have undergone therapeutic abortions; sometimes these after-effects are delayed. Ideas of guilt, self-depreciation and recurrent "pre-occupation centering around the abortion and the general theme of 'I let them kill my baby' might well disturb a poorly integrated personality even to psychotic conditions. To tell a woman she should not continue a pregnancy and have her baby because she is neurotic or psychotic simply increases her feelings of worthlessness. Feelings of love, admiration and respect for the male partner may well be disturbed in the aborted woman to ideas of disgust, hate and disrespect: 'He gave me a baby, then took it away.' The unconscious motivation and even flow of emotions during the readjustments to a normal sexual non-pregnant cycle may result in deeply engrained feelings of hostility toward the husband."[190]

Of women surveyed professionally after legal abortion, 23% eventually suffered severe guilt, 25% mild guilt with symptoms including insomnia, decreased work capacity and nervousness[103]; in another study, 26.4% felt guilt after legal abortions.[198]

GUILT and OTHER PSYCHIATRIC MANIFESTATIONS following abortion were found in up to 55% of European women studied by psychiatrists.[191] The most prevalent psychological disturbances found in 2,771 women studied were "depressive personality developments with self-accusation and guilt complexes, fears of infertility, sexual phobias and other symptoms resulting from unresolved conflicts."[193]

The human manifestations of guilt can take many forms. One couple, Ralph and Dina W.*, "cracked tasteless jokes about it." They admit, "Neither one of us wanted to confront that we had wiped out something alive. So we played games, like in a war, when you end up calling the enemy 'gooks'."[278]

HURT: Other people could never crack jokes about their abortions, so deep is their hurt. Even a decade of society's apparent advocacy of abortion hasn't dimmed what Tyna M. felt even before her abortion was completed. "While I was in the hospital," she says, "there were three (women) in my room, two of whom had a few abortions . . . they were in their early twenties as I was, but their hearts were so hardened.
"The nurse came and gave me a shot to relax me and then they came to roll me down the hall to the operating room. I remember saying, 'Please stop. I've changed my mind; I want to keep my baby.'
"Their reply was now, now, it will be over before you know it. The next thing I knew I was waking up very empty and very lost. I would lie there remembering how my body felt full of child and how in one moment of time my body felt dead and empty . . . I see young girls doing what I did and it breaks my heart. If I could only talk with them for just a minute and share with them the hurt I have suffered . . . "[26]

Sharon V. shares similar feelings. "I live for the day when abortion will be stopped. Abortion killed my baby five years ago. I will never get over it."[26]

IMMEDIATE NEGATIVE REACTION was felt by 11 of 17 women aborted for rubella, and 8 of them continued to have a long-term negative reaction.[88]

MARITAL DIFFICULTIES: "Complications are worse with younger women, the mothers of the future. Therefore, any man contemplating marriage should ask his future wife if she has had an abortus provocatus [a provoked, or unnatural termination of pregnancy]; if so, he should realize that his wife might be barren, or that a child could be born prematurely with subsequent brain damage, possibly leading to spasticity. Such discoveries have sometimes resulted in divorce, due to the husband's disappointment following his wife's previous abortion."[101]

In married couples, the stresses attendant to selective abortion may produce "undesirable marital consequences." In a study of families who sought prenatal diagnosis and aborted disabled offspring, two families experienced separations which "produced repercussions which threatened marital stability for many months or even years afterward."[282]

Mrs. Lee's* abortion resulted in "serious marital difficulties." Her husband felt bitter and left home for a week; upon his return "they continued to deal with the postabortion experience separately." Mrs. Lee experienced "sleep loss, nervousness and tension, and finally contacted a psychiatric social worker." Their marriage was "rocky" for eight months after the abortion.[282]

Mrs. F. was a probable carrier for Duchenne's muscular dystrophy. In a sense she set herself up for a letdown by having amniocentesis; she reacted to the news that her preborn was a boy with "crying and a feeling of disbelief that the whole thing was happening." She insisted upon an abortion although her husband was "torn up inside" and felt "this decision came from thin air."

After the abortion Mrs. F. felt "physically and emotionally empty" and was "really sad" for approximately one month. She suffered from weight loss and decreased concentration and "could not pay attention and could not handle being by myself or alone" for three weeks after the surgery. Both "went through a mourning process." Over a year after the abortion Mr. F. said, "I still feel a lot of resentment and anger, but most sadness."

Mrs. F. became pregnant immediately after the abortion. She again waited until mid-pregnancy for a test to determine the baby's sex, and again it was a boy. He was aborted. "Following this second abortion, Mrs. F. stated she was 'on the brink of being hysterical and was really sad for almost a year.' She related this to the experience of the death of something that was very close to her . . . Mr. F. experienced bloody diarrhea and a 'tight stomach'."

Both husband and wife became so uncomfortable around children they were incapable of actively resuming their careers, she as a teacher and he as a youth guidance counselor. Mr. F. also dropped out of his Master's program, spent less time with his friends and in three months, left his wife; they were separated for six weeks.[282]

Mr. and Mrs. H., the parents of a Down's syndrome child, were concerned about a recurrence (according to Dr. Hymie Gordon of the Mayo Clinic, "if a woman has had a baby with Down's syndrome—trisomy 21—there is a risk of not greater than 1% that she will have another baby with the Down syndrome; in other words, the probability is 99% that she will *not* have another with the Down syndrome."[293])

The H's "did not want an abnormal child, even with the more minor problems of Turner's syndrome" which the test indicated. Mrs. H. chose to abort, but suffered afterward from "negative feelings" which didn't fade for four months. Mr. H. says, "In a way you never recover" and the couple has experienced "a significant deterioration of their sexual relationship."[282]

Their troubles bring to light another distress-producing situation which, while not abortion-related, is significant and not often openly discussed. Mrs. H. resents the fact that they delayed childbearing while her husband pursued his career; she feels this delay may be in part responsible for the genetic defects. Mr. H. feels guilty about this, but "has warned his wife" not to talk about it, or else he's liable to get so upset he'll seek a divorce. He "is considering vasectomy, but his wife prohibits this until she is able to resolve her ambivalence about desiring another child." Clearly, their casual acceptance of contraception, amniocentesis and abortion has brought choices, problems and bad feelings to this marriage which might have been avoided if their marriage functioned under a different philosophy.

In our society today there are great pressures toward having "perfect children" who can share in their parents' pursuit of an increasingly higher standard of living. The availability and acceptance of amniocentesis and abortion puts parents who carry defective genes on the defensive, encourages them to seek and destroy the preborn with a disorder. Such parents may see the community as less willing to offer the financial and emotional support which the parents of a handicapped child require. They may doubt their ability to adapt. Driven to ask themselves "why not" rather than "why" abort, they succumb to the lenis lure. Tragically, these parents may become casualties as often as their offspring.

In the emotional upheaval that surrounds the conception of a child with a disorder, it's easy to lose sight of the alternative choice which is felt by many to be more humane for the infant, and which is potentially less traumatic and risky for the mother. There is no shame attached to placing a child for adoption, even if the parents are married to each other, and even if they have other children. It takes intelligence and good common sense to know when raising a child would be too difficult, impossible, or simply not in the best interest of the child or the family. Our social welfare system has spent decades developing a system of caring for children who are conceived into such situations; there is no need to abort them. Professional adoption counseling could have provided the emotional support necessary for these couples to allow the pregnancies to continue and avoid the turmoil and grief that beset them after selective abortion.

Mrs. B. was a carrier for a genetically-linked bleeding disorder, so a male child would have a 50% chance of being affected or being normal. When amniocentesis showed her preborn was a boy, she was "very depressed and upset"; yet instead of seeking help in coping with the pregnancy and professional guidance in deciding whether to place the child for adoption or raise him, she opted for abortion. Not unexpectedly, she and her husband were "very depressed" afterward. They rationalized their decision by putting it into their minds "that he was a bleeder" although they had no way of knowing this for certain.

Here were parents caught up in the genetic counselling mechanism. When Mrs. B. became pregnant again, she automatically had another amniocentesis; it showed that this baby, too, was a boy. But because there was a breakdown in the system (their doctor was away on vacation) they were able to break away from the "inevitable" outcome with happy results. "The negative experience of the first abortion and the excuse" of the doctor being away "combined to dissuade them from proceeding with the abortion, although [and this is significant] they 'probably would have done it if our doctor had been there.' This child is not afflicted . . . " Had the doctor been around, these

144

weary, distraught parents, bereft of hope, would have aborted a perfectly healthy son.[282]

The bottom line, particularly as regards the status and importance of informed consent, is this: the families in this study "all received excellent counseling regarding the genetic and technical facets of amniocentesis, but *without discussion of the psychological aspects of the procedure* [emphasis added]. An intelligent decision requires the input of all available data, and ignorance of the psychological aspects of selective abortion precludes a fully informed decision . . . It must be the responsibility of the counselor to convey the experiences of others to the patient in order to promote a well-considered decision and to allow preparation for the consequences of that decision."[282]

MENTAL HARM: "Mental harm to abortion patients," according to Sandra Haun of Women Exploited (a prolife group whose entire membership is women who have experienced induced abortions) "may be under-reported since very few women would return to the abortionist for consolation."[192]

NEGATIVE EXPERIENCE: In a second-year followup of teenage girls, 12 described their abortions as a negative experience and indicated they would not have another abortion.[121]
"Immediate negative response to abortion is not uncommon." Up to 43% of 500 women studied showed immediate negative response; the long-term negative response was as great as 50%. Up to 10% of women develop serious psychiatric complications.[283]

NUMBNESS: Many women, particularly teenagers, seem to be unaffected by an induced abortion. But some psychiatrists believe that this numbness—emotional paralysis—is an adverse reaction meriting psychiatric attention.[198]

OVERWHELMING GUILT AND ANGUISH: "The premature spontaneous termination of a wanted pregnancy can be a psychologically and emotionally disturbing experience for any young woman. When such a premature delivery results in the loss of a wanted baby, and is found to be due to damage caused by a previous surgical termination, then the guilt and anguish experienced can be overwhelming."[47]

145

PARTICULARLY PRONE to PSYCHOLOGICAL DISTURBANCES are "motherly women" and those "talked into abortion" by others. Those with the least chance of becoming disturbed are women "with little motherliness" and the feeble-minded.[193]

PSYCHIATRIC DISTURBANCES: An examination of research into the psychiatric consequences of premeditated abortion suggests that the relationship between abortion and psychiatric disturbance is far from simple. Up to 14% of women seek psychiatric help after abortion; up to 10% are hospitalized. A study of 188 women who had abortions "found that women with a history of any psychiatric disturbance were three times as likely to have some psychiatric disturbance afterwards as those who did not report psychiatric disturbance in the past."[280]

PSYCHIATRIC ILLNESS: The failure of abortion providers to make certain that a woman has all the available data with which to make an intelligent decision—information on prenatal development, the abortion method, complications and adverse effects both physical and psychological, knowledge of other women's experiences, alternatives, and ample time to go through the decision-making process and be able to give informed consent—can have catastrophic consequences.

According to an article in the *American Journal of Psychiatry,* a number of women "will experience true psychiatric illness after abortion. It is desirable, but difficult to predict with any degree of certainty, which women will develop postabortion psychiatric illness . . .

"The literature on abortion and our clinical experience both indicate that there is a greater likelihood of postabortion psychiatric illness in situations in which any of the following elements are present: coercion, medical indication, concurrent severe psychiatric illness, severe ambivalence [i.e. when the woman wants a baby, sees this preborn as her baby, or feels she is its mother], and the woman's feeling that the decision is not her own [and even sometimes when it is her own]."[283]

Accordingly, a woman should *not* abort if:

1. a doctor says she is too mentally unstable to continue the pregnancy

2. a doctor says she or the preborn is too physically ill to allow natural termination of the pregnancy

3. the family says she should have forced termination
4. the family says she shouldn't have forced termination
5. the positive help of Birthright, or another emergency pregnancy service, could support her until natural termination.

A doctor and two social workers who have dealt extensively with women suffering serious psychiatric complications of legal abortions chose the following four case histories from more than 500 patients to illustrate individual problems caused by legal abortion.

A 21-year-old single woman, Megan McG.*, felt socially aborted by her family, "that they wished to be rid of all her problems as quickly as they were rid of her first pregnancy. . . . After the procedure (she) began a pattern of heavy drinking, in which she went to a bar, drank to the point of exhaustion, spent a day in bed recovering, and then repeated the pattern. One night, after a fight with her parents, she had intercourse with a family friend without contraceptive protection and she became pregnant."

She denied to herself that she was pregnant until "the pregnancy was too advanced for abortion; her baby was due around the anniversary of her (prior) abortion. . . . Her pregnancy was discovered only after her regression to an enraged state and psychiatric hospitalization." The fact that some women cope well with unplanned and even illegitimate pregnancy suggests that a woman make her choice only after careful thought and after being given the alternative of carrying the pregnancy to term.[283]

Laurel* was an attractive, good-humored, 27-year-old career woman who saw herself as "happy-go-lucky with no awareness that things can go wrong in life" until she discovered she was pregnant. Panicked, she made a tragically all too common mistake—she didn't want to think about it until after the abortion. Because so very many women react the same way, understanding Laurel's thought process, her decision, and its consequences are crucial for women considering abortion and professionals dealing with such women.

Laurel's "avoidance of emotional conflict strongly interfered with her decision-making about the abortion. . . . She could not stand the idea of discussing her decision. . . . Only afterward did she acknowledge her longing for a baby and her

147

religious reservations about abortion. At the time of her decision, she allowed herself no consideration of these issues and removed herself from an evaluation process that would have forced such consideration." [This demonstrates the need for informed consent legislation that requires abortion providers to inform women of both the nature of pregnancy and abortion and the possible adverse effects of forced termination and that includes a waiting time sufficient to enable the woman to evaluate all the implications, at least 36 to 48 hours.]

Laurel's "wish to settle the issues of intimacy by quick action rather than slow growth" resulted in anxiety, sexual difficulty, and a need for professional help (she spent several months in group therapy). "After the abortion she was preoccupied with her body, particularly her abdomen. She felt pain, bloating, and gurgling in her lower abdomen, and was afraid she had cervical or uterine cancer. She no longer enjoyed sex and was terrified of pregnancy even though she took birth control pills with fanatic regularity . . . "[283]

Krista*, 23, was an attractive secretary who "had been living with her boyfriend for a year. She was using contraception sporadically and assumed they would marry if she became pregnant." When she did, and he backed down, she "denied [to herself and to others] being disappointed by his decision." After a "social work evaluation" she submitted to an abortion.

"This case demonstrates again the development of post-abortion psychiatric illness in a relatively healthy woman. It furthermore illustrates a challenge to abortion counseling—that of a woman who professes to a firm decision when she is actually deeply ambivalent." A year after the abortion "she contacted the social worker. Although she and her lover had been married for several months, she had become sexually unresponsive. She had been unable to reach orgasm since a month after the abortion. She willingly accepted referral to the psychiatrist. . . .

"The major focus of the treatment was her anger at her husband over the abortion. She retold the story of their decision: Upon learning of the pregnancy, he had become quite upset about the responsibilities of marriage and a baby. He was open about this and his preference for abortion; however, he also stated that he loved and would marry her if she wished. This made her deeply angry—she felt he was a coward and was asking her to shoulder all the responsibility. She decided to have an abortion, but experienced this not as a decision, but rather as

148

something she was forced to do. She strongly desired a baby at that time." Her "postabortion frigidity" remained until 15 sessions of psychotherapy had been completed.[283]

Candice*, the 22-year-old mother of an 18-month-old child, had borderline intelligence. Because of her low IQ and the fact that she suffered from a congenital disease (which had not prevented her from reaching adulthood, marrying, and becoming the mother of a healthy child) she became a victim of the type of genetic counseling that seeks to cleanse the world of potentially defective people. "Undue pressure was put on this woman by the genetic counselor, the surgeon, and her family." Because of her circumstances she was conned into an unnecessary and unwanted abortion!

Her mid-trimester pregnancy—the preborn developed nearly enough to survive if born—was aborted by saline infusion. Candice asked to see her baby; the little boy was shown to her.

Forty-eight hours later, when she told her husband about it, he "became upset because he had wanted a boy. A few hours later the patient became agitated; she cried, was unable to sleep, and demanded to see her son. She ranted uncontrollably about her baby . . . in the denial stage of an acute grief reaction. . . . Her denial of the abortion and her agitation continued and she was transferred to a psychiatric hospital. She was not felt to be psychotic, but of limited intellectual and ego resources to deal with her grief." [Grief is, after all, a natural maternal response to a dead child.]

A woman with no previous history of mental illness developed a near-psychotic postabortion grief reaction. Why? She hadn't wanted to get rid of her baby, who was already making his presence known to her. She knew she was his mother! *"The most clearly recognized contra-indication to abortion is a decision based solely on coercion"* [emphasis added]. In other words, an excellent reason for allowing a pregnancy to continue is a decision to abort based on other people's ideas that the pregnancy should be aborted.[283]

"In all the cases of postabortion (psychiatric) illness we have presented there were compromises in the decision-making process."[283]

PSYCHOLOGICAL REACTIONS to abortions may also occur in the woman's partner, relatives, and others close to her.

Some authors have questioned the effect on children's personality development upon learning that mother or an older sister has had an abortion.[194]

PSYCHOLOGICAL SCARS: Carolee, a cashier in a fashionable hotel restaurant, bitterly regrets her abortion. "It was so painful I couldn't help crying. I still don't like to talk about it, but I want you to know, I want everyone to know, I am permanently scarred emotionally. It affects my relationships; I can't get away from it."

Rosa T. also bears a burden of mental anguish from an abortion that cost her several internal organs and eight months' hospitalization. Rosa will never be normal again: she is physically scarred from multiple surgeries needed to correct the ravages of her "safe legal abortion." She lost her spleen and all her reproductive organs, her voice is changed and she readily admits having psychological scars that will last a lifetime.[246]

PSYCHOSIS: "Even in our contemporary society, with relaxed sexual mores and widespread therapeutic abortion, some individuals do feel guilty about abortion. One may attempt to rationalize, intellectualize, or otherwise defend against the guilt, but one cannot escape one's superego . . . Psychiatric difficulties following abortion do occur" even though some "physicians may be reluctant to recognize that a 'therapeutic' procedure may produce morbidity."[145]

"We have seen a number of patients who did have emotional difficulties after a therapeutic abortion. The purpose of this communication is to report two cases in which patients clearly functioned well before the abortion and experienced psychoses precipitated by guilt over the abortion. We do not believe that environmental or other factors contributed to the psychoses":

Marilyn*, a 17-year-old honor student, was chosen to attend a summer-long program in the field in which she excelled. "This was the first time she had been away from home for an extended period; she met her first boyfriend, fell in love, and became pregnant. She visited a sister in a northern city and obtained a therapeutic abortion without her parents' knowledge." Months later "she developed lethargy, malaise, nausea with occasional

150

vomiting. Thorough physical evaluation failed to reveal any organic cause for the symptoms. A short time later she complained of feeling bloated, excessive weight gain, breast engorgement and tenderness. On the eve of the first anniversary of her therapeutic abortion, she experienced an overt psychosis and was referred for psychiatric care.

"The mental status examination revealed marked regression, visual hallucinations, and psychotic thought processes . . . The regression was so severe that she had fecal incontinence and smeared the feces on herself and around the room . . . Psychological testing revealed a marked amount of guilt . . . Treatment with an antipsychotic drug was begun . . . She was able to attend school . . . However, each time her menstrual period began, she rapidly regressed to psychotic behavior with fecal smearing and visual hallucinations . . . After a 5 month hospitalization, she returned to her usual level of functioning . . . "[145]

Norma* was single, 24 years old, and "employed in a position of great responsibility. She became pregnant and obtained an abortion in her third month of gestation. Six months later, 'at the time I would have had my baby,' she experienced insomnia, anorexia [loss of appetite], agitation and severe depression that necessitated psychiatric hospitalization.

" . . . The patient paced constantly and had pressured speech . . . She was markedly ambivalent . . . She had a visual hallucination of 'seeing babies in their mothers' arms' . . . In the hospital she was treated . . . then able to talk about her profound guilt over both the pregnancy and the abortion." She remained confined for a month.[145]

REGRET: "There are few women, no matter how desperate they may be to find themselves with an unwanted pregnancy, who do not have regrets at losing it. This (is a) fundamental reaction governed by maternal instinct . . . if the indication for the termination was flimsy and fleeting, she may suffer from a sense of guilt for the rest of her life."[194] "As many as one-fifth of the women allowed therapeutic abortions later expressed regret for accepting the procedure."[195]

RISKS: "Termination of pregnancy is not without psychiatric risks . . . "[196]

RISK of EMOTIONAL REACTIONS following abortion is "greatest in cases in which a legal abortion can best be justified from the psychiatric standpoint. It may be said that legal abortion stands out as a fairly ineffective psychiatric therapeutic means. Women who are psychically vulnerable risk a deterioration in their emotional condition after therapeutic abortion."[197]

SELF-REPROACH was felt by 14% of women studied at the time of abortion and again 2 to 3½ years later—11% had serious self-reproach and self-regret; 10% "continued to feel the operation unpleasant"; 1% suffered gross psychiatric breakdowns.[20]

SENSE OF LOSS: "There is a much greater sense of loss following abortion in teenage girls than in the 20-to-30-year-olds. Also, the older adolescent (15-18) suffers a much greater reaction than does the very young girl aged 13 or 14. Although an accidental consequence, pregnancy often fulfills some kind of need, and if the girl loses the pregnancy (and eventually the boyfriend) the sense of loss at six months postabortively can be quite immense . . . these girls care and react internally more than we realize."[189]

SERIOUS PSYCHONEUROTIC OR PSYCHOTIC REACTION is "undoubtedly" caused by termination of pregnancy.[1] "There is some agreement that women with diagnosed psychiatric illness prior to abortion continue to have difficulty following abortion."[191] Four to nine percent of women who have a legal abortion can expect "severe and prolonged or chronic side effects."[193]

SHOCK: Many women don't know how abortions are done, and many referral agencies don't tell their clients what to expect. Shock is a fairly common reaction of saline abortion patients who haven't been prepared for the abdominal injection, the uncomfortable thrashing and convulsions of the preborn as it dies, and the birth-like expulsion which mimics natural delivery except that the infant is smaller and is covered with bruises. Compounding her trauma is the likelihood that she will be alone when this takes place.

"All I was prepared for was an injection," Kate complained. "They never told me it would go straight into my abdomen. It scared me to death!"

SUPPRESSED REMORSE was expressed by psychosomatic symptoms such as abdominal discomfort, vomiting, pruritis vulvae, dysmenorrhea, frigidity, headache, insomnia and fatigue in women studied four months after legal abortion.[58] Suppressed remorse can also make itself known by ulcers—

Six weeks after the uneventful abortion of a four month pregnancy, Gina* began vomiting blood. In the hospital tests showed she had bleeding ulcers. Based on her medical history, Gina's doctor linked the problem to repression of her feelings about the pregnancy and the abortion, and recommended a therapist who helped her work through her emotional problems.

Gina was on the road to recovery when she took a clerical job in a hospital. "For a time focusing on other people's situations helped me forget my own," she says somberly. "But soon it began to gnaw at me. There were so many tragedies: teenagers coming in alone, hugely pregnant and wanting abortions, parents pushing their daughters to have abortions when they wanted to have the baby. Husbands and boyfriends would be sitting in my office loudly insisting on abortions, threatening to walk out if they didn't get their way; and of course the women who got threatened most often had little children in tow. I wanted to reach out to these people and talk to them about it, but that wasn't my job. I was embarrassed to approach them, so I said nothing but I got more and more uncomfortable. Soon my symptoms began to recur." For the sake of her health, on the advice of her therapist, Gina gave up her job.

SYMBOLIC SUICIDE: Women who dislike themselves or who have a poor self image or other emotional problems use various means of harming themselves. Some turn to booze, some try to eat their way into oblivion, others identify with their preborn children and experience induced abortion as a symbolic act of self-destruction. Fifty instances of such symbolic suicide were discovered by psychiatrists treating women for problems other than abortion-related distress; these women had never realized they harbored strong feelings about past abortions until intensive psychiatric therapy began to uncover their hidden pain. Each woman mourned the loss of the child she hadn't allowed to be born.[279] This possibility should figure in every woman's pre-abortion decision-making process.

TRAUMA: Some degree of trauma, including anxiety and depression, usually accompanies an elective abortion.[198]

"Every woman—whatever her age, background or sexuality—has a trauma at destroying a pregnancy. A level of humanness is touched. This is a part of her own life. She destroys a pregnancy, she is destroying herself. There is no way it can be innocuous. One is dealing with the life force. It is totally beside the point whether or not you think a life is there. You cannot deny that something is being created and that this creation is physically happening," states Dr. Julius Fogel who has been advocating and performing abortions for years. He has become deeply concerned about the "psychological effects of abortion on the mother's mind."

He continues, "Often the trauma may sink into the unconscious and never surface in the woman's lifetime. But it (abortion) is not as harmless and casual an event as many in the proabortion crowd insist. A psychological price is paid. It may be alienation; it may be a pushing away from human warmth, perhaps a hardening of the maternal instinct. Something happens on the deeper levels of a woman's consciousness when she destroys a pregnancy. I know that as a psychiatrist." [100, 103]

Another psychiatrist, Dr. William E. Sorrell, explains, "Any abortion is an emotionally traumatic experience, and is sometimes a precipitating and unsuspected cause of a typical psychotic reaction." [103]

"Results strongly indicate that induced abortion in women pregnant for the first time, especially very young women, is far from an innocuous procedure. It remains to be proved that new techniques can make it safer. The psychological trauma is, at any rate, inevitable . . . " [260]

Even abortion on psychiatric grounds may cause more harm than good, according to Dr. Nicholas J. Eastman, carrying with it "a degree of emotional trauma far exceeding that which would have been sustained by continuation of pregnancy." [103]

"The selection of an instillation technique commits the woman to the potential psychological trauma of long and painful labor and delivery, frequently unattended and in a facility far from home." [110]

A psychiatrist working with a group of 50 women who had *not* come to him with abortion-related problems, discovered after prolonged therapy that these women were unearthing long-buried emotional reactions to long-ago abortions. Intrigued, he decided to pursue the matter. He made a comparison between them and 72 women in therapy *because of* abortion trauma. An intensive investigation brought some very startling conclusions to light, including sharp differences between the groups.

Those who had suppressed negative feelings following their abortions expressed an intense pain, bereavement, and a sense of identification with the preborn. These feelings existed even though the woman believed the abortion had been her only choice. Although this appearance may have been deceiving, that reasoning apparently blocked the emergence of their deeper feelings.

When the suppressed emotions began to surface, it was learned these women had been rejected by their mothers and were identifying with them, each taking on her mother's infanticidal desires and acting them out by aborting her baby.[279]

Psychiatrists have found that subconscious ambivalence about elective abortion is extremely common. A woman who has positive feelings about herself and her preborn child will have a strong commitment to life. However she may also have tangible problems which move her to consider abortion. The evidence drawn from women who have been in this situation should be used by pregnant women in their decision-making process: whatever the reality of her physical situation, the pregnant woman may unconsciously regard abortion as an act of infanticide. Through the process of identification, an induced abortion may be an act of symbolic suicide committed to gratify an unconscious need to reject the child. This possibility should be raised in each instance of a woman considering abortion, so any underlying feelings can come to the surface and be expressed. Failure to do so can set the stage for a traumatic re-appraisal of the abortion decision at some future time.

"Complications are inevitable: they can be reduced but not totally eradicated . . . Comprehensive descriptions of the management of abortion-related complications are, for the most part, lacking in the medical literature. Modern texts of obstetrics and gynecology often provide little or even faulty information about the technique of abortion and the management of complications." [57]

7

HIDDEN
DANGERS

AMBIVALENCE: A need to know has been established. A woman exposes herself to serious psychological trauma when she fails to heed her own feeling that abortion, for whatever reason, may be wrong for her. Even a far-fetched reason, such as wanting a baby when raising a child seems impossible, is an important indicator that abortion may be a poor choice.

"Reports of postabortion psychiatric illness . . . indicate there is a high risk in abortion when any of the following elements is present: strong ambivalence, coercion . . . and the woman's feeling that the decision was not her own."

Some women "who had been *certain* about their decision [to abort] later felt some unhappiness." A team of doctors reporting instances of postabortion psychiatric illness stated, "We feel that these women actually had deep, unconscious ambivalence about their decisions. They often wanted the child, but felt that their life situation made this impossible . . . It does seem that a strong desire to have a baby, which may be concurrent with a woman's certainty that she is not prepared for a child at the time, contributed to this reaction."[283]

Aborting women frequently have the same hopes and expectations for their preborns as women carrying to term, and they "appear to mourn its loss."[283] More than one investigation has found that "the ambivalence about pregnancy termination continued after the procedure."[152]

157

These women, as well as women considering abortion today, probably could have found a place in their lives for their babies, with adequate help and encouragement. In most instances, once the hurdle of the decision to accept the pregnancy has been passed, things fall into place and the pregnancy becomes a positive experience. Instead of unhappiness after the abortion, the woman feels a measure of contentment after the birth and, with continuing support if necessary, can integrate the child into her life physically and emotionally, whether she raises the child or gives him "a chance for a better life" through adoption.

COERCION: "On September 30, 1977 an abortionist attempted to coerce me into an abortion," states Pat Goltz of Arizona. "His excuse was that I had experienced hemorrhage the night before. Although my vital signs remained stable for 10 hours and blood loss was minimal during that time, he stressed that I must have a D&C or face the possibility of further hemorrhage. He told me he thought I had miscarried and that if by some rare chance I was still pregnant, it would be impossible for me to carry to term.

"He made no attempt to determine the cause of the hemorrhage or whether or not I was still pregnant. He ordered me to stay in bed and the sides of the bed were put up. He gave me two and one half hours to think about having the D&C . . . He didn't inform me of any complications that might arise from the operation, nor at any time did he use the term 'abortion' to describe the operation, nor did he indicate that to be pregnant means to be carrying a baby and that a D&C would deprive me of that baby. I received no counseling.

"Although my doctor and the entire nursing staff attempted to intimidate me with the possibility of hemorrhage, I made the decision not to have the operation and went home . . . My pregnancy progressed normally.

"This is what the 'right to choose' has meant to me: that I was asked to make a decision which would have affected my entire life while I was in a debilitated condition, alone, in 2½ hours, without counseling, with erroneous and inadequate information, and after being subjected to intimidation. My health and life would have been *put at risk* . . . "

CONCEALING INFORMATION about a prior abortion from the obstetrician caring for a subsequent pregnancy can endanger a woman's life and that of her preborn child. Several

158

women in one group studied asked the abortionist not to tell their regular doctor about the abortion. "It seems reasonable to assume that these patients will not admit their termination during a future pregnancy . . . which could thus be jeopardized." Other reports have likewise documented this tendency.

"It must be impressed on the patient that she must not keep her future obstetrician ignorant of previous termination. This becomes even more important if the cervix was lacerated or the uterus perforated . . . We have seen cases in which this failure to provide information has ended in near disaster, not only for the fetus but for the mother as well."[281]

DANGEROUS, INEPT AND ILLEGAL PRACTICES flourish inside some abortion clinics in flagrant defiance of state guidelines and accepted medical standards. Experts agree doctors should schedule abortions a minimum of 15 minutes apart, but in clinics where doctors are paid by the number they perform, quickie abortions are common. Doctors have been known to race one another, competing for big bucks in the game of Who Can Perform the Most Abortions Today.[241]

Although most physicians limit themselves to 15 or 20 abortions per day, others may perform six to eight per hour. Doing too many may be monotonous, fatiguing the doctor and endangering the woman's health; but the profit motive may prompt a precarious pace—dozens and dozens a day.[246] How is a woman to know whether her abortionist is trying for the world landspeed record?

Aides, medical assistants and counselors may be hired without checking for references or credentials. Reporters investigating for their newspaper had no trouble getting jobs in abortion clinics. Unqualified and untrained, their responsibilities included giving injections, removing IVs, counseling frightened women and assisting in surgery. One reporter called it quits after being told to draw someone's blood.[248]

During an investigation of dangerous medical practices, these undercover reporters found forms recording the woman's post-abortion condition *were filled out before the abortion took place*. Despite the fact that women were both calling and coming in to report serious complications, clinic employees routinely marked patient records "no complications."[249]

159

Cost-cutting methods can cost patients adequate care: some clinics lack proper handwashing facilities and improperly store drugs. Owners at times refuse to admit state health officials for inspections while continuing to admit as many women as possible for abortions.[243]

Postoperative care, say the experts, is absolutely essential to safeguard against serious infection and other life-threatening complications that may follow legal abortions. Money, say some abortionists, is the prime essential. Dana*, trying to comfort her pale and pain-racked daughter Dale*, spent five hours trying to get help from clinic personnel. The doctor demanded cash before he would touch the girl again; he refused to take a check or send a bill later. When mother and daughter persistently refused to leave the clinic, the doctor called the police and had them thrown out.[243]

DECISIONS, UNDECIDED: Rushing into an abortion, "getting it over with as soon as possible," is *not* the same as making a decision to abort. "Precipitous action," as psychiatrists term hasty abortion, actually avoids making a decision. Such flight from reality may land a woman on an operating table, but abortion can't remove old problems, and several new ones may lie ahead.

In the *American Journal of Psychiatry*, a psychiatric team reported, "In all of the cases of postabortion illness we have presented, there were compromises in the decision-making process. The woman in case 1 appeared to comply with or resist parental wishes rather than making her own decision. In case 2, decision-making was avoided entirely by precipitous action. Complying with the wishes of another made it possible for the patient in case 3 to avoid feeling responsible for her actions. This process was heavily rationalized. The woman in case 4 was severely ambivalent and reluctant. She may have been pressured by the medical staff. . . . Our work suggests that inability or reluctance to make a decision, with resulting continued ambivalence, can trigger severe symptomatic response in the postabortion period."[283]

The community must not be indifferent to these documented instances of serious psychiatric illness following ill-considered or impulsive legal abortions. To protect vulnerable women from such tragic "responses" to impetuous choices, there is a growing trend toward informed consent legislation. Legislators and women's groups are becoming increasingly aware that an ounce of prevention—informing the woman about the stage of development of her preborn and the difficulties of removing her prematurely from the womb, the known complications of legal abortion and the experiences of other women, substitute options and community support, and giving her sufficient time to reflect on the facts and possibilities, to consider and perhaps reconsider before making her final decision—is worth considerably more than the proverbial pound of cure which in these four reported cases was extensive psychiatric hospitalization and therapy.

It is difficult for a woman to resist the lenis lure, particularly if her resistance is low because of the situation making pregnancy a problem and if she's experiencing the morning sickness and depression commonly caused by early pregnancy hormone changes. Informed consent legislation may prevent exploitation through legal abortion by acting as a brake to impulsiveness and preventing her being pushed into an abortion against her will.[101] Some women may feel they have no choice but to abort; for them Birthright centers and other crisis pregnancy facilities have sprung into existence (see Chapter 12 for details). Having no financial or political interest in an abortion decision, their trained volunteers offer caring, confidentiality and a quiet place where a woman can ask herself, "Is this what I really want?", a place where she can find ample support to enable her to carry the pregnancy to term. Thoroughly examining alternative means of dealing with the problem situation is a necessary element in the decision-making process.

HAZARDOUS HYPODERMICS: Abortion providers boast confidently the safety of legal abortion, but is faith in "the system" which provides the opportunity for women to exercise their right to choose abortion justified, or are they being gullible? Some have found their confidence misplaced in clinics where syringes may be filled in quantity, by unskilled aides, under less than sterile conditions; storage for several days invites infection. Eyewitnesses have reported seeing aides recklessly replace caps fallen from the needles of prefilled, stockpiled syringes, totally unconcerned that such dirty practices may endanger the health of clinic patients.[248]

NONCHALANCE: Gretel*, the 28-year-old wife of a university lecturer, pregnant for the first time, was advised by her physician that an abortion was less complicated than a birth. Without thoroughly investigating she acceded to his dictum and underwent a legal abortion. While recovering on vacation she became ill, was found to be suffering from an incomplete abortion, and had to undergo surgical womb scraping. Afterward the surgeon asked her why, if abortion was less complicated than birth, she had been given a prescription for an antibiotic; he explained such medication against infection is never given following birth. After lengthy discussion with the doctor Gretel came to realize that she had, through a lack of knowledge, been misled about pregnancy termination.[101]

QUESTIONABLE COUNSELING: In our "get back to nature" culture, it is difficult to define what drives a woman to seek unnatural termination of pregnancy. The woman wanting abortion may be a mass of insecurities, panic-stricken, poverty-stricken, socially aborted by her family or lover, alone with nowhere to turn. She may be confused by the demands of school, her employer, her friends, and the biological reality just beneath her skin.

She may be disbelieving, thrilled, angry and desperate all at once. One thing she is not likely to be is patient. Although the alarm reaction to pregnancy is normal, she may not know this; she may be unaware of her own inner strength, temporarily out of touch with that resiliency women have that helps them bounce back.

Counseling such a woman is no easy task. She may deliberately or unintentionally conceal pertinent feelings and facts.[283] In anxiety and haste she may forget critical health information; she may not remember, for example, a serious reaction she had as a child to novocaine or to other medication. She might forget about the heavy bleeding that followed a tooth extraction, or purposely not mention it, fearing that such information would be an obstacle. ("If they find out about my tendency to bleed, they'll be afraid to go ahead".)

If ever a person needed legal protection from those who would exploit her predicament, she is the one. Regrettably, the newly-found rights that give her a choice may at the same time deepen her confusion and obstruct consumer protection laws designed to assist her.

State regulations may require clinics to counsel abortion patients but some will make a mockery of their mandate. Counseling may be looked upon as "merely a courtesy, part of the abor-

tion procedure that the patients are expected to go through."
How a woman really feels may never come up; the clinic may
feel satisfied if it makes its patients feel comfortable, however
temporarily.[278]

Instead of probing motives, fears and misgivings, and actively pursuing nonviolent solutions to the woman's problems, some
clinics offer no real counseling at all. Others make feeble attempts with groups of 10 or more women in five minutes or less;
and in states where abortion is unregulated, even that attempt
may not be made.

At one clinic a counselor was ordered by her supervisor to
stop talking with a distraught client and get back to the busy
reception desk. If staff members do have time to talk, they may
be under orders not to say anything to scare women away: not to
enumerate possible complications, not to mention pain, not to
answer too many questions for fear prospective patients will get
nervous and leave. [241, 250] And just beyond the doors of an ever-
increasing number of abortion clinics are watchful pro-lifers,
ready for the opportunity to offer housing, counseling, medical
care and friendship to women who change their minds about
aborting.

While pro-life pregnancy services are always ready to
describe abortion procedures, those that perform abortions
usually aren't, and patiently evade a woman's every attempt to
learn what will happen. Clarise* recalls asking repeatedly how
her abortion would be done. "They would only say it wouldn't
take long and I shouldn't worry about it. They never did give me
an explanation."

On her first day as counselor at a prominent legal abortion
clinic, an investigative reporter was trained to counsel by her
supervisor. These were her instructions:

1. Don't tell the patient the abortion will hurt
2. Don't discuss procedure or the instruments to be used
3. Don't answer too many questions
4. Don't try to talk about birth control

That clinic is owned and operated by two men who have no
qualms about being in the abortion business. At a staff meeting
they instruct their people to vigorously sell abortions over the

phone, using whatever tactics necessary to beat out the competition.

To compete they advertise heavily and sell women on services they rarely deliver. For example, they offer prospective patients private counseling. But in the clinic, counseling is done in groups of 10 and 12 women at a time—many of whom are unprepared for abortions. Women are made to feel it's best they do not know, and those who are embarrassed to bring up their fears are not encouraged to do so.[258]

During a five-month investigation it was learned that some abortion profiteers advertise under a number of different and deceptive names to entice women into their posh clinics. There telephone sales pitches are monitored more carefully than a doctor's operating techniques. Every trick in the book is used to peddle abortions and women who do come in for help may be swindled by entrepreneurs who pay commissions for every abortion sold. [250, 258] Expertise in smooth talking comes in handy for those liberated lovelies who don't mind selling out their sisters; 39% of women interviewed four months after their abortions said their pregnancies had been wanted.[152]

Despite occasional weak protests to the contrary, it's a fact that the so-called counselors in many abortion clinics are little more than pitchwomen, many of whom have betrayed their own maternity, who are hired to sell abortions. The tools of their trade include ruthlessly slanted surveys which claim that "ambivalence about abortion is no reason to counsel against it" and purport to prove that "women need emotional support after their abortions far more than they need preabortion counseling."[152] This offer to substitute a pound of consolation for an ounce of foresight needs to be exposed for the fraud that it is. It's more like shoving a blind woman in front of a moving truck and then offering her a bandaid, than guiding her safely through a dangerous intersection. The proabortionist's arrant offer to substitute postabortion reassurances for eclectic examination before it's too late will be of little help to women tormented for the rest of their lives, and no help at all to those permanently disabled or killed by a legal abortion.

Distraught pregnant women desperately want to believe that abortion is quick and painless, that you can get it over with fast so that chapter of life can be closed forever. And just as

164

desperately clinic counselors want to believe that those pregnant women wouldn't be calling or coming in if they didn't want an abortion. Abortion mills are a fantasy land where the fragile feelings of frightened women frequently get trampled in the press of business.

Women need to be told they *can* deal with their problems; they need to be reminded that they are intelligent, capable, and resourceful. They need to be offered the medical, legal, emotional and material support that will make resort to the violence of an abortion unnecessary. They need to know that they are persons of worth and dignity and this is especially true when they arrive at that frightening forté of femininity, carrying a new life, pregnancy. If they come to an abortion provider for counseling, they should be helped to make a decision that is right for themselves, not right merely for the clinic's investors and employees; they cannot and must not be made pawns in the social abortion controversy.

QUESTIONNAIRES—CAUSE FOR CONCERN: Many people place great confidence in the results of questionnaires as precision indicators of how legal abortion affects women emotionally. The findings of a team of Canadian doctors test the reliability of such questionnaires and the validity of our faith in them.

Two groups of women who had deliberately aborted their pregnancies were compared. Fifty women in psychotherapy were interviewed in depth and 72 located through general practice answered questionnaires dealing with the difficulty of making the choice to abort and emotions experienced subsequently.

Based upon questionnaire results alone, one would assume abortion is as harmless as the feminists insist; however, evidence from the interviews is at odds with that conclusion. There were distinct discrepancies between the two. And the doctors wondered why.

It turned out that the survey was cold. It touched the women only superficially, so they answered unemotionally, without reaching down within themselves and searching for their inmost feelings. Two factors thus played a role in creating the discrepancy between the results: awareness of deep feelings and the ability to express them. The women from psychotherapy were in touch with their emotions and the other women weren't. The doctors believe that if the same questionnaire had been given

165

before psychotherapy was begun, their answers would have been similar to the questionnaire group's responses. It was the getting in touch with themselves on the deepest levels that enabled the women to identify their true feelings (these are referred to in this book under the headings Symbolic Suicide and Trauma).

Therefore, regardless of who sponsors a survey, or how well designed it is, caution should be used when interpreting the responses, particularly if policy decisions are to be based on it. The next time your favorite magazine publishes the results of a survey or questionnaire on abortion, remember that the doctors who published this information in a medical journal did so believing that the profound regret expressed by women in psychotherapy is likely to be a more reliable indicator of the way a woman will react to elective abortion than average question-naire responses indicate.

Induced abortion is not a panacea for all the problems created by a pregnancy. While many factors may tempt a woman to abort her baby, it may be in her best interest to seek other ways of dealing with her problems.[279]

RECOVERY—SWIFT BUT NOT SO SURE: Some clinics have such small recovery rooms that patients still in pain are forced to leave within 15 minutes to make room for the next woman.[242] Recovery bed sheets may not be changed with fanatic regularity so stuporous women may be covered with sheets bloodied by the previous occupant.[248]

After waiting several hours for an abortion, Lola was given just a few minutes in the recovery room. Despite feeling groggy and unsteady she was instructed to dress and leave. "This is abortion on demand all right," she said later. "I have the abortion and they make the demands." Lola huddled on the dressing room floor for half an hour.

Another end-of-the-day patient who spent time on the floor was Tanya, ordered out so beds could be made up for the next day.[241]

A registered nurse who underwent a clinic abortion com-plained they gave her only 10 minutes to recover by making it plain the bed was needed. She felt worse for a teenager who, despite having a rough time, got the same treatment. An aide who complained about the women being moved out of recovery too soon was invited to take a hike if she didn't like it. She didn't, and did.[248]

166

REFERRAL RIPOFFS have become less common as legalized abortion has become more widespread, but it may be worthwhile to bear in mind the experience of the past. Referral services are those which, for a fee, direct women to doctors or clinics that perform abortions; they generally offer little in the way of pregnancy testing and nothing remotely resembling competent counseling. Some charge exorbitant fees but refer women only to particular clinics with which they are financially affiliated. In the absence of abortion regulations law enforcement agencies are reluctant to take action against all but the most flagrant abuses.[250,252]

With second trimester abortions, hot-line counselors have been instructed to do nothing for the customer until they see cash. Women without money in one locale were sent to see the owner of a loan company who was quite helpful—at 30% interest. Women who changed their minds learned what had been paid to the referral service as an "abortion deposit" somehow became a counseling fee, non-refundable of course.[250]

Adrienne*, a 27-year-old secretary, called a toll-free number from a newspaper advertisement for women with "problem pregnancies." She was given an address and told to take $75 with her. In a well-appointed office she talked with a man who set up an out-of-town abortion and gave her instructions not to eat before the surgery. No options were discussed, no dangers mentioned, no procedures explained in the 20 minute, $75 meeting.

Her fiance and a friend went with her for the abortion. Although her appointment was for 10:30 a.m. the doctor didn't arrive until 5 p.m. Meanwhile she was examined by another doctor who estimated the pregnancy at 18 weeks. Mentally prepared only for the abortion of a 14 week gestation, Adrienne responded that if it were 18 weeks she didn't want to go through with the abortion; she was reassured that the abortionist would double-check.

Neither Adrienne nor her boyfriend could pinpoint when things began to go wrong although she remembers the doctor's eyes being red-rimmed and swollen and her boyfriend can't forget the doctor's abnormally long fingernails. In a procedure room the doctor examined Adrienne in silence; he was rough and she was scared. The still of the room was shattered as the doctor barked an order, then darkness descended on Adrienne as the anesthetic was administered. She awoke in a recovery room bleeding heavily, wounded emotionally as well as physically.[255]

SCHEDULING UNNECESSARY SURGERY: Virtually everywhere that investigators have "tested" abortion clinics by submitting male urine for pregnancy tests the results have come back positive; not every time, but too many times. Women with negative results have been sold abortions they didn't need, suffering severe complications they weren't prepared for. Clever operators have even turned a supposedly simple examination into a fast abortion. Mikki* submitted a urine sample and was told to undress and get up on an examination table. Knowing that the test results were negative, the doctor came into the room and silently examined her, ignoring her question about the test results. After a brief examination he turned on the machine and "aborted" her empty uterus.[257]

Four women who had undergone surprise abortions said they never learned if they were pregnant before their wombs were suctioned. One wasn't even given the test result afterward, and helplessly confesses she wouldn't have gone through with the procedure if she had known it was too early for a clear indication of pregnancy. Another woman, who didn't find out until afterward that her test result had been negative, angrily asked how women are supposed to know whether they're pregnant if doctors don't tell them, and how women can be certain doctors aren't just financially abusing them.

Only a good internal examination by a doctor and a carefully controlled test on urine samples can confirm pregnancy. Some clinics routinely sell confused women a procedure to "extract the menstrual blood" when a pregnancy test turns up inconclusive or negative. This "menstrual extraction" is essentially the same as an early abortion but isn't as thorough or effective in ending pregnancy because it's usually done on women whose periods are only a week or two late, when the embryo (if there is one) is so tiny that it may be easily missed by the suction device. Experts say the risks and discomfort are as great as with an abortion performed later in the first trimester. Most women who submit to "menstrual extraction" aren't pregnant in the first place; according to a professor of obstetrics and gynecology, as many as 80% are done needlessly. Jeana was duped into such a pro-

168

cedure and within a week developed such severe pain she couldn't walk. She was hospitalized with a severe infection. [241, 257]

UNREGULATED CLINICS: One never knows where unsterile conditions and haphazard clinic care will pop up. Incompetent and unqualified doctors and paraprofessionals perform abortions in a fraction of the time experts say is safe, sometimes without waiting for pain-killing anesthetics to take effect, sometimes on women who aren't even pregnant. Nonlicensed personnel are performing duties that should be done only by trained professionals, such as writing prescriptions and giving examinations and injections. [244]

Clinic operators often challenge laws that don't suit them. The Board of Health tried to close down one clinic after at least two deaths and an alarming number of serious complications; the clinic owner appealed the case and won! The Court struck down as unconstitutional the city's attempt to safeguard women by regulating clinics; the abortionist made millions. [243]

In lawsuits filed by former patients, one legal abortionist has been charged with such grisly acts as leaving heads behind during abortions, slicing the insides of wombs and tearing a piece of scalp from a baby who was later born alive. [255]

Another doctor's license was revoked, but the state failed to make any public announcement of the fact. The clinic continued business as usual, the doctor's practice unaffected by the revocation. A public health official later admitted it might not have been a bad idea to inform the public of the clinic's status. [242]

Sometimes a doctor who operates an unsafe abortion mill in one state will fly on weekends to another state to do abortions in another unsanitary facility. This type of abortion profiteer hires ex-convicts as assistants and uses his influence to have charges against the man dropped; his unsafe techniques cause women to develop serious complications. This kind of abortionist is charged with failing to have qualified personnel administer general anesthesia and with permitting unlicensed medical personnel to perform abortions and internal examinations. This kind of abortionist has slick attorneys to help him wiggle out of indictments. [255]

UNSANITARY CONDITIONS: Sterile conditions are sadly lacking in some clinics; either blood isn't wiped up between patients[248] or rooms are inadequately cleaned and not disinfected. They just don't take the time to remove such objects as bloody towels before the next girl is brought in.[241]

Some abortionists pay equally poor attention to their own cleanliness. In numerous clinics doctors go from one abortion to the next without washing their hands.[241]

During a series of inspections at one legal abortion clinic, health officials found[246]:

dirty, worn, deteriorated, even rusted instruments
recovery room beds made with dirty linens
supposedly clean instruments encrusted with matter
sterilizing being done with plain water or household
    detergent

Elsewhere an investigator observed a doctor stop short, halfway out of the clinic, and come back to do just one extra abortion. He removed his coat, entered the procedure room and began an abortion without attending to any of the expected amenities, like changing from street clothes into surgical scrubs.[245]

VITAL SIGN FRIVOLITY: According to medical experts it is essential to measure vital signs—breathing rate, heartbeat, blood pressure, pulse and body temperature—before and after any surgical procedure including abortion. Before, to make sure the patient can tolerate anesthesia and the procedure; after, to detect excess bleeding, shock or other life-threatening complications. But in some clinics, if the technician trained to take blood pressure isn't there, blood pressures simply aren't taken.

On the abortion assembly lines, workers invent vital signs. "Don't take it, just fake it" could have been the motto of the clinic where untrained aides were told to fill out charts themselves. During her first day as a nurses' aide, Jacqueline* was told it wasn't necessary to take pulse and respiration; she could enter anything on the chart.[248]

After surgery vital signs are even more crucial. A high temperature can mean infection; a weak heartbeat could mean shock. At one clinic, temperatures weren't taken for weeks because the batteries in the recovery room thermometers were dead (apparently they didn't believe in the old-fashioned, do-it-yourself type). For blood pressure readings nurses instructed aides to write down something a bit higher than it had been before the abortion. [241, 248]

For the section on the patient's chart titled Progress Notes a standard formula indicating no problems was used; these jottings bore no relationship to the patient's actual condition and any possible mention of nausea or dizziness was omitted. [248]

"Uncomplicated induced abortion represents evidently no guarantee against complications in a later pregnancy . . .

"Harmful effects on later reproductive performance are of greater importance for women whose first pregnancy was terminated by induced abortion than for those women who already have a family.''[260]

8

COMPLICATIONS FOR OTHER CHILDREN IN THE FAMILY

The natural environment for all preborns conceived by a woman is the same. If that environment is assaulted by the induced abortion of one child, it can become a hostile environment for the next child. This is what we mean when we say "trauma of the reproductive tract is responsible for miscarriages in women who have aborted a first pregnancy"[260] or when we talk about "poor reproductive performance." Unnatural termination of pregnancy affects the prenatal development of the child conceived afterward; it can alter the mechanism of natural pregnancy termination, adversely affecting the next baby's birth. It can also have an effect on children living at home with a woman, and on her children who survive subsequently.

APGAR SCORES are GENERALLY POORER in newborns of mothers who have had an unnatural termination of pregnancy; these infants also demonstrate a greater incidence of disturbances in the neo-natal period.[45]

BATTERING: "Abortion weakens the instinctual bonds of restraint against the occasional rage felt toward those dependent on parents for care, and diminishes the social taboo against attacking the defenseless, so that the response to cries of distress is more likely to be a blow than a caress."[274]

A woman who has experienced abortion is more likely than

other mothers to batter her living children, according to a Maryland child psychiatrist who is studying the characteristics of potential child abusers.[200]

CONGENITAL HANDICAP can be caused by faulty development of the placenta which was caused by damage to the endometrium during a legally induced abortion.[61]

DAMAGE: Induced abortion changes the environment in which the next child will be living and developing; these changes are responsible, at times, for "poor reproductive performance and the birth of damaged and handicapped children."[62, 172]

The excessive number of babies born prematurely or dead in pregnancies following elective abortion has been linked to pathological changes in the uterine environment which influence implantation and the ability of the preborn to survive.[30]

DEATH: "For those individuals who have had abortions, the incidence of abortion [miscarriage] and late fetal losses and prematurity in subsequent pregnancy continues to be a matter of concern, irrespective of the specific methodology utilized for the interruption of pregnancy."[267]

Interest in the health consequences of induced abortion has resulted in a few studies of the long-term health effects. Findings indicate that legal abortion may predispose women to increased prenatal losses and premature birth in subsequent pregnancies. [173, 281] In other words, the wanted child conceived after a forced termination of pregnancy may be lost by early miscarriage or premature birth. [172, 281] Your chances of losing a wanted baby may double[25] or even quadruple[77] after a legally induced abortion.

Stillbirths and miscarriages[237] were the outcome of planned pregnancies for:
5% of women who had carried their last pregnancy to term
8% of women whose last pregnancy had been aborted by suction
10% of women who had D&C abortion of their most recent pregnancy

A number of studies show "a high incidence" of second trimester miscarriage "in pregnancies after vaginal termination

174

. . . Perinatal mortality has doubled and the incidence of premature labor has increased in Hungary since the introduction of a liberal policy (on abortion)."[281]

In England doctors noted "an apparent increase in the number of women admitted . . . in premature labor" and were prompted to carry out a survey. They compared the second pregnancies of 211 women whose first pregnancies were artificially aborted with pregnant women whose first pregnancies had aborted naturally. They found significantly more first and second trimester miscarriages and premature deliveries in the forced abortion group than in the spontaneous abortion group. "There were 9 perinatal deaths among the 29 premature deliveries in the termination group. None of these was due to fetal abnormality. Several other infants are being followed by pediatricians, who expect a high morbidity or delayed mortality in this group. Indeed, at least two infants have already died in early infancy. In contrast, there were 3 abnormal infants among the prematurely delivered infants in the spontaneous abortion group."[281]

LOW BIRTH WEIGHT: D&C abortion appears associated with reduced birth weight in subsequent pregnancies, a finding consistent with the World Health Organization's study of the effect of previous abortion on pregnancy.[237]

Other studies have made similar findings, particularly when the cervix is dilated byeond 12 mm. [260, 309] The weight of the newborn after 36 weeks of pregnancy may be reduced significantly. When the first pregnancy was forcibly terminated, weight of the newborns proved to be lower compared with babies born to women whose first pregnancies had terminated naturally.[260] In another study of pregnancies following elective abortion an equal percentage, 6.7%, of babies born following suction and following D&C suffered from abnormally low birth weight. Furthermore, the number of babies affected jumped from 6.4% to 10.8% when the mother had had more than one previous abortion.[309]

Conchatta's* first husband was an alcoholic. She divorced him shortly after her daughter's birth. She moved around from job to job, from man to man, and chose to abort her second and third pregnancies. Then she met Rico* and found with him a contentment she had never known before. They married and moved into a large, comfortable apartment, and Conchatta

175

settled down to the life of a homemaker and mother. A couple of years later she and Rico decided to have a baby.

There is an unpredictability about legal abortion; sometimes the curette twists both ways, cutting off life from the wanted pregnancy as it did the inconvenient pregnancy. Unfortunately for this couple, their happiness was shattered by the birth of a baby affected with severe growth retardation.[260]

The growth limitation occurring after an induced abortion may possibly be due to intrauterine adhesions or other pathological processes which limit the capacity of the uterus.[260]

MATERNAL-INFANT BONDING DEFECTS: The stress of a previous abortion may cause a delay in preparation for the infant and retard the all-important bond that must form between mother and baby.[300]

PERINATAL MORTALITY: Death occurring in the period before, during or just after birth is 50% higher among infants whose mothers have had an abortion. [95, 201] Elsewhere the figure has been put at more than one hundred times maternal mortality.[61]

"Data from 25,958 consecutive UCLA deliveries" showed "abnormal live births—defined as infants with either birth weight under 2501 grams, gestational age less than 37 weeks, or congenital anomalies—significantly increased as the number of prior abortions" increased. The perinatal death rate "increased more than threefold among women with at least one prior premature birth and at least one prior abortion."[201]

PLACENTA PREVIA: Scars in the uterus can prevent implantation of the placenta in its proper place. In this life-threatening complication, the placenta (the preborn's organ which roots to the wall of the womb and through which he derives nourishment) obstructs the opening of the birth canal, making a cesarean section necessary if the lives of baby and mother are to be saved. The c-section increases the risk of uterine rupture in subsequent pregnancies and makes cesareans necessary for later births.[77]

PLACENTAL ABRUPTION: An unnatural separation or tearing away of the placenta from its proper place in the uterus can occur in pregnancies following D&C or saline abortion, perhaps because the placenta attempts to root in scar tissue. This condition makes cesarean section delivery necessary in the affected pregnancy and in future pregnancies.[64]

PREMATURE LABOR: 5% risk if you have never aborted; 14% risk after one abortion; 18% risk after two; 24% risk after three. [43, 44]

"Evidence from Hungary suggests that the incidence of premature labor due to cervical damage is trebled in post-abortion patients."[21]

PREMATURE DELIVERY: No fewer than ten research studies indicate that following induced abortion women deliver babies of a younger gestational age than normal.[309] "Several recent reports citing increased rates of prematurity among women who have had induced first-trimester abortion suggest that forceful cervical dilatation may result in cervical incompetence in future pregnancy."[297] A lengthy report published in the *International Journal of Gynecology and Obstetrics* concludes, "There seems little doubt that there is a true relationship between the high incidence of induced abortion and prematurity."[28]

To induce abortion, the cervical muscle must be forced open. "Mechanical dilatation of the cervix is still commonly undertaken before suction curettage for termination of first-trimester gestation. The resultant trauma, manifest by visible cervical lacerations, tenaculum tears (rips in the cervix made by the sharp, hooklike instrument used for grasping and holding the cervix while rigid rods are being shoved through the cervix to force it open), and uterine perforations, is commonly observed . . . Microscopic cervical tears occur in a *substantial majority* of patients undergoing mechanical dilatation. The increased rates of prematurity and cervical incompetence would appear to be related to forceful cervical dilatation since the physiologic dilatation occurring with term delivery does not appear to be associated with increased prematurity rates."[297]

In other words, even though the cervix opens wider during childbirth of a full-sized preborn, this natural dilatation does not cause the prematurity of subsequent babies which is seen following the forceful opening of the cervix for unnatural "delivery" of a much smaller preborn in induced abortion.

Even the D&C for spontaneous miscarriage does no harm to the cervix because it is naturally soft and open at that time. But when a normal, well-rooted placenta and growing preborn are to be taken from a firmly closed womb protected by a long "green" cervical muscle, the task of dilatation is quite difficult. Some muscle fibers are torn, permanently weakening it. Stanford University Hospital reports that as many as 1 in 8 women aborting first pregnancies by suction require stitches in the cervix because of damage done during dilatation.[30]

This weakening frequently results in an "incompetent cervix" which can be understood by picturing the uterus, or womb, as an upside-down draw-string bag; the cervix is the opening of the bag and the cervical muscle is the draw-string. To protect the inhabitant of the womb, the cervix must remain tightly closed until relaxed by hormones at the natural end of pregnancy. Normally the cervix is long and narrow; to see how far it must be forced open, see Chapter 13.

In an incompetent cervix, the damage done in prying the cervix apart to induce abortion leaves it unable to close completely, or so weak it isn't strong enough to hold the weight of a growing baby; it opens before the infant is developed enough to survive and the baby literally falls out. This is part of the reason for the great increase in spontaneous miscarriage and premature delivery after legal abortion. Normally only 5% of all babies are born prematurely; this jumps to 40% in women who have had an abortion. [61, 101] Delivery before 37 weeks of pregnancy more frequently follows D&C abortion than suction abortion and occurs twice as often among women who have aborted more than one pregnancy.[309]

Concern has been expressed for the causal relationship of "forceful cervical dilatation for legal abortion" to "subsequent increased rates of cervical incompetence, prematurity, stillbirth, and spontaneous abortion. . . . A correlation between the number of induced abortions and a subsequent increased percentage of premature live births" has been widely reported.[297] This cause-and-effect relationship between induced abortion and subsequent abnormal outcome of pregnancy is shown in the "increasing evidence that aborting a first pregnancy yields a considerable increase in the births of prematures in subsequent pregnancies. Prematurity has long been known to be associated with an increased incidence of cerebral palsy, mental retardation and forms of damage to the central nervous system such as learning disabilities."[68]

In one study 30% of 143 women who had an abortion later delivered prematurely, compared to only 11.2% of 143 control women who had not ever had an abrotion. So prematurity in wanted children went up threefold for women who had first trimester abortion of a previous pregnancy.[68]

Prematurity is the *leading cause* of mental and motor retardation in the United States.[202]

"Prematurity was a direct or contributory cause in over 50% of deaths during the first month of postnatal life. The death rate of premature babies ran about 30 times higher than among full-term infants. If premature infants survive, they face a higher frequency of mental retardation, neurologic diseases and blindness."[32]

In actual numbers some 1,000,000 pregnancies are surgically terminated every year in America; if even 250,000 of them (which is a VERY conservative figure) were first pregnancies, and 8% of these mothers were to deliver a subsequent "wanted" pregnancy before the 32nd week of that baby's gestation, we would have at least 20,000 such premature deliveries per year; and if 10% of these develop the expected complications of prematurity, we will be adding at least 2,000 cerebrally palsied and mentally retarded people to our population per year![68] It is entirely possible that the number of diseased and handicapped babies killed by abortion will ultimately be less than the number of surviving "planned" babies made handicapped by their premature births, a direct result of the previous legal abortions of their mothers.[33]

The United States is not alone in suffering these effects of liberal abortion. According to a report in the *Wall Street Journal,* infant mortality rates in the USSR have risen from 22.9 in 1971 to 31 in 1976. One explanation given for the increase is "the high rate of abortion (which) may have caused a higher proportion of premature births in later pregnancies and hence higher infant mortality."[203]

An article in a journal sponsored by the Hungarian government referred to research evidence considered conclusive by the

179

government "that artificially induced abortions predispose (women) to premature births in subsequent pregnancies." Professor Jenö Sárkány's study "of perinatal and infant morbidity statistics revealed a striking increase in physically and/or mentally handicapped babies among these born to mothers who had had a therapeutic abortion previously."[284]

A group of Scandinavian women who had aborted their first pregnancies was compared with a group who had delivered their first pregnancies. Ten of the aborted women delivered a second pregnancy prematurely compared to only three of the term delivery women. "Only in the study group" (the abortion group) was there a birth in the second pregnancy of an infant weighing between 500 and 1000 grams (2500 is normal).[260]

PSYCHIATRIC PROBLEMS OF CHILDREN WHOSE MOTHERS HAVE ABORTIONS include immediate reactions of anxiety attacks, nightmares, increased aggressiveness, stuttering, running away, death phobias, increased separation anxiety, sudden outbursts of fear or hatred of the mother, even suicide attempts. Late reactions range from isolated fantasies to pervading, crucial and disabling illness.[49]

RISK of DAMAGE to an INFANT'S CENTRAL NERVOUS SYSTEM is "much more than one hundred times the risk of damage to the mother's" in children conceived after a legal abortion.[61, 135]

Rh BLOOD DISEASE: When the Rh blood factor of a preborn is positive and the mother's is negative, a mingling of even a few drops of their blood can cause the mother's to develop antibodies. In the next pregnancy, this "sensitized" blood of the mother's will react against an Rh positive baby by identifying him as an invader in the body and attempting to destroy him. A baby in this predicament is in danger of losing his life to the Rh blood disease erythroblastosis fetalis. Such tragedy can be prevented by injecting Rh negative women with Rh immune globulin (RhoGam) immediately after an abortion (or birth).
Unfortunately, many abortion providers don't provide such testing, or the results are inaccurate so the condition goes undetected. (See Isoimmunization)
"The importance of abortion as a cause for preventable sensitization warrants scrutiny. Reported rates of Rh immune

180

globulin utilization for elective abortion have varied widely, with some documented at a very disappointing level (only 42% in one study)." Awareness of the need for Rh screening and treatment to prevent sensitization will result in decreased death rate of preborns conceived after induced abortions.[229]

SPONTANEOUS ABORTION AND PREMATURE DELIVERY IN THE 2nd AND 3rd TRIMESTERS: "The most recent multi-center study, sponsored by the World Health Organization, indicated that spontaneous abortion was, in fact, more common among previous aborters than non-aborters."[271]

"A significantly higher rate of late spontaneous abortion and premature delivery was found" in a group of 137 women with legal abortion of their first pregnancy compared with 129 women who delivered their first pregnancy. "The induced abortion group (had) the highest frequency of late spontaneous abortion and premature delivery and in addition, a trend toward earlier spontaneous onset of labor in their second pregnancy. There was a conspicuous decline of the reproductive performance in the third and fourth pregnancy of the induced abortion group . . . They showed an increased rate of spontaneous primary and premature rupture of the membranes and also a definite trend toward lower weight of the newborn, especially beyond 41 weeks of pregnancy."[260]

Two women in this group aborted first *and* second pregnancies; "both suffered late spontaneous abortion in the third pregnancy" and the fourth pregnancy of one of them "had a particularly unhappy outcome—a stillborn, small-for-dates" baby.

These results confirm three previously published reports of "an increased rate of late abortion and premature delivery and also a trend toward earlier onset of labor in the second pregnancy after legal abortion of the first."[260]

"The findings of a significantly increased and increasing rate of late abortion indicate that the termination of the first pregnancy had represented a major trauma."[260]

TEENAGERS: THE EFFECTS OF ABORTION ON LATER PREGNANCIES

Among teenagers, the effects of abortion on later *wanted* pregnancies appear to be even worse than among women in general. "The cervix of the teenager, pregnant for the first time, is invariably small and tightly closed and especially liable to damage on dilatation." This quote appears in the 1975 National Academy of Sciences study "Legalized Abortion and the Public Health," page 61. It was made by Dr. J. K. Russell. From 1960 to 1971 he kept records on 62 pregnant teenage patients: 50 of the girls had abortions, 11 gave birth and one miscarried. After their first pregnancies he kept track of the girls. The results of their *subsequent* pregnancies are as follows:

	OUTCOME OF SUBSEQUENT PREGNANCIES	
	Teenagers Who Aborted 1st Pregnancy	Teenagers Who Had Baby 1st Pregnancy
Total Subsequent Pregnancies.............	53	9
Terminated by Abortion................	6	0
Total WANTED Subsequent Pregnancies.........	47	9
Miscarriages...................	19	0
Stillborn...................	1	0
Premature Births— Survived Infancy....	5	0
Premature Births Ending in Infant Death....	2	0
Term Deliveries Ending in Infant Death....	4	0
Total WANTED Pregnancies Ending in Defective Birth or Infancy......	31 (66%)	0 (0%)
WANTED Pregnancies Ending In Normal Birth and Healthy Infancy....	16 (34%)	9 (100%)

Figure 7

182

"The scope of the problem of abortion complications is large, both numerically and economically. For example, in 1975 some 77,000 women in the United States sustained complications of legal abortions and 29 died. Excluding the indirect costs of lost productivity, the estimated direct cost of treating these 77,000 women was over $19 million."[271]

9

THE PUBLIC ASPECT
OF THE PRIVATE ACT:
ABORTION ON THE JOB

Some women face abortion in situations other than their own pregnancies; it touches their lives through friends, neighbors or family members, or when they are hospital patients. Others are confronted by it on entering medical or nursing school, and on the job as doctors and nurses. Even as the pregnant woman has a right to know how abortion has affected other women who have experienced it, the woman health-care worker has a right to know how legal abortion has affected others in the health professions.

Some nurses find it difficult to accept that necessary surgery is pushed aside to make room on the operating schedule for elective abortions; also upsetting is the purchase of abortion gadgetry before other equipment needed for inpatient care. Others have developed intense anxiety over which patient should be cared for at a given moment—the woman threatening to spontaneously abort (for whom the nurse is involved in saving premature life) or the woman in the next bed about to abort because of the salt poison or prostaglandin given to induce the abortion which takes a premature life.

Following a prostaglandin injection, Zina* went into a gynecological ward to await the abortion delivery of her 20-week-old preborn. Only a thin screen separated her from the

185

other patients, women being treated for infertility. When the baby came out and began to cry, many of the patients and nurses burst into tears.

"I heard the child cry," said a staff nurse. "So did the other patients. It was horrifying." Another nurse who was on duty in the ward at the time said, "Everybody was upset. Many patients were crying. What made it worse was that some of the women desperately wanted children. It took weeks for all of us to get over it."[290]

Many nurses find abortions extremely distasteful and are particularly vexed when their duties include handling the dismembered body parts of aborted infants.

Because so many health professionals find induced abortions grotesque, many states guarantee nurses and doctors the right to refuse to assist in them without jeopardizing their jobs. Trudy S. is a registered nurse who works in the maternity unit of a New Jersey hospital; several years ago she notified her superiors that she would have nothing to do with abortion procedures. "I've met some nurses who had thought they could work on an abortion patient," she says. "But after the first one they changed their minds. They had nightmares."[289]

But another New Jersey nurse, Beverly Jeczalik, lost a lawsuit against the hospital that transferred her from maternity to emergency following her request not to assist in any more abortions. Beverly, a new mother herself, devoted to the positive birthing experiences of her maternity nursing duties, hadn't thought much about abortion until the day she had to singlehandedly assist in the delivery of a baby killed by an instillation abortion. It was not a pleasant experience.

Despite the fact that a 1974 conscience law should give hospital personnel the right to be excused from participating in such procedures, Beverly was dismissed from her chosen field. "The hospital called to tell me I could never ever work in maternity again. Sure nurses have the right to refuse, but once they exercise that right, they can't work where they want to any more."

Her unsuccessful attempt to sue for reinstatement has left her frustrated but it hasn't changed her mind about abortion duty. "We just couldn't make them understand how it is there. In our hospital, on the maternity floor, young children are running around visiting their mothers and new siblings; fathers are holding their infants. A nurse has to go from helping one mother breastfeed to picking up a dead baby delivered from a saline abortion—it's too much for a maternity nurse to handle.

"On the other hand, what can she do? Stick her neck out and risk her job? Have her professional status affected? Or get sick in her stomach and have dreams?"

Couldn't she get a job somewhere else? "How?" Beverly asks. "I answered a newspaper ad for part time work in a hospital nursery; when I told them my name, they started giving me the run around; they said the job was full time. A prolife nurse's right to choose may look good on paper, but there will always be an excuse why I can't work."

Beverly would like to see the decision appealed, not for her own sake, but because such a precedent could result in discrimination against nurses throughout the state.

Ronald DeM. is Executive Vice President of a hospital where second trimester abortions were performed until several years ago when its nurses objected. Last year the hospital sought to reconsider its policy, but was unable to because, of seventy nurses he interviewed, "Not one would participate in a second trimester abortion. . . . It tears these nurses up."[289]

Nurses who have participated in many abortions have reported nightmares and researchers documenting this have concluded that "regardless of one's religious or philosophic orientation, the unconscious view of abortion remains the same . . . that unconsciously the act of abortion was experienced as an act of murder."[205]

Physicians are no more immune. "D&E often involves greater emotional strain on the clinician and staff. It forces them to deal with the fetus in an intimate way that many find distasteful."[273] "A major part of the aversion to the procedure comes from its technical difficulties, and most especially from an appropriate feeling of revulsion for the dismembering of a fetus with . . . crushing forceps. . . . It is much easier to perform amniocentesis, to inject a solution, and then leave the hours of labor and delivery of a dead fetus to the patient and her nurse."[277]

There have been many reports of increased depressive reactions and breakdowns among guilt-ridden doctors. [206, 207] Resident doctors in obstetrics and gynecology have expressed their dissent at having to spend "inordinate portions of their learning

187

time carrying out too many distasteful abortions."[208] It seems a robot-like constitution is needed when carrying out large numbers of abortions.[209]

One doctor who has since given up performing abortions remembers the incidents that led to his decision. "Called upon to perform a number of abortions on women suspected of having rubella in early pregnancy, I was faced with the realization that as a physician, I was treating a disease by killing the patient with that disease . . . At precisely the same time we were called upon to perform abortions, we were also performing the first intrauterine fetal transfusions for Rhesus disease. How was I to rationalize vigorous efforts to treat and save one human fetus with a congenital disorder on one day and on the next kill the fetus with a congenital disorder that I could not correct?"[210]

"Second trimester vaginal abortion is a difficult procedure, requiring not only an accurate estimation of fetal size, skilled use of laminaria, and adequate instrumentation, but also considerable experience and expertise . . . The emotional impact of these abortions on the surgeon and the entire staff cannot be underplayed. The surgeon is clearly the instrument of termination and must be absolutely certain of her commitment." The use of "mechanical methods to dilate the cervix before a second trimester abortion requires a commitment from the physician to monitor the patient during any subsequent pregnancy because there is an increased incidence" of loss of the wanted preborn and "increased incidence of premature cervical dilatation in the later pregnancies of these women . . . Although surgical second trimester abortion is 'much harder' on the physician, the chemical methods are 'harder' on the woman."[211]

Even medical textbooks caution against removal of the dismembered preborn through the long, narrow cervical canal. Physicians are warned their skills will be taxed to the utmost in the attempt, especially if the body is torn off and the head bobs about in the uterus.[212]

"All too often I've been asked to do the dirty work (the abortion) only to then have the girl whisked out of any ongoing care we arranged for her," says an ob/gyn/abortionist who specializes in young girls. "The physician who does abortions on teenage girls is the answer to every mother's prayer when her daughter gets pregnant. But once this nasty little social problem is resolved . . . if the subject of contraception is introduced for parental approval, the physician is made to feel as if he or she is encouraging or reenforcing sexual immorality."[189]

Clinicians are advised to take the time to see a teenage girl by herself to determine carefully whether or not she should be aborted. Many pediatricians, family doctors and ob/gyns do not separate the mother from the girl. If this separation does not take place, the physician gets the mother's side of things. The girl naturally has to go along under pressure. "Have the girl in by herself, first, and get *her* story . . . explore *her* feelings. It doesn't take very long to detect ambivalence and this is a critical warning sign. SUCH GIRLS POSSIBLY SHOULD NOT HAVE AN ABORTION." [emphasis is theirs][189]

"Forms relieving physicians from responsibility for complications are not legally binding." That was the State Supreme Court ruling in the case of a Knoxville, Tennessee doctor and his patient who received a botched legal abortion. The woman, who had signed such a release, subsequently complained of nausea and ill health but was told everything was fine. She later gave birth to the child who had managed to elude the abortionist.

In ruling the legal disclaimer invalid, the Court stated, "A professional person should not be permitted to hide behind the protective shield of an exculpatory contract. . . . We do not approve of the procurement of a license to commit negligence . . . "[213]

"If termination of pregnancy were as safe as so many advocates of liberal abortion maintain, a patient suffering as a result of the operation could claim that professional negligence was responsible for her subsequent distress or disaster. Such claims [however] would generally be grossly unfair. There would be a great sympathy for a 16-year-old girl whose uterus was torn beyond repair; for the married woman with gut resection and peritonitis; for the mother in monthly distress following hysterotomy because of implantation endometriosis in her abdominal wall, vagina, or bladder; for the anxious infertile wife who knows that the tubal damage which now denies her the baby she desires is the delayed price she is paying for her teenage abortion. But the fact remains that none of these situations may be the result of negligence. They are complications which, though well known to, and well documented by, those with wide experience of an operation which is neither simple nor safe, are seldom mentioned by those who claim that abortion is safe and merely an extension of contraceptive techniques."[21]

10

A DIFFERENCE
OF OPINION

Initially abortion was espoused as a means of assuring the privacy of a woman's reproductive organs when she declined to share them with a newly-conceived life. Increasingly it's seen as a fool-proof way of removing offspring from, not only the body, but the life of a woman. Currently a difference of opinion exists among abortion advocates themselves as to what a woman's rights entitle her; legislators, politicians, doctors, courts, and women activists all have their own, often conflicting, versions.

While most women suppose that the right to an abortion includes the right to removal of the preborn, alive or dead, from their wombs, the authors of OUTPATIENT SALINE ABORTION didn't see it quite that way. "We believe that fetal death fulfills the essential obligation we have undertaken," they said, quite astonished to "have come under pressure to 'do something' for the unusual patients who have not fallen into labor many days after saline instillation."

Although the women were acutely anxious to get it over with, the doctors "resisted this pressure" feeling that once the preborn's body was dead, their job was done. Thus, in this instance, 13 women were left walking around, still visibly pregnant, who had had legal abortions performed by competent physicians who kept reassuring them that an abortion had, indeed, been performed satisfactorily. Understandably these women were confused and upset. Their doctors, not wanting to face the "psychologic pressure to do something further to initiate labor," sent the women home.[180]

The nurses working with these doctors seemed to have ideas of their own, too, about dispensing medication to relieve pain for women in abortion labor. Despite the fact that most abortions are paid for in cash, in advance, in good faith by women who have every right to expect this includes analgesics, some women never receive the drugs they ask for. Suffering women repeatedly requested, even begged for pain killers, in vain. Their doctors verified, "By the time most patients could persuade a nurse to get the medication, the patient was completing the abortion."[180]

Women choose abortion believing that termination of pregnancy is an exact science and that the abortionist knows what he or she is doing. Often this faith is not justified. In clinics and hospitals medical directors may assign doctors who have little or no related experience to perform abortions; residents who audition well are allowed to practice their techniques by operating solo on unsuspecting women.[245]

Experienced doctors experiment, too. They may, as the number of complications and their severity increases, modify procedures. One group of abortionists, for example, attributed many of their cases of incomplete abortion to a possible effect of "oxytocic agents after passage of the fetus."[141] During the next few hundred abortions they perform, these doctors will try withholding oxytocic agents, or decrease their dosage, in an attempt to reduce the incidence of this problem. Maybe it will work and maybe it won't. How is a woman to know whether her abortion procedure will be a time-tested method or a trial run?

There are also differences of opinion over how much should be taken from a woman during an abortion. Caldeena had been pregnant for a while when she was sent by a referral service to an abortionist "who specializes in borderline cases." General anesthesia put her to sleep for the surgery. She awoke in a hospital, where she had been taken for repair of a hole gouged in her womb during the abortion, minus not only the pregnancy but her appendix and her ability to have another baby as well. The surgeon claimed the abortionist had told him the woman wanted to be sterilized. "I don't know where he got that idea," Caldeena fumed. "I think I would have liked a baby some day." After a heated conversation with the abortionist she

192

related his belief that she "should be glad the surgeon threw in the appendectomy for free, and he couldn't see the sterilization as anything but a bonus!"

A distinct diversity divides doctors on the long-term effects of widespread induced abortions. "Through several years of controversy and debate that involved the medical profession as well as the public in the United States, the sinister remote effects of therapeutic abortions have never been mentioned," broods Doctor Leslie Iffy. "Unawareness among the profession of this danger was reflected by the fact" that a pre-1973 statement strongly advocating the legalization of abortion, signed by "100 prominent professors of obstetrics and gynecology, contained no reference to potential effects [of induced abortion] on perinatal and infant mortality and morbidity . . .

"In the same spirit, in his Address to the College [in 1973] the President of the American College of Obstetricians and Gynecologists projected an almost 50% decrease in infant mortality rates in the forthcoming 10 years and suggested that 'simply postponing pregnancy . . . could drop infant mortality rates by nearly 30%.'

"Since much of the 'postponement' would be the result of artificially induced abortions, in the light of the East-European experiment (where surgical evacuation of the pregnant uterus has resulted in catastrophe) the *actual probability* is that perinatal and infant mortality and morbidity rates, rather than declining by half, *would increase significantly* in the forthcoming decade . . . despite current efforts and improvements in technics and methodology of perinatal care . . .

"It is undesirable and dangerous . . . for the [medical] profession to base its stand on philosophical and political considerations, since only medical ones can claim preferential consideration over those of theologians, lawyers, politicians or the layman."[284]

The Supreme Court's 1973 decision to legalize abortion throughout pregnancy was based in part on its opinion that abortion was safer than childbirth—a finding based, according to Dr. Albert Altchek, on one carefully controlled series of legal abortions performed in New York State. Eight months after the decision, Dr. Altchek, who had been active in promoting legalized abortion, expressed concern that the margin of safety achieved in that series "might not necessarily hold true if the floodgates of completely unsupervised abortion" were suddenly opened nationwide. He predicted[230] that the medical profession would "sadly record a far greater morbidity and mortality rate" if the stringent practices which had led to the recorded safety were abandoned.

He cited the "continuous careful scrutiny" of the New York City Department of Health and "restrictions in actual practice" which were enforced despite the lack of state or federal restrictions on surgical intrusion into the natural state of pregnancy. Among the "unrecognized significant reasons for the good results" he listed:

1. Whereas the state law allowed abortions anywhere, when two deaths occurred in New York City as a result of abortions performed in medical offices, the Department immediately forbade office abortions.
2. Abortions were permitted in clinics not connected with hospitals *only if* they were properly equipped and within 10 minutes distance of a hospital; "even then many clinics were summarily closed and entrepreneurs found that this was not the easy way to make money."
3. The Department let it be known that clinic physicians should be obstetrician/gynecologists.
4. "It was thought wise if only those obstetrician/gynecologists who were interested in developing their technic (sic) and in continuing to do abortions would actually start."
5. Immediate recognition of the need for exploratory surgery and handy facilities in which to perform it are necessary. Hospital abortions afford the easy opportunity for this, the convenience of overnight observation, and the availability of a general surgeon in the event of bowel injury.
6. Although state law permitted abortions in women who were up to 24 weeks gestation, most New York City hospitals set a 20 week limit.
7. "The worst defect is lack of good followup. There may be unreported deaths or serious complications. The incidence of potential long-term complications, such as incompetent cervix or traumatic intrauterine adhesions, is completely unknown."

How do these rigid restrictions which produced that un-

194

equalled safety record which so impressed the Supreme Court justices, compare to restrictions in force today? And to the safety record we are achieving now?

1. States are prohibited from directing where first trimester pregnancies can be aborted; abortions are performed anywhere the operator decides to set up shop, from medical offices to storefronts.

2. Abortions are performed in facilities without emergency equipment or life-saving supplies such as blood; a critically injured woman may be left unattended or driven past closer hospitals to a more distant facility.[107, 115] Entrepreneurs have found fly-by-night referral services and storefront abortion chambers excellent ways to get rich quick.

3. States are prohibited from directing who may perform abortion during the first trimester of pregnancy; in some places surgery may be performed by paramedical or non-medical personnel, or by a physician inexperienced with the organs of female reproduction.

4. Doctors who are uninterested in abortion careers are called upon to abort pregnancies; legislation has even been proposed which would penalize doctors who refuse to surgically interfere with a normal pregnancy. Hospitals that have neither the personnel nor the special equipment needed to perform abortions have been judicially (perhaps injudiciously) forced to provide this type of delicate surgery. Can economic, political, or legislative pressure tactics really result in quality care for women? Or is it possible, even likely, that such pressures will create a climate more hostile than hospitable for the unsuspecting woman seeking abortion?

5. In many abortion facilities the lack of emergency equipment causes life-threatening crises; no attempt is made to observe postoperative patients beyond 15 minutes to an hour; counseling is given by women whose chief qualification is having had an abortion themselves. In some facilities women are released before labor begins following saline injection; profiteering legal abortionists and pharmaceutical drug pushers are agitating for blanket acceptance of prostaglandins so abortions can be self-induced at home completely without the benefits of medical management; these precarious practices unques-

195

tionably endanger women. "Complications such as uterine rupture probe the question of safety in performing midtrimester abortions as outpatient procedures without constant medical supervision and emergency surgical back-up at hand."[259]

6. There is no limit to the gestational age at which a preborn can be legally aborted; it can be done at any time right up until maximum maturity.

7. Often followup is not a concern of the abortionist nor is it attempted; only 4 of 10 women return to the abortionist when complications develop; society is deprived of valuable knowledge by which to judge the total effect of permissive abortion practices.

It is little wonder that Dr. Altchek, who has personally performed over 5000 abortions, is dismayed at the paradox by which the New York City Health Code regulations—after yielding the "good" statistics that were the *basis* of the Supreme Court's ruling—*were themselves declared unconstitutional* by that very same ruling! Never again will such safety be secured for the simple reason that the means of achieving it have been banned, the methods have been outlawed. The Supreme Court created a Catch-22 vortex that is submerging us deeper and deeper in a mire of misery and senseless death.

To make matters worse, courts from coast to coast have struck down informed consent legislation and consumer protection bills which would have regulated abortion in ways reasonably related to maternal health (as required by the Supreme Court). At a time when more women are dying from legal abortions than from illegal, and the same pattern of complications is repeated in all areas of the country, one might reasonably ask why the Surgeon General hasn't officially declared that legal abortion may be hazardous to a woman's health, and required posting of notices to this effect on the front doors of abortion facilities.

"This University (the University of Alabama Medical Center in Birmingham) has had an inordinate number of referrals of patients with complications from evacuation abortions performed after 14 weeks of pregnancy. Retained products of conception, infection, and hemorrhage are complications that are prevalent throughout the country and explain the reason this technique has not achieved. . . . popularity . . . There are inherent risks and problems associated with this procedure . . ."[263]

11

YOU HAVE A
RIGHT TO KNOW . . .

about Abortion: "There is no harmless method."[61] "Induced abortion, at any period of gestation, exposes the woman to a risk of complications which is always larger than zero."[67]

about Menstrual Extraction: "The existence of an ectopic pregnancy or a mole would have catastrophic results."[37]

about Early Suction Abortion: "The powerful suction necessary to accomplish the procedure satisfactorily does pose a serious hazard. The risk of uterine perforation is present even for the most experienced operator."[53]

"Taking only long-term complications, the incidence was 14.4% when suction was used."[61]

about D&C Abortion: "Taking only long-term complications, the incidence was 17.7%."[61]

about Mid- and Late-Term Abortion: "THE MEDICAL SOCIETY OF THE STATE OF NEW YORK WOULD LIKE TO CAUTION ALL PHYSICIANS THAT AN ABORTION PERFORMED AFTER THE TWELFTH WEEK OF GESTATION IS FRAUGHT WITH TREMENDOUS DANGERS" (emphasis is theirs).[60]

"Major abdominal operations (hysterotomy and hysterectomy) have complication rates up to 40.3 times higher than suction curettage."[271]

about Saline Abortion: of 300 women: 10% required blood transfusions; 13.3% had fevers; 31 required additional surgery; 64.8% were in labor 24 to 36 hours; 14.3% were in labor for 36 to 48 hours; 5% were in labor for more than 48 hours; 1.7% needed major surgery to complete the abortion.[53]

about All Extra-Amniotic Methods of Abortion: "Most fetuses are born alive."[66]

about Early Complications of Abortion: These kinds of complications are much more frequent in the young woman pregnant for the first time[89] and "up to two times more frequent in poor women."[63]

"In a series of 73,000 abortions one woman in every 20 had early complications; one in every 200 had major complications."[63]

about Abortion's Effects on Subsequent Pregnancies: "There appears to be a positive correlation between previous abortion and placenta previa, abruptio placentae, cervical incompetence, and prolonged labor."[28]

"Any patient who has had a previous history of an abortion should be regarded as a high risk patient."[61]

about Your Future: "Throughout the crucial stages of human reproduction, from conception to weaning, the risk of death to the child is more than 100 times the risk of death to the mother. So it is the consequences *to subsequent children* of surgical interference with the delicately adjusted reproductive system of women that is primarily at stake; the health of the woman is also at stake."[61]

"It would be wise for young women and their (future) husbands to assume that induced abortion is neither safe nor simple, that it frequently has long-term consequences, may affect subsequent children, and makes single women less eligible for marriage."[61]

"To those contemplating an actual abortion—think of the consequences, and talk openly to several people before accepting the need for the operation. Information is needed." [101]

"An intelligent decision requires the input of all available data, and ignorance . . . precludes a fully informed decision . . .

" . . . convey the experiences of others to the patient in order to promote a well-considered decision . . . " [282]

12

MAKING AN
INTELLIGENT CHOICE

In the absence of long-term observations, the rhetoric of choice and untested hypotheses weighed heavily in women's abortion decisions. The basis of a "need" to abort is elusive. Economic and social factors may play a role, however these fail to encompass the social ramifications of long-term effects such as colostomy or sterility and the economic burden on families in which the mother dies from her legal abortion or is hospitalized with complications. Continuation of the pregnancy may appear more difficult at first, but all adjustments take time and the advantages may be numerous.

Like any other major vaginal or abdominal surgery, abortion annot be induced more safely than natural termination can be allowed to occur naturally. In addition to its medical risks, abor- ion is expensive. Extrapolating from complication rates, treat- ment expenses and the cost in human time and suffering, we pro- ject that the savings in overall abortion costs would justify natural termination as a viable choice.

The psychological costs of abortion are more difficult to assess. Waiting for amniocentesis results prolongs the emotional turmoil inevitably surrounding a problem pregnancy. Childbirth spares the woman much of the psychological trauma of induced abortion.

Since publication of the Supreme Court decisions which claimed to be based on the safety of abortion, much abortion advertising has stressed safety, although the basis of that belief was weak and limited; sound basis for its existence is lacking. On the contrary, the overwhelming weight of evidence challenges the validity of such suppositions. One major roadblock to safety is the physiological and psychological inability of woman's body to adequately adapt to the abrupt termination and the inability of even the most skilled physician to completely control her body and its reaction to the shock. As documented in Chapter 3 most pregnancy/childbirth deaths are confined to a small group of high-risk patients. For the average woman elective abortion is far more hazardous than childbirth, a common method of pregnancy termination which can be tolerable even for the woman choosing adoptive parenthood for her child. Well-designed birthing rooms maximize the opportunity for the woman to have a positive, healthy childbirth experience.

If your doctor has advised you to abort your baby, he more than likely had a reason, but that does not mean an abortion is necessary or best for you or your baby. Remember that many very fine doctors believe abortion is never, ever required. Past presidents of the National Right To Life Committee have been doctors; one is a surgeon. There are national organizations of prolife physicians; one is limited to obstetricians and gynecologists. The world's leading pediatric surgeon, doctors who established the sciences of fetology and genetics—none of these eminent professionals have ever recognized a *need* for forced pregnancy termination. Their advice would be to get a second opinion from a doctor who has no vested interest in abortion. The doctor who sees himself caring for two patients instead of one will undoubtedly handle the mother's health problem differently from the doctor who would subject her to the stress of unnecessary surgery. A competent prolife doctor will be able to assess the situation objectively and make recommendations that will allow for the treatment best for both mother and baby; no one has to get hurt.

In order to make an intelligent choice all available information must be evaluated. Getting an abortion is probably one of the biggest decisions you'll ever make; but unlike getting a gas guzzler, you can't take it back if it proves unsuitable. Once this transaction is made, you're stuck with it for the rest of your life; and while a car dealer will provide you with glossy photographs of interiors, and glowing reports of performance and options before the sale is made, an abortionist probably won't—unless required to by law.

Evaluating the information about abortion and its potential complications as well as your other options may be confusing, but it is of critical importance to your mental and emotional well-being. All of your feelings, past and present, about motherhood, babies, responsibility—whatever is pertinent to *you*—must be taken into consideration. Any reluctance, compromise, haste, even unintentionally repressed feelings can trigger severe emotional reactions after the abortion when it's too late to go back and undo the damage.[283]

No abrupt termination of a complex, natural, on-going physiological process can be so simple that it is entirely free of risk. The wise woman will balance the presumed benefits of an operation she considers advisable with its disadvantages, both immediate and long-term. Making an intelligent choice involves contrasting the artificial with the natural, the abrupt with the gradual, the violent with the non-violent. It requires judging whether aborting the pregnancy or allowing it to progress naturally carries the greater risk to life and health. Without full knowledge of these risks, this decision cannot be made sensibly or responsibly; the experiences of other women must be taken into account.

Having read this book you know abortion has innumerable catastrophic, even lethal effects. *These things happen.* They have happened before and they will happen again. No doctor, no clinic, no hospital can guarantee a nice, safe legal abortion without any direct, indirect, immediate or delayed bad effects. In fact, they can't even guarantee a woman will live through it. This choice cannot be made lightly because it's a matter of life and death.

Two factors may help temper a hasty, potentially regrettable, abortion decision. One is a finding by experts that *a majority of women* who initially reject a pregnancy will have accepted it by the end of the second trimester. [101, 302] The other is the fact that the alarm reaction to pregnancy is *normal*, and is as much a component of the desired pregnancy as of the unexpected pregnancy. It is an integral phase which has been found by psychologists to be essential—or at the very least functional—for reorganization; it has been described as a "readying of the circuits for new attachments" and a "positive force for the mother's adjustment."

In recent months increasing numbers of women have come forward to say they chose abortion believing they were taking charge of their lives, only to learn through the experience that they had submitted to an invasion of their privacy bordering on rape. The women who feel they were sold out by the lenis lure describe their abortions as acts of violence which left them feeling degraded, invaded and bereaved. Their message to other women is that the situation making pregnancy a problem can become worse by aborting.

A woman can control her body and her life by keeping the pregnancy but not the infant. She can choose termination at its natural time, in dignity, without surrendering herself to the multiple threats of invasive surgery. Giving up the products of conception at 40 weeks doesn't have to be any more traumatic than giving it up at 8, 10, or 16 weeks.

So if you've been thinking, "I don't want to have a baby," you're off the hook. You can carry the pregnancy to term and not have a baby. Allowing your pregnancy to continue *doesn't* mean you're going to have a baby. It means you're going to complete your sexual cycle, which is natural and healthful. It means you're controlling your body instead of submitting to mechanical manipulation of it. Staying pregnant means keeping your body safe from the risks of unnatural, forceful, surgical intrusion. And it means that among the tens of thousands of people who already want your baby, someone is going to get the gift of a lifetime.

It is true, one person's gift can be another's problem. It's normal to want to escape from problems. In a woman's hour of distress, abortion looms larger than life, the Great Escape's towering exit sign. In a moment of fear, instead of facing her total situation, a woman can reach for the quick fix, the surgical solution. Too many find out too late they're trapped, and once done, an abortion cannot be undone.

When pregnancy is a problem, it's a human problem and requires a human solution. *All pregnancies terminate;* when you're pregnant, the only way you can become unpregnant is by delivery, by nature or by force, before term or at term, giving life or taking life. In terms of the risk to life, the most rational choice of method for terminating pregnancy is normal childbirth.

For this reason it's always better to investigate the positive alternatives first. If you think you need an abortion, contact a local BIRTHRIGHT or other emergency pregnancy service center (which may be called Lifeline, Heartbeat or Soul), the National Office of BIRTHRIGHT (609-848-1818), the National

Pregnancy Hotline, your State Division of Youth and Family Services, an adoption agency, or the maternity department of a hospital. Finding out the positive alternatives available to support you through your pregnancy won't hurt you or cost you anything; not finding out *can* hurt you—it could cost you your health, your future, or even your life.

The farther along a pregnancy is, the older the preborn gets, the larger s/he becomes. Forced termination thus becomes increasingly more difficult, more complicated procedures must be employed, and complications are more common, with an inevitable increased mortality rate. [113]

13

APPENDIX

The cervix of the woman pregnant for the first time is more difficult to open than that of a woman who has given birth. The cervix which has never had the opportunity to efface (shorten) and dilate (open) itself naturally, is very long and thin, more rigid than supple, and very tightly closed; it will not yield easily to the metal rods of increasing diameter used to pry it apart—as far as 18 mm[305]—to induce abortion.

Even in the woman who has delivered an infant before, dilatation can be difficult. When the obdurate cervix has once been broken down, it may permanently lose the muscle tone necessary for effective performance of its natural function.

Figure 8 accurately illustrates the preborn's size by the end of the first trimester and in the second trimester of pregnancy; it demonstrates how wide the cervix must be stretched for removal of the preborn referred to technically by scientists and doctors as "the fetus."

A research biologist tells us the term "the fetus" is encountered "too often . . . implying a certain uniformity. . . . We tend to lose sight of the fact that *there is no such entity as the embryo or the fetus* since these [terms] include all the stages of development which are most dynamic and ever changing. An embryo at 7 hours postconception is very different from an embryo at 8 hours postconception . . . "[288]

To clarify, in "Research On The Fetus" [1975, p. 1-1 & 11-3] the National Commission for the Protection of Human Subjects of Biomedical and Behavioral Research stated, "The human embryo from conception to delivery . . . is an organism—even in

209

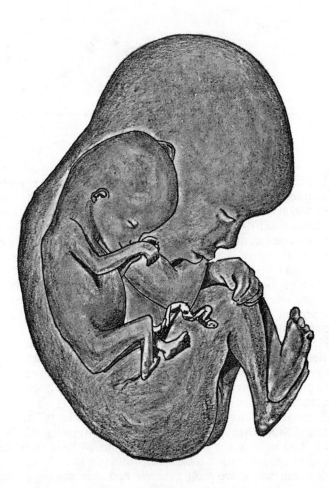

Figure 8

The preborn, life size, at three and four months

utero. Though it is composed of tissue, it is not merely tissue, unlike muscle or skin or collagen. The assertion that the fetus is a part of the mother is simply false. It is a different organism, no matter how dependent it is on the mother. The fetus, in its varying stages, is a self-developing, self-changing whole, which assimilates and transforms food supplied by the mother, and grows and differentiates itself according to the plan encoded in its own DNA. It becomes, on its own and from within, progressively more organized—i.e., possessed of organs that contribute to the maintenance and functioning of the other organs and of the whole. It has a unique genotype, different from that of the mother and those 'parts' of her which are truly herself and 'her own.' The fetus is a distinct organism right from its start.... It is a living organism until it dies or is killed."

"If a Government makes abortion on demand legal it must accept some responsibility for what follows, both to patients aborted and to society as a whole."[21]

14

REFERENCES AND BIBLIOGRAPHY

1. *Spontaneous and Induced Abortion,* WHO Technical Report Series, No. 461, 1970, p. 40

2. *Handbook on Abortion,* Dr. & Mrs. J. C. Willke, 3/73, Rev. p. 68

3. *Id.,* p. 72

4. *Ibid.,* no. 78 at p. 85 and 93

5. *Ibid.,* no. 1, p. 38

6. *Avulsion of the Ureter from Both Ends as a Complication of Interruption of Pregnancy with Vacuum Aspirator,* C. Dimopoulos, et al., J. Urol 118(1):108, July 1977

7. *Therapeutic Abortion: A Review of 567 Cases,* P.H. Brenner, et al., Calif Med 115:20-27, July 1971

8. *Lacerations of Cervix and Perforation of Uterus in Artificial Interruption of Pregnancy,* K. Poradorsky, Cesk Gynek 25:682, 1960

9. *Changes in the Blood Coagulation in Artificial Abortion,* V. P. Skipetrov, Vop. Okhr. Materin. Det. 11:69, 1966

10. *Induced Abortion in New York City, A Report of Six Separate Studies,* R. E. Hall, Am J Ob and Gyn 110: 601-611, July 1, 1971

11. *The First Year of Experience in Colorado with the New Abortion Law,* W. Droegemueller, et al., Am J Ob Gyn 103:694-702, Mar. 1, 1969

12. *The Immediate Morbidity of Therapeutic Abortion,* M. A. Carlton, et al., Med J Aust 2:1071-1074, 5 Dec 70

13 . *Maternal-Fetal Microhemotransfusion as a Result of Induced Abortion,* J. Gellen et al., Orv Hetil 107: 732-4, 17 Apr 66

14 . *Abortion in New York State Since July 1970,* H. S. Ingraham & R. J. Longood, Clin Obstet Gynecol 14: 5-24, Mar 1971

15 . *Ibid.,* no. 12

16 . *Complications of Hysterotomy,* S. V. Sood, Br Med J. 4:495-496, 11/21/70

17 . *Early and Late Sequelae of Abortion,* E. Midak, Pol Tyg Led 21:1063, 1966

18 . *Japan's 22 Year Experience with a Liberal Abortion Law,* XIIth International Congress of FIAMC, Y. Hayasaka, October 11-14, 1970

19 . *Termination of Pregnancy,* D. Potts, Brit Med Bull 26:65-71, Jan. 1970

20. *Induced Abortion on Psychiatric Grounds, A Follow-Up Study of 479 Women,* M. Ekblad, Acta Psychiat Neurol Scand Suppl 99:238, 1955

21. *Legal Abortion: A Critical Assessment of Its Risks,* J. A. Stallworthy, et al., Lancet 1245-1249, 4 Dec 71

22. *Ibid.,* no. 2, p. 76

23. *Ibid.,* no. 78 at p. 96

24. *Abortion Surveillance 1976,* Center for Disease Control, p. 8-9, August 1978

25. *Abortion in Czechoslovakia,* M. Kuck, Pro Roy Soc Med 62:831-832, 1969

26. *Two Women Tell About Their Abortions,* Voice for the Preborn, Sept.-Nov. 1979

27. *Ibid.,* no. 1, p. 27-28

28. *A Critical Review of Legal Abortion,* J. Jurokovski and L. Sukarov, Int J Gynec & Obstet 9:111-117, May 1971

29. *Course of Delivery of Women Following Interruption of Pregnancy,* R. Slumsky, Cesk Gynek 29:97, 1964

30. *Spontaneous Abortion and Fetal Abnormality in Subsequent Pregnancy,* A. Gardiner, et al., Br Med J 1016-1018, 22 Apr 78

31. *Ibid.,* no. 2

32. *The Challenge of Prematurity,* D. Cavanaugh, Med World News, Feb. 1971

33. *Ibid.,* no. 78, at p. 92

34. *Research in Prostaglandins,* Worcester Foundation for Experimental Biology 1(3):2, Dec. 1971

35. Life Science Library—GROWTH by James M. Tanner, Gordon Rattray Taylor and the Editors of *Time-Life* Books

36. *Ibid.,* no. 34 and *Population Report—Prostaglandins,* Geo. Washington Univ. Med. Ctr., Series G, No. 1, 4-73 and No. 2, 6-73

37. Dr. Albert Altchek, *Emergency Medicine,* Sept. 1973

38. Testimony given before the Royal Commission on Human Relationships, Sidney, Australia, by T. W. Hilgers, M. D., May 21, 1975, p. 37

39. *Maternal Death Due to DIC after Saline Abortion,* S. R. Lemkin & H. E. Kattlove, Ob Gyn 42(2):233-235, Aug 1973

40. *Analysis of Placenta Associated with Saline Abortion: Clinical Considerations,* G. S. Berger, et al., Amer J Ob Gyn 120:484-488, Oct. 15, 1974

41. *Ibid.,* no. 38, at p. 42

42. *Complications Caused by Difficult Removal of Laminaria Tents,* J. P. Gusdon, et al., Amer J Ob Gyn 8:680-691, Sept. 1971

43. *Consequences of the Legalization of Induced Abortion in Eastern Europe,* A. Klinger, Ther Umsch 27:681-692, Oct. 1970

44. *Id.,* no. 29

45. *Past Abortions and the State of Consequent Pregnancies,* W. Dziewnska, Ginek Pol 44:1003-11, 1973

46. *Glioma of the Uterus: A Fetal Homograft,* P.A.R. Niven, Amer J Obstet Gynec 115:534-538, Feb. 15, 1973

47. *Cervical Incompetence: Aetiscogy and Management,* B. G. Wren, Med J Aust 1146, Dec. 29, 1973

48. *Uterine Rupture Following Attempted Saline Abortion with Oxytocin in a Grandmultiparous Patient,* D. A. Horwitz, Ob Gyn 43(6):921-922, June 1974

49. *Children's Disturbed Reactions to Their Mothers' Miscarriages,* A. C. Cain, et al., Psychosom Med 26: 58-66, 1964

50. *Induced Abortion Mortality:* CA 1967-1973, G. K. Stewart

51. *Maternal Mortality Associated with Legal Abortion in New York State:* July 1, 1970 - June 30, 1972, G. S. Berger, C. Tietze, and S. H. Katz, Ob & Gyn 43:315-326, 1974

215

52. Testimony by Pat Goltz, International President, Feminists for Life, Inc., before the Senate Subcommittee on Constitutional Amendments, Aug. 21, 1974

53. *Abortion: Medical Aspects in a Municipal Hospital,* D. P. Swartz & M. K. Paranjpe, Bull NY Acad Med 47(8): 845-852, Aug. 1971

54. *Air Embolism and Maternal Death from Therapeutic Abortion,* R. A. Munsick, Ob Gyn 39(5):688-90, May 1972

55. *Abortion Tragedy in Hospital,* H. Koblin, Los Angeles Free Press, Sept. 15, 1972, p. 13

56. *Abortion: The Personal Dilemma,* R. F. R. Gardner & W. B. Eerdmanns Publ Co., 1972, p. 213

57. *Management of Uterine Perforation Following Elective Abortion,* S. M. Freiman & G. Wulff, Ob Gyn 50(6):647-649, Dec. 1977

58. *Interruption of Pregnancy and Guilt Feelings,* D. Beck, Schweiz Med Wschr 94:357, 1964

59. *Influence of Interruption of Pregnancy on the Sexual Life of the Woman,* J. Cepelak, et al., Cesk Gynaek 25:609, 1960

60. *State M.D.'s Clarify Abortion Stand,* R. Klemfuss, Med Soc Press Release, Mar. 26, 1970

61. *Some Consequences of Induced Abortion to Children Born Subsequently,* Margaret and Arthur Wynn, Foundation for Education and Research in Child Bearing, London, 1972

62. *Air Embolism and Maternal Death from Therapeutic Abortion,* R. A. Munsick, Ob & Gyn 39(5): 688-690, May, 1972

63. Reprinted with the permission of the Population Council from "Joint Program for the Study of Abortion (JPSA): Early Medical Complications of Legal Abortion," by Christopher Tietze and Sarah Lewit, *Studies in Family Planning* 3, no. 6 (June 1972).

64. *Id.,* no. 63

65. *Id.,* no. 63

66. *Induced Abortion: A Factbook,* C. Tietze and D. A. Dawson, Reports on Population/Family Planning, # 14, p. 33, Dec. 1973

67. *Ibid.,* no. 66 at p. 38

68. Testimony of Dr. Andre Hellegers before the Senate Subcommittee on Constitutional Amendments, April 25, 1974

69. *Abortion Surveillance 1972,* Center for Disease Control, April 1974, p. 5

70. *Family Practice News,* Int Med News Service, 5/15/74, p. 18

71. Dr. Bohumil Stipal, Czechoslovakia's Deputy Minister of Health, 1974

72. *Second Trimester Abortion After Vaginal Termination of Pregnancy,* Wright, et al., Lancet, June 10, 1972, p. 1278

73. *Rhesus Isoimmunization After Abortion,* S. Murray and S. L. Barron, Brit Med J 3:90, 1971

74. *Ibid.,* no. 63

75. *Maternal Mortality Associated with Paracervical Block Anesthesia,* G. S. Berger and C. W. Tyler: Center for Disease Control; E. K. Herrod: County of Erie, Dept. of Health, Buffalo, NY

76. *Management of Retained Placenta Associated with Saline Abortion,* G. S. Berger and C. W. Tyler, Center for Disease Control; T. Kerenyi, Park East Hosp, NY City

77. Testimony of Dr. W. J. Godfrey before the Senate Subcommittee on Constitutional Amendments, June 26, 1974

78. *Handbook on Abortion,* Dr. & Mrs. J. C. Willke, Rev. 1975, p. 95, 96

79. *The Situation of Abortion in Finland,* M. Olki, Internationale Abortsituation, Abortbekampfung, Antikonzeption, Leipzig, 1961

80. *Termination of Pregnancy,* D. Potts, Brit Med Bull 26:65-71, 1970

81. *The Findings of an Inquiry Into the First Year's Working of the 1967 Abortion Act: Conducted by the Royal College of Obstetricians and Gynecologists,* Brit Med J 2:529-535, 1970

82. *Abortion—Death Before Birth,* J. R. Stanton, cited in testimony by Senator James Buckley before the Senate Subcommittee on Constitutional Amendments, 3/6/74

83. *The Abortion Experience,* Osofsky, #3, cited in testimony by Congresswoman Bella Abzug before the Senate Subcommittee on Constitutional Amendments, 3/6/74

84. *Report of Selected Characteristics on Induced Abortion Recorded in New York State* July 1, 1970—June 30, 1971, H. S. Ingraham, NY State Dept. of Health, Oct. 1971, p. 1

85. *Ibid.,* Tables 7 and 15

86. *Ibid.,* no. 21

87. *Ibid.,* no. 1

88. *Psychologic Reaction to Therapeutic Abortion,* K. R. Niswander & R. J. Patterson, Ob Gyn 29:702-706, May 1967

89. *Artificial Termination of Pregnancy in Czechoslovakia,* A. Kotasek, Int J Gynaec Obstet 9:118-119, May 1971

90. *Deaths from Paracervical Anesthesia Used for First Trimester Abortion,* Grimes and Cates, New Eng J Med 295(25):1397-1399, Dec. 16, 1976

91. *Predicts Highest Abortion Morbidity Yet to Come,* McDonald and Aaro, Fam Practice News, Sept. 15, 1974

92. Survey conducted by the American Assn of Pro-Life Obstetricians and Gynecologists, National *Right to Life News,* July 1974

93. C. E. Olsen, H. B. Nielsen and E. Ostergaard, Int J Gynec and Obstet 8:823, 1970

94. *Ibid.,* no. 61, citing C. Zwahr (1972) and J. Hoffman & E. Ziegel (1962)

95. *Ibid.,* no. 61, citing *Perinatal Mortality,* N. R. Butler & D. G. Bonham, Livingstone, 1963

96. *Abortion in a Changing World,* R. E. Hall (ed), 1970, 2 vols., Columbia Univ Press

97. *Séquelles des Opérations Gynecologiques Dans Deurs Rapports Avec la Gravidité,* R. Palmer, Rev. Franc Gynec 67:2-3, 175-180, 1972

98. Ian Donald, Professor of Midwifery, Glasgow Univ., The Scotsman, March 9, 1970

99. *Ibid.,* no. 23, citing the 1968 Nagoia Survey

100. *A Psychological View of Abortion,* A Commentary by Colman McCarthy, St. Paul Sunday Pioneer Press, Washington Post, March 7, 1971

101. *A Critical Evaluation of Legal Abortion,* M. Harry, World Med J 23(6):83-85, 1976

102. *Vascular Coagulation Seen in Saline Abortion,* Hospital Tribune Report, Hospital Tribune, Oct. 30, 1972, p. 8

103. *Deaths and Near Deaths with Legal Abortions,* M. J. Bulfin, presented at the ACOG Convention, Oct. 28, 1975

104. *Urologic Complications of Legal Abortion,* R. A. Watson, presented to the annual meeting of the Amer College of Surgeons at Louisville, KY, Mar. 18, 1977

105. *Laminaria Tent: Relic of the Past or Modern Medical Device?,* B. W. Newton, Am J Ob & Gyn 113:442-448, 1972

106. Sup. Ct. CA-7603-76; also CA-7902-76, CA-3214-75, CA-2917-76, CA-2631-77, CA-3817-74, CA-3048-74, CA-3226-72

218

107. *Woman Sues Clinic Over Abortion Complications,* Dallas Times Herald, p. 1, 23, June 20, 1978

108. *Abortion Deaths "Happening Every Day,"* J. Boland, The Wanderer, Oct. 27, 1977

109. *Clinic Client Dies in Hours;* $1 Million Lawsuit Readied, *National Right to Life News* 4(10):1, 3, Oct. 1977

110. *Gestational Age Limit of 12 Weeks for Abortion by Curettage,* D. A. Grimes & W. Cates, Am J Ob Gyn 132(2): 207-210, Sep. 15, 1978

111. *Committee on Maternal Welfare Report,* J. F. Jewett, New Eng J Med 290:340-341, 1974

112. *National Right to Life News,* Mar 1978, p. 8

113. *Deaths Caused by Pulmonary Thromboembolism After Legally Induced Abortion,* A. M. Kimball et al., Am J Ob & Gyn 132(2):169-74, Sep. 15, 1978

114. *Ex-Abortionist is Probed by U.S. Attorney,* T. S. Robinson, *The Washington Post,* p. C 1, C 5, Oct. 26, 1977

115. Sup. Ct. CA-556-75 subsequently removed to U.S. Dist. Ct. CA-75-1156

116. Abortion Surveillance 1975, Center for Disease Control, April 1977

117. Testimony of M. J. Bulfin, M.D. before the U.S. Senate Subcommittee on Constitutional Amendments, Hearing Record part 2, p. 797

118. *Abortion and Maternal Deaths:* Editorial, Brit Med J 2(6027):70, July 10, 1976

119. *Medical and Surgical Complications of Therapeutic Abortions,* G. K. Stewart and P. Goldstein, Ob Gyn 40:539-548, 1972

120. *Laceration of the Ascending Branch of the Uterine Artery: A Complication of Therapeutic Abortion,* R. I. Lowensohn & L. T. Hibbard, Am J Ob & Gyn 118(1): 36-38, 1974

121. *Follow-up of 50 Adolescent Girls Two Years After Abortion,* H. Cvejic, et al., Canadian Med Assn J 116:44-56, Jan. 8, 1977

122. *Fatal Uterine Rupture During Oxytocin-Augmented Saline Induced Abortion,* D. A. Grimes, et al., Am J Ob Gyn 130(5):591-592, March 1, 1978

123. *A Review of 700 Hysterotomies,* B. J. Nottage & W. A. Liston, Brit J Ob & Gyn 82:310-313, April 1975

124. *Committee on Maternal Welfare Report,* J. F. Jewett, New Eng J Med 288: 47-48, 1973

125. *Saline Abortion and Lupus Erythematosis,* J. F. Jewett, Reprinted, by permission of The New England Journal of Medicine 294(14):782-783, April 1, 1976

126. *Surveillance of Abortion Program in New York City: Preliminary Report,* J. Pakter, et al., Clin Ob & Gyn 14(1):291, March 1971

127. *Therapeutic Abortion Using Intraamniotic Hypertonic Solutions,* D. N. Menzies & D. F. Hawkins, J Ob Gyn Brit Cwlth 75:215-218, 1968

128. *Surgical Disease in Pregnancy,* H. R. K. Barber & E. A. Graber, "Surgical Aspects of Abortion," W. B. Saunders, Phila, Pa 1974, p. 491

129. *Abortion Deaths Associated with the Use of PGF2α,* W. Cates, et al., Am J Ob & Gyn 127(3):219-222, 1 Feb 77

130. *Termination of Second Trimester Pregnancy Using PGF2α,* ACOG Technical Bull No. 27, Apr 1974

131. C. W. Tyler and W. Cates, Am J Ob & Gyn 131(2): 230-231, May 15, 1978

132. *Maternal Deaths Associated with Cervical Block Anesthesia,* G. S. Berger, C. W. Tyler, E. K. Harrod, Am J Ob Gyn 118:1142-1143, 1974

133. Morbidity and Mortality Weekly Report, p. 75, March 4, 1977

134. *Elective Abortion: Complications Seen in a Freestanding Clinic,* G. Wulff, Jr. and S. Freiman, Ob & Gyn 49(3):351-357, Mar 1977

135. *Reported Live Births Following Induced Abortion: 2½ Years Experience in Upstate New York,* G. Stroh and A. Hinman, Am J Ob Gyn 126(1):83-90, Sep. 1, 1976

136. *Ibid.,* no. 126

137. *Rupture of the Bladder Secondary to Uterine Vacuum Curettage: A Case Report and Review of the Literature,* S. N. Rous, F. Major and M. Gordon, J Urol 106:685, 1971

138. *Contraceptive Technology* 1974-1975, Fam Plann Prog, Dept of Gyn and Ob, Emory Univ School of Medicine, Atlanta, GA, p. 57

139. *Abortion in Hawaii:* 1970-1971, R. G. Smith, et al., Hawaii Med J 32(4):213-220, July/Aug 1973

140. *Coagulopathy with Midtrimester Induced Abortion: Association with Hypersomolar Urea Administration,* R. T. Burkman, et al., Am J Ob Gyn 127(5):533-536, March 1, 1977

141. *Intraamniotic Urea and PGF2α for Abortion: A Modified Regimen,* R. T. Burkman, et al., Am J Ob Gyn 126(3):328-333, Oct. 1, 1976

142. *Electroencephalographic Changes After Intra-Amniotic PGF2α and Hypertonic Saline,* R. P. Shearman, et al., Brit J Ob & Gyn 82:314-317, Apr 1975

143. *Laparoscopic Sterilization with Therapeutic Abortion vs. Sterilization or Abortion Alone,* A. Weil, Ob & Gyn 52(1):79-82, July 1978

144. *Abortion in Hawaii,* Fam Plan Perspec 5(1): (Table 8) Winter 1973

145. *Psychoses Following Therapeutic Abortion,* J. G. Spaulding and J. O. Cavenar, Jr., American Journal of Psychiatry, 135(3):364-365, March 1978. Copyright, 1978, the American Psychiatric Assn.

146. *Term Delivery Through a Spontaneously Occurring Cervicovaginal Fistula Following Second-Trimester Surgical Repair,* J. T. Harrigan & D. Karbhari & A. Halpern, Am J Ob Gyn 128(8):912, Aug. 15, 1977

147. *Major Extra-Peritoneal Bleeding Complicating Amniocentesis: A Case Report,* J. R. McBride, et al., Am J Ob Gyn 130(1):108, Jan. 1, 1978

148. *Detroit News,* Feb. 17, 1978

149. *Continued Pregnancy After Failed First Trimester Abortion,* W. L. Fielding, et al., Ob & Gyn 52(1):56-58, July 1978

150. *Failed Abortion in a Separate Uterus,* C. R. McArdle, Am J Ob Gyn 131(8):910, Aug. 15, 1978

151. *Failed Termination of Pregnancy Due to Uterus Bicornis Unicollis with Bilateral Pregnancy,* M. A. Pelosi, et al., Am J Ob Gyn 128(8):919 Aug. 15, 1977

152. *Abortion: Subjective Attitudes and Feelings,* Ellen W. Freeman, Reprinted with permission from Family Planning Perspectives 10(3):150-55, May/June 1978

153. *Medical Abortion Complications: An Epidemiologic Study at a Mid-Missouri Clinic,* D. K. Nemec, et al., Ob & Gyn 51(4):433-436, April 1978

154. *Culture and Treatment Results in Endometritis Following Elective Abortion,* R. T. Burkman, et al., Am J Ob Gyn 128(5):556-559, July 1, 1977

155. *A Safer Method for Paracervical Block in Therapeutic Abortions,* R. McKenzie & W. L. Shaffer, Am J Ob & Gyn 130:317-320, Feb. 1, 1978

156. *Uterine Rupture Following Midtrimester Abortion by Laminaria, PGF2α, and Oxytocin: Report of Two Cases,* D. Propping, et al., Am J Ob Gyn 128(6):689-690, July 15, 1977

157. Manchester, NH Union Leader, June 2, 1978 quoted in *National Right to Life News,* Oct. 1978, p. 2

158. Stephen E. Lindstrom, M.D. in National Right to Life News, Sept. 1977, p. 5

159. *Pregnancy—Specific Beta—1—Glycoprotein and Chorionic Gonadotropin Levels After First Trimester Abortion,* M. Mandelin, et al., Ob & Gyn 52(3):314-317, Sep. 1978

160. *Catecholamines During Therapeutic Abortion Induced with Intra-Amniotic Prostaglandin F2α,* W.E. Brenner, et al., Am J Ob Gyn 130(2):178-182, Jan. 15, 1978

161. *Midtrimester Abortion by Intraamniotic Prostaglandin F2α; Safer than Saline?,* D. A. Grimes, et al., Ob & Gyn 49(5):612-615, May 1977

162. Ob Gyn News, p. 12, March 15, 1977

163. *Complications Following PGF2α—Induced Midtrimester Abortion,* J. H. Duenholter & N. F. Gant, Ob Gyn 46:247-250, 1975

164. *Early Rupture of the Gravid Uterus,* E. J. Lazarus, Am J Ob & Gyn 132(2):224, Sept. 15, 1978

165. Dr. Margaret White at the Royal College of Physicians, The Liverpool Echo, May 25, 1976

166. Brit Med J, p. 587, Sept. 4, 1976

167. *Dilatation and Curettage for Second-Trimester Abortions,* Hodari, et al., Am J Ob Gyn 127(8):852-853, Apr. 15, 1977

168. *Ureterouterine Fistula as a Complication of Elective Abortion,* J. J. Barton, et al., Ob & Gyn 52(1-Suppl):81S-84S, July 1978

169. *Hysteroscopic Management of Intrauterine Adhesions,* C. M. March, et al., Am J Ob & Gyn p. 653-657, March 15, 1978

170. *Failed Prostaglandin F2α-Induced Abortion: A Case Report,* R. G. Cunanan, Jr., et al., Ob & Gyn 49(4):495-496, Apr 1977

171. *Effect of Abortions on Population Held Equivocal,* Dr. Margaret White, Ob Gyn News, March 15, 1977, p. 38

172. *UCI Doctor Warns of Dangers in Abortions,* Dr. D. Kent, Anaheim Bulletin, March 25, 1978, p. A3

173. *Increased Reporting of Menstrual Symptoms Among Women Who Used Induced Abortion,* L. H. Roht, et al., Am J Ob Gyn 127(4):356-362, Feb. 15, 1977

174. *Abortion in Japan After 25 Years,* Med World News, Nov. 1973

175. *Second Trimester Abortions Require Special Skills,* Ob Gyn News, p. 25-27, June 1, 1977

176. *Psychological Effects of Abortion: with Emphasis Upon Immediate Reactions and Followup,* J. D. Osofsky, H. J. Osofsky, and R. Rajan, "The Abortion Experience," Harper & Row, 1973

177. *Induced Abortion and Secondary Infertility,* D. Trichopoulos, et al., Brit J Ob & Gyn 83:645-650, Aug. 1976.

178. Dr. Robert W. Kistner, at the Dallas meeting of the Amer College of Surgeons' Clinical Congress, quoted by Dr. W. F. Preston in the Phila. Bulletin 10/15/78

179. Dr. Luigi Mastroianni, Jr. in the Phila. Bulletin 2/19/76

180. *Outpatient Saline Abortion,* H. Schulman, et al., Ob & Gyn 37(4):521-525, Apr. 1971

181. *Endometrial Ossification Following an Abortion,* M. Waxman & H. F. Moussouris, Am J Ob & Gyn 130(5):587, March 1, 1978

182. *Hypokalemia and Cardiac Arrhythmia Associated with Prostaglandin-Induced Abortion,* R. L. Burt, et al., Ob Gyn 50(1S):45S-46S, July 1977

183. *Artificial Termination of Pregnancy in Czechoslovakia,* A. Kotasek, Int J Gyn & Ob 9:118, 1971

184. *Diagnostic and Therapeutic Hysteroscopy for Traumatic Intrauterine Adhesions,* O. Sugimoto, Am J Ob & Gyn 131(5):539-547, July 1, 1978

185. *The Problem of Women Seeking Abortion,* K. Malmfors, "Abortion in the United States," M. Calderone ed, Harper & Row, p. 133-135

186. *Reflections of a Psychiatrist,* T. Lidz, "Therapeutic Abortions," H. Rosenk, Julian Press Inc., Vol. 22

187. *Psychiatric Indications of Abortions,* D. C. Wilson, VA Med Monthly 79:448-451, 1952

188. *The Psychiatrist's Role in Therapeutic Abortion: The Unwitting Accomplice,* S. Balter, American Journal of Psychiatry 119:312-318, 1962, Copyright 1962, the American Psychiatric Assn.

189. *Problems of Adolescent Abortion,* C. A. Cowell, Orthopanel 14, Ortho Pharmaceutical Corp. publ

190. *Is Therapeutic Abortion Scientifically Justified,* R. J. Heffernan & W. A. Lynch, Lenacre Quarterly 19(1), Feb. 1952

191. *Psychiatric Sequelae of Abortion,* N. M. Simon & A. G. Sentuvia, Arch Gen Psych 15:378-389, Oct. 1966

192. *National Right to Life News,* p. 2, October 1978

193. Professor Peter Peterson, Hannover Medical School, in Deutsches Arzteblatt

194. *Liberal Abortion Laws: A Psychiatrist's View,* F. J. Ayd, The Medical-Moral Newsletter, Spring 1967

223

195. *Abortion in the United States*, L. C. Kolb, Hoeber-Harper, p. 123, 1958

196. Testimony of Dr. Irving C. Bernstein before the Senate Subcommittee on Constitutional Amendments, June 26, 1974

197. *Mental Disorders After Abortion*, B. Jannson, Acta Psych Scand 41:87-110, 1965

198. *Emotional Sequelae of Therapeutic Abortion: A Comparative Study*, Ian Kent, et al., presented to the annual meeting of the Canadian Psychiatric Assn at Saskatoon, Sept. 1977

199. *Pregnancy, Abortion and the Unconscious*, J. C. Sonne, Marriage and Family Newsletter 6 (4,5,6) 1975

200. Pennsylvanians for Human Life, Northeast Region Newsletter, March 1978

201. *Suboptimal Pregnancy Outcome Among Women with Prior Abortions and Premature Births*, S. J. Funderburk, et al., Am J Ob Gyn 126(1):55-60, Sept. 1, 1976

202. *Induced Abortion: A Documented Report*, T. W. Hilgers, Jan. 1973, p. 43

203. Wall Street Journal, June 20, 1978, quoted in *National Right to Life News*, p. 2, Oct. 1978

204. *Abortion Repeal in Hawaii: An Unexpected Crisis in Patient Care*, J. McDermott & W. Char, Amer Journal of Orthopsychiatry 41:620-626, July 1971

205. *Staff Reactions to Abortion, A Psychiatrist's View*, H. D. Kibel, Ob Gyn 39(1):128-133, Jan. 1972

206. *Therapeutic Abortion*, E. J. Connor, Audio-Digest Ob Gyn 17(16), Aug. 18, 1970

207. *A Public Health Physician Views Abortion*, H. Ratner, Il Med J, May 1967

208. *Liberal Therapeutic Abortion: Cure or Cause of Mental Illness*, L. Marder, Audio-Digest Ob Gyn 16(17), Sept. 2, 1969

209. *Medical Hazards of Legally Induced Abortion*, testimony before the Senate Subcommittee on Constitutional Amendments, Hearing Record Part 1, p. 491-505

210. Dr. W. A. Bowes, Testimony before the Senate Subcommittee on Constitutional Amendments, Hearing Record Part 2, p. 209

211. *Second Trimester Abortions Require Special Skills*, Ob Gyn News, p. 25-27, June 1, 1977

212. *Textbook on Obstetrics*, Dr. J. P. Greenhill, 12th edition

213. Knoxville News Sentinel 11/22/77

214. *Oxytocin Administration in Midtrimester Saline Abortions*, N. H. Lauersen & J. D. Schulman, Am J Ob Gyn 115(3): 420-430, 1 Feb 73

215. *Legal Abortion by Extra-Amniotic Instillation of Rivanol in Combination with Rubber Catheter Insertion Into the Uterus After the 12th Week of Pregnancy*, C. Ingemanson, Am J Ob Gyn 115(2):211-215, 15 Jan 73

216. *Posterior Cervical Rupture Following Prostaglandin-Induced Mid-Trimester Abortion*, A. C. Wentz, et al., Am J Ob Gyn 115(8):1107-1110, Apr 15, 1973

217. *Cervicovaginal Fistula Complicating Induced Mid-Trimester Abortion Despite Laminaria Tent Insertion*, J. H. Fischke & H. R. Gordon, Am J Ob Gyn 120(6):852-853, Nov. 15, 1974

218. *Comparison of PGF2α and Hypertonic Saline for Induction of Mid-trimester Abortion*, N. H. Lauersen, et al., Am J Ob Gyn 120(7):875-889, Dec. 1, 1974

219. *Cornual Contraction Ring with Retained Placenta in Mid-Trimester Abortion*, J. R. Niebyl, et al., Am J Ob Gyn 120(4):563-564, Oct. 15, 1974

220. *The Effect of Meperidine Analgesia on Mid-Trimester Abortions Induced with Intra-Amniotic PGF2α*, L. G. Staurovsky, et al., Am J Ob Gyn 125(2):185-187, May 15, 1976

221. *Death After Legal Abortion by Catheter Placement*, D. A. Grimes, et al., Am J Ob Gyn 129(1):107-108, Sept. 1, 1977

222. *Detachment of the Uterine Cervix in Association with Induced Mid-trimester Abortion*, R. T. Burkman, et al., Am J Ob Gyn 129(5):585-586, Nov. 1, 1977

223. *Prostaglandins and Abortions*, World Health Organization Task Force on the Use of Prostaglandins for the Regulation of Fertility, Am J Ob Gyn 129(6):593-606, Nov. 15, 1977

224. *Intra-Amniotic Urea and PGF2α for Midtrimester Abortion: Clinical and Laboratory Evaluation*, T. M. King, et al., Am J Ob Gyn 129(7):817-824, Dec. 1, 1977

225. *Induced Abortion of First Pregnancy: Its Consequences on Subsequent Pregnancy, Labor, Post Delivery Period and the Condition of the Newborn*, Lembrych, Stanislaw, and Labiak, Bronislaw Dist. Ob Gyn Hospital, Opole, Poland (unpub)

225

226. *Cervical Pregnancy: Diagnosis and Management,* D. J. Rothe & S. J. Birnbaum, Ob Gyn 42(5):675-680, Nov. 1973

227. *Mortality Associated with Hypertonic Saline Abortion,* M. A. Schiffer, et al., Ob Gyn 42(5):759-764, Nov. 1973

228. *One Death and a Cluster of Febrile Complications Related to Saline Abortions,* G. S. Berger, et al., Ob & Gyn 42(1):121-123, July 1973

229. *Reduced Dose of Rh Immunogloublin Following First Trimester Pregnancy Termination,* F. H. Stewart, et al., Ob & Gyn 51(3):318-320, March 1978

230. *Abortion Alert,* A. Altchek, Ob & Gyn 42(3): 452-454, Sept. 1973

231. *Comparative Risk of Death from Legally Induced Abortion in Hospitals and Non-Hospital Facilities,* D. A. Grimes, et al, Ob & Gyn 51(3):323-326, March 1978

232. *Observations on Patients Two Years After Legal Abortion,* P. Jouppila, et al., Obstet & Gynecol Survey 30(9):629-631, Sept. 1975

233. *Culture and Treatment Results in Endometritis Following Elective Abortion,* R. T. Burkman, et al., Am J Ob Gyn 128(5):556-557, 1977

234. *Psychiatric History and Mental Status,* W. L. Sands, "Diagnosing Mental Illness; Evaluation in Psychiatry and Psychology," Freedman and Kaplan, editors, Atheneum, 1973, p.31

235. N. Kaplan, J Am Med Assn, p. 89, July 3, 1972

236. *Maternal Deaths from Ectopic Pregnancy in the South Atlantic Region,* 1960 through 1976, W. J. May, et al., Am J Ob Gyn 132(2):140-147, Sep. 15, 1978

237. *Digest,* Fam Plann Perspec 10(1):38, Jan/Feb 1978

238. *The Effectiveness and Complications of Abortion by Dilatation and Vacuum Aspiration Versus Dilatation and Rigid Metal Curettage,* D. A. Edelman, et al., Am J Ob Gyn 119(4):473-477, June 15, 1974

239. *Early Vacuum Aspiration: Minimizing Procedures to Nonpregnant Women,* E. R. Miller, et al., Fam Plann Perspec 8(1):33-38, Jan/Feb 1976

240. *Are You Sorry You Had An Abortion?* M. Rockmore, Good Housekeeping, p. 120-164, July 1977

241. *The Abortion Profiteers: Making A Killing In Michigan Avenue Clinics,* P. Zekman and P. Warrick, Chicago Sun-Times, Nov. 12, 1978

242. *The Abortion Profiteers: Jury Subpoenas Records of Abortion Clinic,* K. Koshner & P. Zekman, Chicago Sun-Times

243. *The Abortion Profiteers: Men Who Profit From Women's Pain,* P. Zekman & P. Warrick, Chicago Sun-Times, Nov. 13, 1978

244. *The Abortion Profiteers: State To Act On Abortion Clinics,* P. Zekman & K. Koshner, Chicago Sun-Times, Nov. 13, 1978

245. *The Abortion Profiteers: Women Take Chances With "Tryout" Doctors,* P. Zekman & P. Warrick, Chicago Sun-Times, Nov. 14, 1978

246. *The Abortion Profiteers: Dr. Ming Kow Hah: Physician Of Pain,* P. Zekman & P. Warrick, Chicago Sun Times, Nov. 1978

247. *The Abortion Profiteers: License All Counselors, Daley Asks,* G. R. Hillman, Chicago Sun-Times, Nov. 1978

248. *The Abortion Profiteers: Nurse To Aide: "Fake That Pulse!",* P. Zekman & P. Warrick, Chicago Sun-Times, Nov. 1978

249. *The Abortion Profiteers: Doctor Loses Court Tests On Two Clinics,* P. Zekman & K. Koshner, Chicago Sun-Times, Nov. 1978

250. *The Abortion Profiteers: Soft Voices, Hard Sells—Twin Swindles,* P. Zekman & P. Warrick, Chicago Sun-Times, Nov. 1978

251. *The Abortion Profiteers: "Get Rich Quick" Name Of Their Game The Same,* P. Zekman & P. Warrick, Chicago Sun-Times, Nov. 1978

252. *The Abortion Profiteers: Two Abortion Referral Firms Are Subpoenaed,* P. Zekman & K. Koshner, Chicago Sun-Times, Nov. 1978

253. *The Abortion Profiteers: 12 Dead After Abortions In State's Walk-In Clinics,* P. Zekman & P. Warrick, Chicago Sun-Times, Nov. 19, 1978

254. *The Abortion Profiteers: Abortion Mills In Huge Kickback Scheme,* P. Zekman & P. Warrick, Chicago Sun-Times, Nov. 1978

255. *The Abortion Profiteers: Infamous Doctor Is Detroit Connection,* P. Zekman & P. Warrick, Chicago Sun-Times, 1978

256. *The Abortion Profiteers: Plymouth A Health Lemon In Motor City,* P. Zekman & P. Warrick, Chicago Sun-Times, 1978

257. *The Abortion Profiteers: Court Takes Dr. Ming Kow Hah License,* K. Koshner & D. McCahill, Chicago Sun-Times, 1978

258. *The Abortion Profiteers: Counseling The Patient: Buy This Abortion,* P. Zekman & P. Warrick, Chicago Sun-Times, 1978

259. *Uterine Rupture: A Complication of Mid-Trimester Abortion,* M. Borten & E. A. Friedman, Prostaglandins 15(1):187, Jan. 1978

260. *Late Sequelae of Induced Abortion in Primigravidae: The Outcome of the Subsequent Pregnancies,* O. Koller and S. N. Eikhom, Acta Obstet Gynecol Scand 56(4):311-317, 1977

261. D. Cavanagh, Am J Ob Gyn 130(3):375, Feb. 1, 1978

262. *Complication of Abortion Performed with a Plastic Suction Curet: Intrauterine Loss of the Curet Tip,* T. W. McElin & T. M. Giese, Am J Ob Gyn 132(3):343-344, Oct. 1, 1978

263. C. E. Flowers, Jr., Am J Ob Gyn 132(8):913

264. *Ureter-Uterus Fistula Following Abortion,* V. W. Hardt & V. Borgmann, Zschr Urol Bd 68:761-764, 1975

265. *Case of Severe Lesion of the Urinary Bladder in the Course of Induced Abortion,* W. Maternik, Pol Prezegl Chir 43(6):1035-1038, 1971

266. *Intravascular Hemodialysis: A Complication of Mid-Trimester Abortion: A Report of Two Cases,* A. Adachi, Ob Gyn 45(4):467-469, Apr 1975

267. *Hypersomolar Urea for Elective Mid-Trimester Abortion: Experience in 1,913 Cases,* R. T. Burkman, et. al., Am J Ob Gyn 131(1):10-17, May 1, 1978

268. *Abdominal Fetus Following Induced Abortion,* E. M. Silverman & S. E. Ryden, Am J Ob Gyn 122(6):791-792, July 15, 1975

269. *The Management of Midtrimester Abortion Failures by Vaginal Evacuation,* R. T. Burkman, et al., Ob Gyn 49(2):233-235, Feb. 1977

270. *Ectopic Pregnancy and First Trimester Abortion,* L. A. Schonberg, Ob Gyn 49(1S):73S-75S, Jan. 1977

271. *Complications from Legally-Induced Abortion: A Review,* D. A. Grimes & W. Cates, Ob Gyn Survey 34(3):177-191, copyright 1979 The Williams & Wilkins Co.

272. *A Cluster of Uterine Perforations Related to Suction Curettage,* S. B. Conger, et al., Ob Gyn 40(4):551-555, Oct. 1972

273. *D&E After 12 Weeks: Safe or Hazardous?,* W. Cates, Contemporary Ob/Gyn, Medical Economics Co. 13:23-29, January 1979

274. *Doctors Note Serious Side Effects on Women Following Abortion,* E. A. Quay, The Wanderer, Nov. 16, 1978

275. *Mid-Trimester Abortion by Dilatation and Evacuation: A Safe and Practical Alernative,* D. A. Grimes, et al., Reprinted by Permission of The New England Journal of Medicine 296(20):1141-1145, 19 May 77

276. *Termination of Pregnancy in the Midtrimester Using a New Technic,* S. T. DeLee, Int Surg 61(10):545-546, Oct. 1976

277. Stubblefield PG, Albrecht BH, Koos B, Frederiksen MC, Williford JF and Kayman DJ: A Randomized Study of 12-mm and 15.9-mm Cannulas in Midtrimester Abortion by Laminaria and Vacuum Curettage. *Fertil*

228

Steril 29:512, 1978. Reproduced with the permission of the publisher, The American Fertility Society.

278. *The Ambivalence of Abortion,* Linda Bird Francke, copyright 1978 Random House

279. *Emotional Sequelae of Elective Abortion,* Ian Kent, et al., BC Med J 20(4):118-119, April 1978

280. *Therapeutic Abortion and Psychiatric Disturbance in Canadian Women,* E. R. Greenglass, Canadian Psychiat Assn J 21(7):453-459, Nov. 1976

281. *Effects of Legal Termination on Subsequent Pregnancy,* J. A. Richardson & G. Dixon, Brit Med J 1:1303-1304, May 29, 1976

282. *The Psychological Sequelae of Abortion Performed for a Genetic Indication,* B. D. Blumberg, et al., Am J Ob Gyn 122(7):799, Aug. 1, 1975

283. *The Decision-Making Process and the Outcome of Therapeutic Abortion,* C. M. Friedman, et al., American Journal of Psychiatry Vol. 131(12) p. 1332-1337, 1974, Copyright 1974, the American Psychiatric Assn.

284. *Abortion Laws in Hungary,* L. Iffy, Ob & Gyn 45(1):115-116, Jan. 1975

285. *Evaluation of a Balloon Dilator to Augment Midtrimester Abortion,* M. Borten, et al., Am J Ob Gyn 130:156, 1978

286. *Induction of Abortion with Prostaglandin F2α,* H. Knabe & F. Lehmann, Fortschritte der Medizin 96(7):360-362, 1978

287. *Mid-Trimester Abortion Induced by Intravaginal Administration of Prostaglandin F2α-Methylester Suppositories,* A. S. van den Bergh & A. A. Haspels, Contraception 17(2):141-151, Feb. 1978

288. *Radiation Biology of the Fetal and Juvenile Mammal:* Chairman's Remarks, Roberts Rugh, U. S. Atomic Energy Commission, p. 381-382, 1969

289. *The War of the Roses,* K. Rein, Reprinted by permission from the July 1979 issue of *New Jersey Monthly.* Copyright © 1981 Aylesworth Communications Corporation

290. *Another Survivor,* J. Rubeck, National Right to Life News, p. 10, June 1979

291. D. W. Louisell, Commissioner, National Commission for the Protection of Human Subjects of Biomedical and Behavioral Research in *Research on the Fetus,* Report and Recommendations, DHEW Publ. No. (OS) 76-127, p. 79, 1975

292. *Ibid.,* no. 291, M. Lappe, p. 33

293. Hymie Gordon, M. D., medical geneticist, Mayo Clinic, from personal correspondence

294. *A Maternal Death Associated with Prostaglandin E2,* S. P. Patterson, et al., Ob & Gyn 54(1):123-124, July 1979

295. *Uterine Rupture with the Use of Vaginal Prostaglandin E2 Suppositories,* R. Z. Sandler, et al., Am J Ob Gyn 134(3):348-349, June 1, 1979

296. *Midtrimester Abortion Induced by Intravaginal Administration of Prostaglandin E2 Suppositories,* N. H. Lauersen, et al., Am J Ob Gyn 122(8):947-954, Aug. 15, 1975

297. *Reduction of Cervical Resistance by Prostaglandin Suppositories Prior to Dilatation for Induced Abortion,* J. R. Dingfelder, et al., Am J Ob Gyn 122(1):25-30, May 1, 1975

298. *Ibid.,* no. 267, Dr. E. C. Flowers, Jr.

299. *Surgical Drugs Feared—Antibiotics Often Found to Be Harmful,* The Bulletin, Phila., PA Aug. 17, 1979, p. 26

300. *Maternal-Infant Bonding,* M. H. Klaus and J. H. Kennell, The C. V. Mosby Co., 1976, p. 46

301. *The Psychological Aspects of Abortion,* David Mall and Walter F. Watts, University Publications of America, 1979

302. *Ibid.,* no. 300 at p. 210

303. *Research in Prostaglandins,* Worcester Foundation for Experimental Biology 2(6):2, May 1973

304. *Clostridial Sepsis After Abortion with PGF2α and Intracervical Laminaria Tents—A Case Report,* S. L. Green & W. E. Brenner, Int J Gyn Ob 15:322-324, 1978

305. *D&E Plus Suction in Midtrimester Abortion,* F. N. Berry & W. F. Peterson, The Female Patient, p. 86-88, Nov. 1978

306. *Most Mother, Child Mortality Seen in Small High-Risk Group,* Ob. Gyn. News 16(10):13, May 15, 1981

307. *From Conception to Birth: The Drama of Life's Beginnings,* Roberts Rugh & Landrum B. Shettles, Harper & Row, 1971

308. *Gynaecological Sequelae of Induced Abortion,* M. Brudenell, The Practitioner 224:893-898, Sep. 1980

309. *Long-Term Sequelae Following Legally Induced Abortion,* E. B. Obel, Danish Medical Bull 27(2):61-74, Apr. 1980

310. *Abortion Deaths Tied to Amniotic Fluid Embolism,* Ob. Gyn. News, Vol. 15, No. 13, p. 3, July 1, 1980

311. *Abortions in Michigan, 1982,* Office of Vital and Health Statistics, Michigan Department of Public Health, March 15, 1983

312. *Test Yourself: Obstetric Update,* American Journal of Nursing, November 1982, p. 1713 & 1790

"The incidence of complications is almost certainly underreported because patients treated outside the hospital are seldom included in the hospital statistics, and sub-clinical infections, which are usually not treated at all, are, by definition, almost never included. Nevertheless, they may well lead to delayed complications such as subfertility and sterility.''[28]

15

INDEX

233

236

237